SWEET
PASS
KEROSENE

Nigeria: A Personal History

by

Ian McCall

Published by
Cross Border Consultants
Greenburn Cot, Auchencrow, Eyemouth TD14 5LS, UK

First edition 2011

Layout by Fantasy Prints Ltd
14 West Street
Berwick-upon-Tweed
Northumberland TD15 1AS

www.fantasyprints.co.uk

ISBN 978-1-4476-3107-1

To the memory of
Mary Blair McCall
1925 - 1967

Contents

Preface

Part 4
THE SOCIAL SCENE

Part 5
MORE ABOUT WORK

EPILOGUE

Preface

It is just over 60 years since I boarded my first flight to Nigeria. I did not know what to expect. So there was no likelihood of my expectations being dashed. What unfolded was a jumble of exciting and, to begin with, chaotic events that took a long time to form any sort of pattern in my mind. It was seen and lived experience rather than observed and analysed events. I have sought to describe the country as I found it and the changes it underwent through the vehicle of my own work there. My work could only make sense in the light of what had gone before. To that extent this is a personal history of Nigeria. In as far as I needed to fill out the information I gleaned in my time in Nigeria, I have gone to the historical accounts in politics, economics and the social environment. These have informed and enriched my personal experiences. They were further highlighted by the vivid memory of others who could look back to a point in time that links history to the present. History and the memory of older people combine to put my own experience in a wider and hopefully more significant context. Because it is personal it includes the social scene which may give readers a view of day-to-day activities on the ground addressed neither by the memoirs of administrators nor by the researches of political and economic historians, the very nature of whose work often obscures vital human details.

The brilliant three-volume work on the rise, the years of its climax and the decline of the British Empire by Jan Morris, focuses largely on India, the jewel in the crown, and on what was to become the dominions and their place at the centre of imperial history. It tends to neglect some of the colonies and the lives that ordinary people lived in these territories. Out of 1600-odd pages, only some four or five refer directly to Nigeria. The proportion is not much higher in Lawrence James's vivid account of the rise and fall of the British Empire. Linda Colley's recent study of the fate of the white people caught up in, and abandoned by, empire, *Captives*, provides an original focus on a review deliberately restricted to the experience of individuals. In his splendidly researched work *The Scottish Empire*, Michael Fry examines the role of the Scots in the flow and ebb of imperialism, but devotes only some ten pages out of 500 to the 'Four Guineas' and appears to have focused on Ghana as a proxy for West Africa. Fry's work concentrates on the Scots who made it to the top. A very readable counterpart to this is Tom Devine's *Empire of the Scots* which focuses on the way empire affected people who, in turn, had an effect upon empire. I eagerly await his next volume covering 19th and 20th centuries which will, I hope, reflect the importance of Nigeria in an Africa today in which one in every five persons is Nigerian. Nigeria was the most populous and potentially the most wealthy territory in Britain's overseas empire outside India. Niall Ferguson, in his *Empire: How Britain Made the Modern World*, traces empire back to money in his scholarly, revisionist treatment of imperial history, but significantly, in my view, mirrors his predecessors in his focus on India and the Dominions.

The generality of these imperial histories can become more focused and animated by the specifics of life as it was lived in Nigeria. This book, while having as its thrust economic and commercial factors as the drivers of exploration and progress, seeks to illuminate some of the historical record while also seeking to depict everyday events in the life of a serving officer. In the process, it encompasses the political developments leading to the achievement of independence. The first day of the new millennium marked 100 years since what is now Nigeria came directly under the aegis of the British government. That rule was to last but 60 years. It is a short span in historical evolution but reflects a sea change in the economic, political, commercial and social environment.

A young man's early experiences colour his later life and it is only to be expected that attitudes, values, identities and worldview formed and transformed in the impressionable twenties will influence the more mature years. So it was to prove for me. My experience was largely confined to the south of the country and for that chance good fortune I shall always be grateful, for there it seems to me lies such a richness and diversity of cultures, language and history that I am moved to put it down insofar as it determined the engaging milieu in which I was to work. It was to provide me with an opportunity to explore and note aspects of the country and its recent history in a way not readily available to foreigners today. It would give me insights too into the fascinating world of pidgin English of which Nigeria, particularly the south of the country, has developed its own impressive variety and which has provided the title for this book. Its emergence and growth are a direct result of the commercial interactions that started with the gold, ivory and pepper trade, were further developed during the days of slaving and extended in the time of the so-called 'legitimate' palm oil trade. It is a product of the country's commercial history and cannot be separated from it. Thankfully, we no longer see pidgin as an illiterate form of English but as a justifiable and creative form of communication that links people who would not otherwise be in meaningful contact.

That I am doing this nearly fifty years on from my time in Nigeria has advantages and disadvantages. Distance in time filters out detail that the subconscious does not particularly want to retain. Unlike the diarist who records matters of concern meticulously on a daily basis, the memory is selective in that only these memories are brought back that leave an acceptable impression, no matter how trivial. Memory is not neutral. It cannot be objective since objectivity is difficult to ascertain, being the sum total of all possible subjectivities. We do not recall so much as reconstruct, rather like football supporters bringing to mind a perceived unjust decision of the referee, in a way that is favourable to the outcome they prefer. What we remember reflects truly what is important to us even if we cannot explain it to ourselves.

As a new recruit much younger than the vast majority of my European and African contemporaries, I learnt much from them. I have tried to capture some of the earlier snapshots and excitements of colonial life, mostly from people who experienced it at first or second hand, for they do much to illustrate the flux of history and to instruct us in what to admire and what to condemn.

I hope too that in the process I have shed a little light on how people lived and perhaps how that life came to colour the expatriate's outlook. In so doing, I hope I have done justice to the political, economic, historical and cultural aspects of the surroundings I was thrown into. To give some order to what I have written, I have grouped the material into five different categories. Such is the interconnectedness of people and beliefs, values and events, the public and the private, artifacts and actions, work and leisure and social structures and authority that where there is interplay between categories I have included the particular chapter under that category into which most of the topic falls.

Part 1 looks at the factors that took me to Nigeria and records early impressions in Lagos during my induction period there and my first glimpses on the spot into the history of the territory. Part 2 explores the historical determinants of the environment I was to work in through examination of the life of King Jaja of Opobo, a man who went from slave to king, whose life is a substitute for the economic and political changes that took place in a relatively short period of time; through the work of Mary Slessor whose missionary work typifies the influence of Christianity on these changes; and the enterprise of George Goldie whose commercial and political acumen did so much to build the political framework of the present Nigeria and to establish the Royal Niger Company, precursor of the mighty United Africa Company. His shaping influence on the country and the company has been obscured by his reluctance to expose his life and work to biographers.

This leads in to the period of ascendancy of the expatriate firms in the economic life of Nigeria and the eventual constitution of the Produce Inspection Service which I was to join and the setting up of the Nigeria Produce Marketing Boards. Part 3 reflects the peripatetic nature of my work in the early years and the unique opportunity I had to witness the Nigerian scene from the privileged position of one whose travels not only took in experiences, places and events that breathed life into history, but also exposed me to the ways of the expatriates and the local people alike. This provided insights denied to more place and desk-bound contemporaries. The social scene and the rituals symbolising attitudes and values are described in Part 4. A further, more generalised view of the work scene is developed in Part 5. The book concludes with an epilogue that looks reflectively on events and relates the lessons learnt in Nigeria to the current scene in the western democracies.

I wish to acknowledge the inspiration of all these people mentioned in the book without whom it could not have been written. Their number is dwindling fast. It has been a great pleasure to recall them. They have had, together, a formative effect on who I am, what my values are and the multiple nature of my identity. I give special thanks to those of them who have read earlier drafts and made suggestions for their improvement. Others with no connections with Nigeria have read them and pointed me in directions I would not have found on my own. Bob Akroyd bent his highly creative mind to approaches other than those proposed by me. Judi Moore made helpful suggestions based on her writer's viewpoint and experience and Tom Bryan gave me most useful advice and encouragement. I am indebted to Dan and Avril Hood for providing me with a copy of the version they hold of the Book of Genesis in pidgin and to Dan for first and second hand accounts of life there during his visits after home rule had been given effect. James Collin brought much needed order to my original draft and displayed unbounded patience in the face of a stream of amendments.

An earlier version appeared on the internet at *www.ianmccall.co.uk*. The reviews quoted on the back cover are from this version.

Any mistakes, inaccuracies, discontinuities or omissions are mine and mine only.

ianmccall375@btinternet.com
February 2011

Part 1

Induction and Early Images

CHAPTER 1

Towards West Africa

There were hardly any people in Scotland in the post-war years, nor in the rest of the United Kingdom I am sure, who did not have some close friend or relative who was thinking of going abroad or was already there. The race for personal space was on. It was repeating what had happened a generation earlier when two uncles of mine went off to find a new life in Canada and India respectively and a third would probably have sought an outlet in which to exercise and develop his talents if he had survived the First World War. A brother of my Aunt Jenny died in Onitsha, Nigeria in 1930 while still a relatively young man working as District Agent for John Holt and Company. Her surviving brother, Uncle Dugald, had served on yachts of the rich and had sailed to faraway places. My Uncle Hugh worked with the Anchor Line sailing between Glasgow and New York and I still have coathangers that he brought back, albeit with the name 'Waldorf Astoria' marked on them. A cousin of my mother's grew tea in Ceylon, now Sri Lanka, at a place called Banderapola. Such a geographic spread of the extended family was repeated right across the land.

Stamp collecting was exciting in such an environment. There was always someone who had a relative in some foreign place who was prepared to make a child's day by remembering he collected stamps. Mrs Petrie had a son in Bolivia and thrust stamps upon me that were so much bigger and more colourful than our own. A neighbour had a relative in Tanganyika which also seemed to have brighter and bigger stamps than ours. Another neighbour, Bob Lockhart, was reputed to have retired at 40 from a job in timber in the Gold Coast. Yet another, Andrew Yuill, nearer my own age, went to work in Burma and soldiered there after the Japanese invasion. There was a house near my grandmother's in Bervie in north-east Scotland which was called Ilo Ilo after the place the owner had worked in; I was to find out where it was only when I went to the Philippines 30 years later. I suppose it was not surprising that I was fired as a young man by such examples and wanted to try what so many of my relatives and friends' relatives had experienced and talked about when they returned.

Fuel was added to this desire by visiting the Far East when I was in the Royal Navy. While I was at Edinburgh University I took a course in social anthropology. This was not a subject related directly to my studies. A broadening of the mental perspective is encouraged by the Scottish educational system and that was one manifestation of this emphasis. I met African students while studying and realised they had different perceptions of Britain and of its role in their countries than the one generally accepted in the United Kingdom. I am indebted to Joe Beckley, a Nigerian student who lived in the same hall of residence as myself, for explaining this to me. It all stimulated further my interest in people and lands I had not seen. It had the added bonus of becoming increasingly relevant to my interests as the years passed, or perhaps it directed these interests.

By the time I had completed my studies at university, I was 26 years old and keen to get work, preferably abroad. I had a hankering for a job related to agriculture without having an agricultural degree but I was aware of commercial opportunities in that sector. My knowledge of agriculture was confined to dimly remembered tales of my mother and my maternal grandmother who was the widow of a farmer in the Howe of the Mearns in north-east Scotland; to visits to my great-uncle Robert Bell who was one of the pioneers of fruit-growing in the Clyde Valley; to my father's large garden - his enthusiasm to 'dig for victory' during the war had even pushed him to take a field from the neighbouring fathers of St Mary's Church; to my experience in my vacations as a labourer in the tomato houses locally, as a commercial salmon fisherman on the River Tay, as a process worker in a canning factory at Wisbech in Cambridgeshire, as an itinerant hand at a County Agricultural Committee camp near Tonbridge in Kent and as one of many foreign workers at the grape harvest in France.

I did toy with the idea of doing a postgraduate Diploma in Rural Studies. While exploring that possibility, I was required to attend, as a result of an earlier expression of interest, a preliminary interview in Edinburgh, for a post in his department, with Andrew Young, who was the Director of the Department of Marketing and Exports, the executive of the Nigeria Produce Marketing Boards. This led to a further interview in Great Smith Street, London followed by the offer of a job subject to a satisfactory medical report.

I was more than pleased to receive a letter of appointment to the Department of Marketing and Exports and subsequently received flight tickets for Lagos. I made arrangements to acquire such gear as was recommended with one or two exceptions and I remember buying a pair of linen sheets at the bargain price of £3 from Ross the Drapers in the Castlegate in Lanark. Mr Ross seemed delighted to have been able to provide some of my kit. I could feel his goodwill. And, of course, he said that he knew my father, code for 'Well done but don't get above yourself'.

I left for Nigeria by air in the summer of 1951. The excitement of ceaseless tannoy announcements of departures to far-sounding places heightened the feeling of excitement I had been experiencing for a week or more before my date of departure. My sister Marjorie, who was doing her midwifery training at Guy's Hospital in London, and Dora Hickey, soon to marry my good friend Ian Orr, were there to see me off. I didn't feel the sadness I felt at leaving my parents for both girls shared with me that desire to see new places and meet different people as they would later demonstrate. I remember the plane revving up at the end of the runway preparatory to take-off and then, with a suitable apology from the captain, returning to the apron for a technical inspection. I had thoughts of the China Clipper planes crossing the Pacific and beloved of Hollywood - had I escaped an incident which, if it had not been anticipated and rectified, could have happened beyond the point of no return somewhere over the Sahara desert?

4

This was my first flight in a civil aircraft. It is quite easy to appear nonchalant when you are a seasoned traveller. It is not at all easy to give the impression of a man-about-the-air-space when you have stubbed out your cigarette in the ashtray only to be told by the person sat next to you that it is for glasses. And also that the ashtray pulls out from the arm of the seat. Tangential thinking was not something I had knowingly practised and I had expected an ashtray to be in the back of the seat in front as in the buses that went to Carluke, Forth and Carnwath from the Horsemarket. The idea that drinks would be supplied on board had not crossed my mind but I didn't find it a trial to adjust to it.

The plane was a Hermes with a maximum cruising height restricted to 16,000. This meant that on the leg to Rome we had to fly down the Alpine passes. The view of the Alps this gave travellers was quite indelibly magnificent. You felt you could have reached out and scraped some of the snow off the mountain sides with the nail of your forefinger. The scale of the mountains was emphasised by the time it took to pass them by. The next leg was to Tripoli where we landed in the dark. My position overlooking the engines allowed me to see the red glow of the exhaust manifolds and the flames issuing from them. My fellow traveller, who had seen me glancing regularly in the direction of the glow in the night sky, assumed I was worried rather than interested and assured me that it was the guarantee that all was well. It was only if I didn't see it that it would be time to worry, he averred.

The man sitting next to me, an engineer with the Public Works Department, told me that the Hermes was a relatively recent innovation and that flights to Lagos were previously from Poole in Dorset by flying boat and that the journey took two days, one night being spent in Malta where passengers were taken off by tender to their hotel. They had dressed for dinner. When the first flying-boats landed at Lagos, the locals who assisted with mooring and re-fuelling, called them 'de canoe de go for up'. The crews used expressions from the sea rather than the language of the air. They went down hatchways rather than stairs to the lower deck; passengers looked down on the countryside they were crossing through ports rather than windows and engineers periodically checked the bilges. My informant did not know whether the cockpit was called the bridge or something else.

It was daylight when we put down at Kano, the last stop before Lagos and the first place I saw in Nigeria. The ground below seemed nothing but sand or scrub as we banked steeply to line up on the runway. When the door was opened to let passengers disembark your entire person was assailed by a blast of dry heat like the draught on sun-reddened knees from the outside of hot air extractors when you walked past them on a ship. We got down from the plane at Ikeja Airport, Lagos, and filed into the terminal building. Gone was the dry heat. Now it was a heat that nearly drowned you and left you struggling to fill your lungs with fresh air that wasn't there. It recalled my time in the Far East a few years earlier, only this was stickier.

The drive in from the airport was a blur of tumbling sensations; a mass of bicycles that ensured car drivers drove nearer to the middle of the road than I had been accustomed to. One cyclist, complete with what I took to be local headgear, was pedalling with his heels and holding aloft an umbrella as a parasol while guiding his bike with his free hand, his robes flowing behind him in the slight breeze he was creating. Another, who obviously did not feel it necessary to protect himself from the sun at that particular time, rode with his folded umbrella hooked over his shoulder by the handle and hanging down his back.

Houses were squeezed into all kinds of chaotic patterns emphasised by the outlines of their corrugated iron roofs and highlighted by the reflections from the newer roofs among them; there were lorries with slogans painted on them; an unprepossessing building with a notice 'Safebirth Nursing Home' affixed; a roadside grave with what seemed to be a memorial stone and effigy of the deceased; the erectness of the women and the gracefulness of their bearing as they moved easily with their loads on their heads; the predominantly blue colours of the clothing worn by people as they weaved their way in and out of the heaving throng; the sealing wax palms pointed out to me in

6

the grounds of Government House with their distinctive red hue at the crown of the trunk; the deep open drains and the new and different smells that wafted through the open car windows. Then came my immediate goal, the Catering Rest House. The very name sounded exotic.

CHAPTER 2

Lagos and the Produce Scene

I started as a Produce Officer in the Department of Marketing and Exports and spent a short time on the Lagos 'beaches'- this was the name given to the places where officially inspected produce was bought, examined and stored prior to shipment - the expression comes from earlier times when palm oil was bought on suitable stretches of sand in the creeks of the Niger delta. There I was introduced to the inspection and grading of produce for export like cocoa, palm kernels, groundnuts, rubber and capsicums under the experienced eye of D. I. Nosiri, one of the first Africans of the Junior Service to be promoted to a senior appointment in the department some years before. Nothing escaped his keen eye and I learnt quickly under his direction. He took time to explain when I had difficulty in adjusting to his particular kind of Nigerian English, reading any confusion in my face rather than wait for the questions that might not come if I had, embarrassingly, to interrupt him too often to ask him to explain what he meant.

He regaled me with tales of his recent visit to England and his visit to a chocolate factory to see Nigerian cocoa being made into chocolate bars and his discussions with the factory management on how the quality of chocolate was determined by the quality of the cocoa. He also mentioned with pleasure a visit in Cheshire to the home of the mother of a colleague, Ted Clunies-Ross. By way of explanation he admitted to certain fears of how he would be received in England and how these had been dissipated by the warmth of his reception. I did wonder if everyone would be as friendly as I had already had some indications to the contrary.

These reminiscences were thrown in between bouts of explanation about rules for the storage of cocoa that had to be implemented and how it was to be transported from store to ship and vice-versa. He emphasised the need to ensure weights as well as quality were correct and introduced me to the local Licensed Buying Agents of the Boards and their buyers. He talked about and showed me examples of fully fermented, slatey, mouldy, weevily and germinated beans and how they might have got into that state like being harvested too early or too late or not having undergone the proper process of fermentation. He explained the processes and problems of grading and considered I had something to learn about suspecting people instead of just inspecting produce.

There was little doubt he had acquired a nose for the unusual and unlikely and seemed to be able to go straight to the heart of a difficulty. I remember seeing him draw a sample of cocoa from a bag of cocoa with his scoop, take another from a different part of the bag and instruct that it should be removed from the stack. When he examined it closely, he found the stitching and seal had been interfered with and the contents had been adulterated. That meant that that particular parcel, as the bags of that particular consignment were referred to, was suspect and would have to be 'turned down', that is, emptied on a tarpaulin on the ground for inspection. It was an action I would myself repeat when we were joined some years later in Lagos by a newly appointed officer.

The beaches were areas close to the shore with land on which produce could be dried, cleaned, mixed, examined, bagged, weighed, sealed and stored and were convenient to land and/or seaborne transport. I developed a callouse on the finger which I put pressure on to cut the cocoa beans with a knife I bought in the market. It was to remain with me for years. Simultaneously, I was introduced to the Produce Inpection Ordinance and the Produce Inspection Regulations made under it which I was later to have an intimate knowledge of. I was quite amazed at the authority which was being invested in the likes of me. I would have the power to license premises as suitable for inspection; to enter premises, search and seize produce or potential evidence without individual warrants where there had been a suspected breach of the regulations; to require persons to furnish information deemed necessary and to convey produce to a designated place for examination. I would also have the authority, indeed the requirement, to prosecute in cases of contravention of the regulations.

The process of learning the nuts and bolts of inspection was somewhat repetitive and boring if you did not or could not see it in an overall context. It was, however, a necessary beginning to what was to become a fascinating job. More diverting for the moment was the office in which I was based in Alakoro Square in the teeming heart of the open air markets within sight of the waterside and the Carter Bridge that connected Lagos island to the mainland. It was all unfamiliar sights and activities and sounds and smells that assailed the awareness and kept up a constant stream of new and exciting experiences that generated a further feeling of expectation.

This was a city which less than one hundred years earlier had been the most notorious of all the slaving ports even after many attempts by ships of the British West Africa squadron to suppress the actions of Portuguese and Brazilian slave ships and the warring Lagos kings who were slaving intermediaries and able frustrators of abolition. Due to its key position in the continuing slave trade which was inhibiting the growth of commerce in the region, the British government annexed the territory in 1861 and declared it a colony the following year - it was a period when Britain, at the height of its imperial glory linked the commercial and the moral. This was manifested in the phrase 'philanthropy plus five per cent' in the words of the arch-imperialist Cecil Rhodes who could not assimilate the fact that the early missionaries saw the economic improvement of people as an article of their faith and a necessary concomitant to the willingness of these people to embrace Christianity.

Lagos' boundaries were later extended to east and west and, during my time there, Lagos and Colony was still a distinct administrative unit. As a result of this, government was established in Lagos which was in due course to become the first city in Nigeria and its first capital. At the same time it became increasingly a prime centre for trade and eventually received resources for the development of its infrastructure which included

10

the clearing of the bar to make it the premier port of the region by the end of the First World War, the building of a railway to the interior which assured its commercial future, the construction of the Carter Bridge which gave it access to the mainland by road and latterly an international airport.

Lagos pulsates and hammers at the senses. Various activities take place in relatively confined surroundings. People squeeze through the throng to examine wares on offer in the market place or to get to neighbouring stalls all cheek by jowl, while others seem to be pressing in directions that take them away from the markets towards the canoe ferries and the notices saying *obinrin/okunrin* - the lavatories for men and women built out over the creek - towards the side streets and the cooked food purveyors frying meat and vegetable offerings in palm oil, dodging the *omalankes,* the ubiquitous two-wheeled handcarts propelled by their sweating owners who braved the frenetic honking of the lorries and the ringing of bells by the cyclists as they sought to negotiate the chaos with their loads intact. All this against a background of stallholders carrying on multiple conversations simultaneously, strident voices extolling their wares, making offers, uttering imprecations, giving warnings and exchanging greetings.

At first, I felt that these exchanges were aggressive but quickly realised that they were not unlike a conversation in Glasgow, Scotland or Alexandria, Egypt. The sounds at first thought to be aggressive are often succeeded by peals of laughter and indicate a habit of talking loudly or having a naturally abrasive-sounding manner of speaking to ears more accustomed to softer cadences, rather than hostile intent. I was reminded of the annual sheep sales in my home town when shepherds from the remoter parts would meet perhaps for the first time since the previous year's sale and carry on conversations across the road oblivious to the people passing by.

The trading is dominated by Yoruba women - the market mammies - who give more in return than they get from demands and taunts of would-be buyers. They always seem to have the last word. Despite the fact that they are clothed in traditional blue *lappas* (the cloth they wrap round their waists and sometimes given the name of 'tie-ties' from the action needed to secure them) and *bubas* (blouses) and big, colourful headties twisted in a knot at the back and with the ends sticking out like big, Minnie Mouse ears, they still manage to stand out from others similarly dressed. It isn't only their repartee. There is an imperiousness, a presence about them that is forbidding. It reminded me of the cartoon in the Weekly News of the school for conductresses with the severe-looking trainer (like the clippie on the 23 tram when I was at university) who took her class under a banner bearing the motto '*Nae impiddens*'- no cheek. The occasional flash of bright colour of the clothes of women who originated from parts of Nigeria other than the Yoruba-dominated lands provided a vivid mixture of tones. And men too, for the odd Hausa from the north stood out because he was usually taller than his southern neighbours and wore lustrous robes and a white turban in simple yet startling contrast to the subdued colours of the clothes, based on indigo dyes, of the locals.

The variety extended to the stalls themselves. Cowpeas and purple egg plants in the food stalls were set off by the red capsicums and the green plantains. Next door would be the witch doctor and his juju objects for the more drastic diseases. These offerings included antlers of the duiker, West Africa's smallest deer with Bambi-like qualities when alive, yellowing animal skulls, fruit-bat wings, bundles of feathers and, hung up on a string, as a fertility fetish a colleague and relatively old hand on the Coast informed me, a bunch of monkey penises that had taken on a sharny-green hue. Then the herbalist with his roots, leaves, and lumps of chalk, who claimed that all his wares had medicinal properties, and the women selling cosmetics to other women that looked like a collection of powders which they used, I was told, to highlight their skin and the eyes. African women usually have very beautiful eyes, something I noticed from the first day; I was surprised they felt the need of cosmetics to enhance their appearance in that respect. Adjacent to these would be the market woman selling her cloths and threads and another tempting shoppers with her pottery wares.

The smells were forever changing. One moment it would be the pungent aroma of the spices on sale or the heady one of the ripe mangoes, the next the less salubrious ones emanating from the open drains. As you moved away from the markets and into the side streets the signs of squalor became more marked. The smells were now predominantly of the sewer variety. Yet the feeling of vibrant activity and bustle was still there; people talking and laughing, an important activity obviously from the number of groups indulging in it; youngsters playing table tennis between the houses with a piece of coloured cloth as the net and empty boxes as the support for the piece of wood that passed for the table; the peals of laughter that followed the description to a group of some funny incident; the businessman rushing with his brief case from the mud house to his Humber Hawk left parked outside; the barber boasting of his superior 'Sami Cuts' and the mother haranguing her disobedient child. Never in the eight years I was to spend in Nigeria would I see a parent strike a child.

At the other end of the spectrum were the shops on the Marina, at that time the principal shopping area for the better heeled. It was up-market and contained stores with names like Kingsway Stores, A.G.Leventis, G.B.Ollivant, Gottschalk's and Union Trading Company. Into these stores went expatriate Europeans, senior African officials and businessmen, and anybody else who had the kind of income to pay the prices asked or not as the case might be. It was relatively close to Ikoyi, an island just off the larger island of Lagos and connected by bridge, where the lowest density housing was and where the majority of government officers and commercial executives lived. As its name suggests, the Marina gave on to the Lagos lagoon where ships occasionally moored and were unloaded and loaded from or on to lighters or by lorry at the limited docking space. But most of the vessels moored at the Apapa wharves on the other side on the mainland which had the latest facilities for lifting, storing, weighing and handling goods to give the speedy turn-round needed in a busy and successful port.

The newcomer to Nigeria very soon learned that certain words occur with a surprising frequency. 'Dash' is a word that comes to Nigerian pidgin possibly by courtesy of the Portuguese ('das' meaning 'Are you giving?') who were the first to attempt to navigate and explore the west coast of Africa giving us place names like Lagos (after the Portuguese port), Forcados after the river so named (river of the swallow tail) and Escravos (river of the slaves). 'Dash' is variously translated as a gratuity or a bribe. In the early days of the Guinea trade, commercial activity was dominated by the Portuguese and a prior form 'dashee' was used right down the Guinea Coast from Cape Verde to Gabon to mean a customary present made to an African chief negotiator before trading began.

The newly arrived expatriate in Nigeria would be confronted by wide-eyed children who would ask him to give them something. 'Oyibo (white man), dash me' they would say. A response to this could be 'Why I dash you? If the answer is 'because you get plenty money', then the action to take is to pass it off with a light remark like 'I no be big master' and smile. This is usually rewarded by a smile which acknowledges that he or she has tried it on and you both share the joke. If on the other hand he says 'I look after your car while you go for Kingsway (Stores)' there is a reciprocity intended that merits the token payment made (before the performance of the implied contract). This trust ensured he would be on hand when you returned hoping he had started a long term relationship to your mutual benefit.

Lagos is an outpost of the Yoruba heartland which is in south-west Nigeria. The Yorubas are the sophisticates of Nigeria and comprise the largest single group of people in that corner of the country. The provinces of Kabba and Ilorin in Northern Nigeria had a majority of Yorubas and were a potential problem between Yorubas and the Hausas from the North. There are other tribes in the south-west but the Yoruba are dominant. They have had contact with Europe since the late 15th century when the Portuguese were exploring the Gulf of Guinea and penetrating up-country from the Bight of Benin. This kingdom, of uncertain origin and of complex organisation, is dominated by a powerful king, the Oni of Ife. Legend has it that the Yoruba migrated from the north and the north-west, probably around the beginning of the 13th century. The Oni is the spiritual as well as the titular head of the kingdom. The present Oni was in fact a member of the Cocoa Marketing Board and a director of the Nigeria Produce Marketing Company in London. In his spiritual capacity people saw him as responsible for the regulation of the supply of rainfall in his kingdom.

The history of the Yoruba people is bound up inextricably with the trade in human beings destined for the sugar fields of the West Indies and South America in which they were the slave masters supreme. The Yoruba kingdom came easily within the influence of the government set up in Lagos because of endemic wars within it which sprang from the unequal distribution of the wealth derived from slavery. In more recent times, they had created a buoyant economy built on the cultivation of cocoa, the good lands for growing cocoa, namely a clayey loam, deep earth to accommodate the cocoa tree's need to put down a long tap root and a well drained but not too acid soil, being largely co-extensive with the Yoruba territory. Their economic well-being was assisted by the work of the women in planting, tending and harvesting food crops and this gave them a standard of living in advance of anywhere else in Nigeria.

One of the people I met in investigating my new milieu was Jock Brunton. Jock was an old hand on the Coast. He was on the point of retirement and I was among the newest and youngest of the recruits. Highly regarded by all those who knew him, he was a fund of information on the Nigeria that was and an unsurpassed raconteur. In one evening of conviviality he asked myself and a recent recruit to the administrative service if we had seen the dip in the Carter Bridge. Of course we had. You couldn't miss it. He had worked on the construction of the bridge which was of some importance in that it was the first road connection between the island of Lagos and the mainland. It was Christmas Eve and they had been busy driving in piles. They were anxious to finish when the last piles were found to be too short. 'Screw them back' was the instruction given. The construction team screwed back the piles until the tops were level with the others and there they stayed. As the bed of the water was China clay, the hole did not fill in and over the years the piles gradually sank into the Iddo Pool under the weight of traffic, leaving the dip which characterised the bridge. It was something Jock would be unlikely to forget in his years of retirement in Dollar.

CHAPTER 3

Saturday Lunch

It was a ritual in Lagos and in the parts I was to live in later and held a fascination for me in these first days. People took it in turns to have others in for lunch on Saturdays. Sometimes it was people from the department or company but most often it was a gathering of friends who finished work about half past twelve and arrived dressed in their working clothes which was a sleeveless dress for women and for men shorts or longs and ties which our hosts might invite us to take off, and of course the knee hose in white or khaki if you wore shorts. When it was your turn to host a lunch it was at first a source of amazement where all the chairs and indeed glasses came from until you realised in due course that they had been borrowed by the stewards from the stewards of the houses of the guests or neighbours. If as a guest you returned home quickly you might find only one chair if you were a bachelor. If you had half an hour on the bed you would return to a room which had recovered its quota.

Hints were given in official publications to people coming out to the coast whether as a government official or a commercial executive (a word with pejorative associations in these days - slick/pretentious, probably fed off the prejudices of some senior officers against those involved in commercial activity), on what you should do to maintain a healthy life style. You were advised to drink eight to eleven pints of liquid a day - and the water wasn't drinkable. Even if it had been boiled and filtered it tasted awful unless laced with something strong.

It was as well that it was possible to buy a crate of Heineken or Amstel or St Pauli Girl at the local store. Later Heineken would set up a brewery in Lagos and introduce Star beer on the market. Star beer quickly became identified with Nigeria and was sometimes referred to by locals as OHMS ('our home made stuff', an acronym originally given to palm wine) and was a good seller in the stores. The up-country store, called a canteen in earlier times and still so-called in smaller stations, was a corrugated iron shed where cold storage did not exist. In the bigger towns like Lagos the stores resembled a West European department store with Kingsway Stores on the Marina based on Selfridges in London. Star was a pretty good drink if you were thirsty or even if you weren't. Coca Cola was supplied by vendors in the city from small two-wheeled hand carts or from fixed ice-boxes and it could also be bought unchilled in the canteens. The vendors of it sold more Coke than all the other brands because it had been chilled rather than for any distinctive taste it had or indeed any addictive properties, certainly to begin with.

Lunch was preceded by a choice of drinks. Best groundnuts or roasted egúsi (melon seeds) were an accompaniment to the drinks. Some old coasters and their wives stuck to gin which suggested it was a 'safe' drink. Women who took it regularly developed a deep, husky 'gin' voice which suggested it might be doing something to their vocal chords or perhaps even their sex hormones. Never were so many women like the actress Glynis Johns with her dry, throaty yet attractive voice. It was occasionally taken as a long drink with water which in the town of my upbringing was the hallmark of established 'drouths' (persons always ready for the drink).

Water, boiled and filtered, was added to a number of drinks and was poured for some obscure reason from an empty Gordon's gin bottle. The bottle was a clear one (there was, and still is, a bottle green one) and presumably so because it revealed that the water itself was clear with no apparent impurities. Beer was also popular not least because it provided the necessary medically recommended liquid intake and was no great hardship to force down. I quickly learned that drinks and food were not 'served', they were 'passed'. My inside smile nearly burst when I first heard a host ask a servant to 'pass water'.

All this was but a prelude to what was to come. Once the throats had been lubricated, and the conversations cut off and new ones initiated by the call to table, we would sit down to await the palm oil chop. *Chop* was the word given to food in general and was also used as a verb in the sense of 'to eat'. Sometimes the 'chop' was dropped altogether and the traditional Saturday lunch was referred to as a 'palm oil'. Being a staple of the region, it was of the highest quality.

A steaming dish of rice would be brought in and placed on the table. It was not the basmati rice beloved of present day afficionados but the standard round ('pudden') rice, preferably unpolished, which is so difficult to drain without the grains clogging together. One old coaster advised on the best way to prevent this happening. That was for the cook to put the boiled and washed rice in a linen pillowslip and swing it round his head vigorously until the centrifugal effect had the desired result leaving nice fluffy servings with every grain separate. Health buffs, even then, got to hear about unhulled rice and it was possible to get this in some postings. Before serving yourself with rice it was customary to apply a liberal serving-spoonful of mango chutney to the middle of the plate. The rice was then piled on top and made into a bed by tapping it with the back of a spoon. It was then in a proper state to receive the palm oil chop.

The meat could be beef or poultry or goat cooked in palm oil with seasonable vegetables like okra, garden eggs (aubergines) and gbúre and was taken round the table by the steward himself. If the number seated was large he was assisted by his 'small boy' who would also bear a dish of the chop. Guests helped themselves to as much as they felt they wanted and then set to on the twenty or so side dishes or sambals without which the palm oil chop would have lost much of its distinctiveness. These consisted of items sprinkled on the meat and vegetables in palm oil like ground peppers, grated copra (sun-dried coconut), ground capsicums, fried plantain, tomato, 'fufu' made from the root of the cassava plant, chopped groundnuts and stockfish.

This last was a prized Norwegian import of dried cod which we took in powdered form and was invariably referred to as 'stinkfish'. It was prized as a distinctive delicacy by Africans and Europeans alike. 'Fine pass stinkfish' was an expression I was to hear from time to time, spoken with a smile, meaning excellent. One consignment was held up in the roads for a number of weeks while the ship carrying it was waiting for a berth at Apapa, the port of Lagos, and the shipment went bad. The ship's master was required by the health authorities to dump the cargo in the water. For days afterwards dead eels were washed up on the shore but no one could prove a direct connection.

Each person mixed the sambals according to his/her taste and finished off what was always a substantial meal. It was said that you didn't really begin to enjoy a palm oil until the sweat was nipping your eyes. A Scots neighbour referred to it as a 'pilaff' meaning it would be more comfortable to strip off the outer garments. After all the spicy additives the palm oil had to be followed by something that cleaned the mouth. This was almost invariably a fresh fruit salad. It brought people back from the culinary high to which they had been exposed and prepared them for returning home. It is interesting to note in passing that similar spices, but with a greater concentration, were taken internally by Nigerians and some Europeans for chest and throat complaints.

It is interesting, too, to note that sambals is a Malayan word and reflects the transferability of members of the old Colonial Service who brought with them the practices and expressions they had become accustomed to in their earlier postings and this at a time when such crossing of taste barriers was not a commonplace. Today with globalisation of business and particularly the food business, this is usual except that much of the unique taste gets lost in the transfer - there is nowhere less appetising than the international hotel restaurant boasting a so-called international menu. The people transferability is reflected in a story told of the two old colonial servants, one from the Audit Department and another from the Forestry Department who met at the Saturday lunch in the house of a third.

'Haven't we met before ?' asked the first.

'Yes, I am sure we have.' said the second. 'Could it have been in Tanganyika in '48?'

'No' was the answer, 'I left there in '47'.

'In Sierra Leone in '50?'

'No I haven't been to Sierra Leone' the other responded.

'Aden in 49 perhaps?' the first suggested. The second shook his head.

'No. I think I remember now. It was in your office at eight o'clock this morning'.

CHAPTER 4

The Pyramids

I have never been to see the Sphinx or the pyramids of Egypt. The size of the pyramids is conveyed well in photographs which show them dwarfing everything around. But you didn't need to go to Egypt for pyramids. They existed in Kano in Northern Nigeria which I had the good fortune to visit in my official capacity during my induction period in Lagos.

Kano is a town very different from the bustling cities of the south of the country. As Geraldine Illes, the daughter of very good friends, said when she saw it on her very first visit 'It's just like the pictures in the Bible'. It is in a general sense. It is also very different. A walled city, albeit crumbling round the perimeter, a process initiated by Sir Frederick Lugard's artillery when he, as High Commissioner for the Protectorate of Northern Nigeria, sent out to take over the Royal Niger Company's sphere when its royal charter was revoked, ordered the shelling of the city as an early step in the subjugation of the Hausas. Its narrow streets snaked across the place seemingly dominated by the water spouts and what looked like battlements topped by decorative upward-pointing fingers rather like the pricked ears of a German shepherd dog.

The walls of the older houses were made of red clay decorated in geometric designs. More modern concrete ones imitated the old style as did more recent ones with mud walls with the decorative work carried out on the cement rendering. Men and women enveloped in robes went about their daily business, their heads covered and their faces too in the case of the women. The muezzin calling the faithful to prayer from his dark tower denoted the prevailing religion and the impressive mosque built by the Public Works Department emphasised its importance. The desert and camels are not far away and you could occasionally get a glimpse of a Bedouin in his distinctive blue gear shyly shopping in the markets and stores. Rocksalt in from the desert and Cadbury's chocolate out.

The Hausa/Fulani are the most numerous of the main ethnic groups having about half of the population of Nigeria. Included in this number are the Bornu and the Nupe and some other minor tribes like the Tiv with whom they live in a tight symbiosis. They have a mutually beneficial partnership, not least the feeling of strength in unity in face of a very different and sometimes seemingly threatening culture in the south of the country. The Hausas are an urban people, their capital Kano being a city of some sophistication. Descended from great centralised monarchies, they are staunchly Muslim. They had not always been so religious. The Hausa rulers had fallen into excesses of good living and were brought back early in the 19th century into the fold of good Muslims after Osman Dan Fodio, of the pastoral Fulani people, overcame them and reintroduced a strict observance of the faith. He set up the Emirs whose descendants were now dominant in the North.

The chiefs there exercised a very considerable authority and had not been noted in the past for giving encouragement to education of ordinary Hausas outside the extended family. As a result, they had come to rely on the more educated Ibos and to a lesser extent the Yorubas to perform the jobs associated with government and with technology. This resulted in townships being built on the fringes of the northern cities, the *sabon gari*, to accommodate the principally Ibo southerners who were more literate but were also *Kafirs* or unbelievers, and on whose literacy and entrepreneurial flair they had come to rely.

Pyramids would not have been out of place here. And there they were. Just outside the city of Kano were vast pyramids dominating the surrounding landscape. But no latterday Carter would enter them to get them to give up their secrets. They consisted of 15,000 tons of bagged groundnuts each. These large pyramids were the output of many thousands of farmers and had been harvested over a relatively short time. They came not only from Nigeria but also from the neighbouring French territories where they are called *arachides,* a word as familiar to some local traders as the English word.

If the price was higher in Nigeria than on their own side of the border, some of the groundnut crop came to the Nigerian side. If the price was lower, some of the groundnuts went the other way. The boundaries between Nigeria and the French colonies of Niger, Dahomey and of Chad and Cameroun were permeable ones, largely because they were artificial in the first place, being fixed by prior claim and by negotiation rather than by any political or cultural analysis. Nigeria and Senegal, in roughly equal proportions, exported the lion's share of the world's exports of groundnuts in the 1950s, Senegal just having the edge.

An annual meeting took place between officials of the two territories responsible for control of prices, held alternately on the French and British sides of the line that divided them. It took place to ensure if possible that there was relative parity of price so that orderly marketing could take place and stability ensue. It was my knowledge of French that got me on to the trip to Kano while still on my initial training in Lagos working in my marketing capacity on what was called the 'groundnut schedule'. The nuts were stored here to await evacuation to the ports of the south, principally Lagos, but also in some quantities to Port Harcourt.

The line was a single track, nearly 800 miles in length and the rolling stock limited. The evacuation of over 800,000 tons in a year was a daunting business which meant holding vast stocks of groundnuts in these pyramids in Kano, sometimes longer than was desirable from the Produce Inspection viewpoint. Significant consignments, although small by comparison, came down the Benue and the Niger by riverboats belonging to UAC Transport or John Holt Transport to Warri where they were transshipped to ocean-going vessels direct or by way of the stores in which they were kept awaiting shipment overseas.

This meant that precautions had to be taken against deterioration in stocks which could affect the price on the terminal markets or if it was bad enough, could result in no demand for the groundnuts. Consequently, the bags containing the nuts were stored on sisalkraft made in Nigeria and precautions taken to protect them from the ruinous harmattan winds coming down from the desert. Only a damage limitation exercise could be carried out. The answer was to get them shipped as soon as possible.

A second hazard was damage from weevils as a result of infestation. This was limited by sheeting the affected consignments in smaller pyramids of about 300 tons, folding in the sheets to ensure the fumigant to be applied to them didn't escape and fumigating the lot. Urgent telegrams would be sent to the headquarters of the Marketing Board in Lagos advising that cold harmattan winds were causing untold damage to stocks, and soliciting the assistance of those in authority to get the railways to increase their efforts to evacuate them.

The very best groundnuts were the Bornu hand-decorticated ones. If marketed in countries like the UK they could have commanded a premium price that was commensurate with the effort in removing the shells. Had the Groundnut Marketing Board not existed, then a private firm or firms might have identified a market segment worth exploiting. There was no advertising telling of the healthful qualities of groundnuts and particularly of groundnut oil as a cooking medium. Like extra virgin olive oil it passes with credit the cholesterol test. In the Sunday groundnut stew it was the basic medium the meat was cooked in.

Nuts were served to accompany drinks at most times and, delight of delights, they were used to make a soup most nights of the week. It was accompanied by sherry or gin peppers. The peppers, capsicums, or Nigerian Birdseye Chillies as they were known variously or officially, were put in the bottom of a bottle containing sherry or gin and left for a few weeks until the combination of the hot spice and the alcohol reached an optimum taste and sharpness. It was then ready to shake on to the soup.

Able Baker, an engineer in the Public Works Department, told the story of when he was working in Onitsha and staying in the Catering Rest House there, he had his own bottle of sherry peppers which was placed on his table at lunch and dinner. A visitor from the United Kingdom leaned across AB's table and snatched the bottle and applied a liberal dose to his dish - and nearly choked. When the visitor had recovered from his paroxysm AB said to him 'Maybe that'll teach you to say "by your leave" next time'.

CHAPTER 5

Lagos Still

After my induction to the grading and inspection of produce and prior to my visit to Kano, I was transferred temporarily to headquarters of the Department of Marketing and Exports in Lagos. The Department was divided into three sections: the Produce Inspection Service transferred from the Department of Agriculture in 1948 when it was set up with its own Produce Inspection Board and underpinning legislation; it was self-contained and easily transferable as would be seen again in four or five years' time. There was a Marketing Division responsible for administering the produce schemes and for commercial relationships with licensed buying agents of the board, and a Shipping Division responsible for storage at the ports and for getting the produce from the ports to the overseas destinations.

My stint at headquarters was to get to know the work involved in the marketing of produce. At that time the jobs of Marketing Officer and Produce Officer were interchangeable, the knowledge of both jobs being seen as a required background for officers performing either function. It was during this attachment that I went to Kano. I was asked if I would like to continue working in the Marketing Division but declined as I was sure I would prefer the outside work. I hadn't come to Nigeria to spend all my time sat behind a desk. I was to have no regrets.

The boards were set up to give a stable environment for farmers who until then had been subject to the vagaries of a volatile market and did not possess the resources to cope with a severe downturn in price. There was therefore a cushioning effect if the market price dropped because the boards accumulated surpluses when revenues were high and released some of them as price support when they fell. This process was assisted by a long-term bull market which saw produce prices increase steadily and vast surpluses accumulate. At the same time there was a need to maintain and improve quality to cope with an increasingly demanding and competitive market, particularly the competition from the neighbouring French and Belgian territories where mammoth, efficient plantations preducing palm oil and rubber, and to a certain extent cocoa, were encouraged at the expense of the traditional social organisation. There was also increasing competition from Asian countries.

The boards financed research institutes to improve the practice of husbandry and the quality of crops and their storage within Nigeria - the West African Stored Products Research Unit and the West African Institute for Oil Palm Research were financed jointly with the Gold Coast (to be known as Ghana in a few years time). They also established production units to process peasant crops more efficiently. Add to this the development of high yield strains giving six to seven times the oil content, free distribution of seedlings by the Department of Agriculture and the export potential can be imagined. By such means the boards intended to preserve peasant production and existing social structures and simultaneously ensure the ability of Nigeria to compete with other countries in the world commodity markets

Away from the hurly-burly of downtown Lagos, I began to have space to look around rather than just experience sensations. Space to read the papers and take note of the what was happening, not to pass judgments at this stage I kept telling myself. I remember being initially appalled at the apparently seditious stance taken up by Dr Nnamdi Azikiwe ('Zik'), leader of the Ibo-dominated National Council for Nigeria and the Cameroons and his paper the *West African Pilot*. I vaguely resented the anti-European stance reflected in every issue and found that new entrants like myself had that kind of initial reaction.

Those of us who joined at that time had come, in the summer of 1951, with a kind of post-war idealism and the possibility of a worthwhile career helping Nigeria forward into the autonomous and prosperous future British governments had envisaged for it for a long time. At the same time, it was difficult to conceive of myself as a young, educated Nigerian like Joe Beckley, my fellow student at university, who would not want a say in the running of his country and who would not resent the presence of foreign rulers even if their declared intention was to grant eventual autonomy to the people. But this constant vituperation from the press was something we had not expected. If we had known to ask Yorubas about the *West African Pilot*, they would have told us that they too came under the fire of Zik's editors and that the paper was pro-Ibo and against the rest. Fortunately, all Nigerians were not like the impression formed of them from the papers which were responding politically on behalf of a group of educated and politically motivated persons who felt there was no other way to further their views as the ballot box did not meet their aspirations.

There was, however, a small core of educated Africans whose antipathy to the white races compelled them to ignore Europeans when they met or who went out of their way to be rude. I remembered Andrew Young's advice to be in control always despite provocations and resisted the temptation, if not to plant one on them when they became intolerable, certainly not to inflame the situation by saying something cutting. It was easier to take this kind of behaviour from clerks in the post office or from people in humble posts who did not know any better.

The very different backgrounds of the Hausa/Fulani who inhabited large swathes of the north, the Yoruba who lived in the south-west and the Ibo who predominantly populated the south-east of the country, and the three-way suspicions these differences engendered, provided problems of cohesion. As I arrived, a new constitution was being implemented after long consultation with interest groups. The Macpherson constitution was aimed at preserving the unity of the country. A House of Representatives was set up at the centre with the members from the more populous North being exactly balanced by the combined numbers from the East and the West together with a Council of Ministers comprising 6 officials and 12 Africans. This was the first time the North had been represented at the centre.

Regional Assemblies, previously advisory bodies, were now enlarged and given legislative and financial powers over a considerable range of subjects. It was they who chose representatives from their ranks to look after their interests in the House of Representatives. This house could reject any legislation passed by the Assemblies. The Governor retained reserve powers. Dr Azikiwe of the NCNC chose to stand for one of the Lagos seats and was returned to the Western House of Assembly. Traditional chiefs and British-trained lawyers were no longer acceptable to his party as representatives of the people even though they were black; nor would institutions be acknowledged as democratic because of the colour of the skin of those occupying parliamentary benches. They wanted nothing less than the immediate removal of colonial rule. Any means of tarnishing the British reputation in the eyes of as yet non-aligned fellow Nigerians was considered a legitimate tactic in pursuing this end. As I came to know some of the people embracing this philosophy, I realised that the press action was not a personal one and that some of the adherents to their viewpoint were quite charming people.

I discovered that Badagri, a drive of just a few hours or so west of Lagos, had been one of the main ports in the time of the slave trade. It was the place Richard Lander had returned to after his trek with Hugh Clapperton on his journey of exploration from the West African coast to Sokoto in the desert region of what is now Northern Nigeria. Clapperton, a native of Annan in Dumfriesshire had earlier crossed from the North African coast to Lake Chad which washes the shore of what is now north-east Nigeria. So he was the first European to cross the African continent. He died of fever in Sokoto in 1828 and was buried by Lander, his servant, who showed himself to be a man of mettle by assuming control and returning to Badagri against all the odds.

He appealed for assistance to the captains of Portuguese slave ships stood by to receive slaves from the barracoons or fenced depots where the slaves were assembled. But for his pains they put out the rumour that he was a spy and within hours he was hauled before Adele, King of Badagri, where he was sentenced to drink a draught made from sasswood bark, a poison from which no one had recovered for a number of years. Dressed in his best for the occasion he swallowed the poison and made his way back dizzily to his hut where he took an emetic when nobody was looking and vomited up the poison. This was proof to his judges that he had not come with evil intentions and from then on he was supplied with all he needed until he was able to board a British ship, but not before he saw what might have been his fate. That was the sight of the fetish tree where the bodies of the less fortunate victims of the trial by ordeal were hung after their hearts had been eaten by the king.

Lander was to return to Badagri with his brother from his native Cornwall two years later in a successful attempt to prove conclusively that the Niger flowed into the Bight of Benin and not into Lake Chad or the Nile as people had earlier believed. He followed the route he had taken with Clapperton and returned down the Niger by canoe to Brass in the Niger Delta, braving all sorts of hazards on the way. He it was who heralded the possibility of water communication on the Niger and its tributaries and the water-borne trade that would follow. In the process he discovered the remains of an earlier intrepid explorer, Mungo Park, at Bussa on the Niger. Like Park, he himself had a violent death on the river. Park is commemorated suitably in his native Selkirk.

Badagri was at the end of one of the slave routes to the coast from the north of the Yoruba country. Surprisingly, there is still evidence of the slave barracoons from where slaves were sent in earlier times during the early period of Portuguese maritime dominance in the 15th and 16th centuries, initially to Portugal and later to what is now Ghana. There the gold mining Akan tribes preferred, or even insisted on, receiving part of the price of their gold in slaves and the Portuguese operating out of their base on the island of São Tome obliged as did British, French, Dutch, Danish, Brazilian, American and Swedish slavers two centuries later. By then the Americas were the destination of West African slaves in a triangular trade whereby ships from European ports took goods to West Africa to exchange for slaves who were carried across the Atlantic and sold for cash. With this money they purchased cargoes of sugar and molasses, cotton, rum and tobacco and loaded them for eventual sale in Europe after disposal had been made of the human cargo.

Gold was the lure of the early explorers. The Company of Scotland, fated to be ruined by the promotion of the Darien Scheme, did make one journey to West Africa returning at the turn of the 18th century with a cargo of the precious metal out of which the Darien *pistoles* were made – the last gold coins struck in the old Scottish Mint. The Guinea Coast gave its name to the *Gulf of Guinea*, to the English *guinea coin* (21 shillings or £1.05) and later to the slave ships or *guineamen* that plied their trade in human beings with the willing compliance of local chiefs for whom slavery was part of the economic system, as well as to *guinea-corn* or local millet, *guinea-worm,* a parasite which causes filaria, a most painful condition, and *guinea-fowl*, or '*dinda bird*' in pidgin English, which was a good source of food in the bush.

The children of the Badagri area knew the sad history of the slaves and showed the infrequent visitor to their town the manacles and chains used to restrain them, totally ignoring the fact that the Badagrians at the time of Lander ran five slave 'factories' and were hard taskmasters while awaiting the arrival of the Portuguese slave ships.

These youngsters would pose for photographs unasked and would wind chains round their wrists and ankles, one of them even holding aloft a branding iron which in the slaving days had been heated in wooden fires and dipped in palm oil so as not to stick to the skin. They assumed that the handful of visitors calling there in the course of a year would see them as the descendants of slaves when in all probability they were the descendants of the enslavers. It is an old ploy to play the victim when you want to be considered sympathetically. The enslaved people had been snatched from their homes by raiding parties and driven to Badagri on an infamous slave route from Ilorin.

Badagri spanned an area between British and French influence and had been a place where British traders from the oil rivers and French traders from Dahomey frequently interacted at the turn of the 20th century. Dahomey is now the Republic of Benin, a state which is not inclusive of the age-old city state of that name situated in Western Nigeria. It was given the designation of the ancient kingdom to dignify it although it included only a small portion of the medieval empire of Benin. The indigenous population of Benin City, known as the Edo or Bini people were indeed related to a relatively small number of people in the new state but had been cut off politically from them in the 'scramble for Africa'. It is close to Whydah or Ouidah in French, which was the equivalent of Badagri in the French colony and is immortalised in Bruce Chatwin's classic novel of the continuing Brazilian connection from the slave trade days, *The Viceroy of Ouidah*. Chatwin's story nicely leaves us to assume the arbitrary nature of the border between Dahomey and Nigeria and its permeability as the characters move easily from one country to another driven by their relationship to a Brazilian who had become the friend and blood brother of the mad king.

The space to look around applied equally to the social milieu in which I found myself. Another recently appointed colleague and I were invited to coffee and a drink after dinner by a senior colleague. We had coffee and a quick brandy. Then our host stood up, rubbed his hands and said 'Well, tomorrow is another day'. I have long admired the urbanity of some of my countrymen of a certain upbringing. I liked the way that they smiled and said 'I'm sorry?' when they didn't catch what you were saying, head half turned, eyebrows raised in question and an ear half inclined to catch your response, rather than the bald 'I beg your pardon?' or 'Could you say that again?' This particular person lacked that kind of graciousness. People who pride themselves in calling a spade a spade tend to become boors as they grow older. Thankfully, such people were the exception. I prefer to remember the others who were the epitome of hospitality. Particularly, I liked the custom in informal situations of handing you the open whisky bottle to help yourself. It had a symbolism that appealed to the sense of hospitality handed down to me by my parents.

The residential area of Ikoyi, where I was first accommodated in a non-catering rest house after a brief stay in the catering one, was of a very typical colonial design with the older houses being big with outside balconies and situated in large compounds. The newer houses were smaller but still with largish compounds. Some of the houses, and the better ones at that, were owned by the big companies who were responsible for the upkeep. Government quarters were the responsibility of the Public Works Department. Many of the new ministers from the House of Representatives, particularly the Northerners, declined to live there as there was not enough accommodation for their wives and retinue. They preferred to find more suitable quarters in the town.

An unexpected sight was the cutting of the grass in government-owned properties by prisoners from the local jail. One man would beat out an appropriate rhythm with his own cutlass and a piece of metal and the others would cut the grass with cutlasses more willingly as a result. They were even known to sing as they worked. The sole warder never seemed to have any trouble with them and the prisoners themselves were invariably well-behaved if understandably taciturn except when in song. It was said that many of them lived better in prison than outside. This gave rise to the tale that when two men lagged behind on the way back to prison, the warder called *'Run, quick quick or we go leff* (leave) *you-o'*. And the prisoners, fearful of being denied return to prison, complied at the double, calling out *'Makee no leff we, sah'* (Don't leave us, sir).

When I first arrived in Lagos I noted a particular facility for using the English language in a punchy way. Now I had time to view a poster which caught the eye. It advertised a coming attraction - *Grand Dance Yaba Rex Saturday Night* with the added injunction *No Knicker*. 'Knicker' is the name given to shorts as distinct from the dressier longs. So the Yaba Rex was trying to set standards. Once you started to think in the Nigerian way, such linguistic licence was not seen as such and was not so apparently funny.

When confronted by official English, my erstwhile staff tended to become flummoxed because they found the written language of the expatriate plus the civil-service-speak an unfamiliar medium. My very first disciplinary procedure was in Lagos where I was delegated at the instance of Daniel Nosiri, presumably to get me used to the idea, to call for the representations of a member of the junior staff as to why disciplinary action should not be taken against him for acting contrary to Standing Instructions. These were free interpretations to meet local needs of the general guidelines in Colonial Regulations and Financial Instructions as well as the Produce Inspection Ordinance and Regulations. Apart from having to acknowledge receipt of my missive by return, he had to submit his defence within 24 hours in quadruplicate - and that before the era of the photocopier.

So the longer his defence, and such defences were invariably long, the longer the agony of writing it three times more plus a copy for himself. Despite my short time in Lagos and my relative youth, he assured me I was his father and his mother and that I was already aware of his diligence. If he were condemned now I would perhaps be succeeded by someone 'who knew not Joseph'. For good measure he suggested that any punishment would be 'ultra vires (beyond your powers)'. The biblical reference, the appeal to the emotions and the embellished language are all devices that reinforce the spoken rather than the written word.

The legal tradition is prized in the south of Nigeria, legal expressions being used freely by people without training in the law. The parenthesis was probably an insurance against the contingency that I did not know the meaning of the phrase. If this was Nigeria, then it was getting to me through its capital and the people I was meeting there. The personal files of staff that came before me revealed to my amazement that before and during the war government officers had the authority to fine staff for misdemeanours, subject to approval by senior officers.

The nature of these happenings and those I was to experience in the future were largely shaped by events that started at a much earlier point in time and developed over the years. It is to these we now pass.

Part 2

Through a Century of Change to the Working Environment

CHAPTER 6

Jaja (1): The Produce Trade and Traditional Authority

The story of King Jaja of Opobo is a microcosm of developments in the world of palm oil production and distribution for export in the nineteenth century. Palm oil was by far the first of the commodity exports and gave the name of 'Oil Rivers' to the Niger delta. It was many years later followed by crops like cocoa and groundnuts from what was to become Nigeria. Jaja's life illustrates the tensions that arose between the white traders and African middlemen after centuries of working together amicably and how these interacted with the growing authority of the consuls overseeing the 'informal' empire, the sole legal legitimacy of which was based on an agreement signed by the European powers at the end of a conference in Berlin in 1885. Prior to that date individual powers had taken it on themselves to keep a watching brief on the interests of their traders in West Africa. The Berlin Conference agreed to areas of influence. Subsequent boundaries were the result of the ambitions of individuals and national groups, power plays and negotiation.

As a youth, Jaja, an Ibo by upbringing, was snatched by strangers and sold to the Aro, a tribe notorious for having an extensive network of alliances that enabled them to sell slaves along routes which they controlled. The Aro sold him on to new owners. He was bought by a trader from the royal canoe house at Bonny on the Imo River just east of the Niger Delta and connected to it by means of a series of creeks. A canoe house was a trading and fighting unit capable of manning and maintaining a war canoe. It was also a social and administrative system within a grouping of canoe houses that made up the so-called 'city states' of the eastern delta with names like Brass, Nembe, Bonny and Akassa. These grew and thrived in the era of the slave trade because they had an advantageous position near the sea-coast and possessed a good anchorage. By offering slaves the rights of the house and granting them advancement on the basis of individual merit subject to their giving their allegiance in return, they were readily integrated into the community. Each canoe house had rules for the behaviour of its members and was responsible for ensuring that the members met their obligations to the city state which might include supplying labour for a special project like erecting defences or serving when needed in the war canoe. A war canoe could contain up to 50 persons.

Jaja became a noted trader on behalf of his house while still a young man. He had the confidence of the head of the canoe house who recommended him to one of the European traders who in turn entrusted goods to him. The wealth of the area was founded on the 'trust' system. This was the practice by which the captain of a trading vessel, or a person designated as the manager of the enterprise, handed over goods to the local trader, usually a chief or the chief's nominee, on which prices had been fixed. In return the chiefs were expected to deliver quickly the value in slaves, or, after the abolition of slavery in British spheres of interest, palm oil to an equivalent value.

So successful was Jaja that no one was surprised that he was offered the headship of the Annie Pepple House on the death of the incumbent. The Ibo slave was now a Bonny chief responsible for a war canoe. Jaja set about surrounding himself with able young people whom he as chief would introduce to the European traders from the ships. These entrepreneurial young men would then set forth perhaps fifty miles up-river and either buy palm oil in exchange for the goods or use some of the trust goods to sub-contract purchases. In addition, Jaja began to think strategically. He established a special relationship with neighbouring communities like the Ogoni and the Ibibio whose goodwill he might need in the future for the advancement or the protection of his trade.

But further change was already taking place that would alter for ever the structure of trade in the Delta economy. Bonny's 'open door' policy meant in effect that while it was thriving on the increasing sales of palm oil fuelled by the new industrial processes being developed in the United Kingdom, it chose at the same time to provide with slaves those nations which had not yet abolished the trade like France, Brazil, Portugal and the United States of America. As a result of a treaty between Spain and Britain, British warships could seize Spanish slave ships north of the equator if carrying slaves or the equipment of slavery like manacles. Under this agreement a warship of the British West Africa squadron seized four Spanish ships in Bonny waters. This was during the minority of the King of Bonny. The Regent ordered the arrest and imprisonment of the British party which was having a parley on shore with some traders and the Spanish slavers for what he saw as unwarranted challenge to the city-state's sovereignty. When various other ships of the West Africa squadron arrived the Regent ordered the release of the prisoners.

The British government eventually paid compensation to Bonny for loss of the slave trade. As a result a British consul was appointed to regulate relationships with local rulers. His remit was to further the interests of the British commercial community which can be seen as a first step to what Bonnymen would see as a series of actions increasingly prejudicial to their own interests. The man appointed was called Hewett. He had been a successful European trader.

Meanwhile Jaja's success as a chief attracted impoverished canoe houses to seek affiliation with his. This earned the antagonism of the dominant Manilla Pepple canoe house whose adherents perceived the Annie Pepple canoe house as overbearing and as offering a direct challenge to their traditional supremacy. The young king, a first among equals, was not strong enough to keep the competing factions apart nor was the British consul who was ignored. The situation was exacerbated by a fire which destroyed most of the living quarters of the Annie Pepple house which prompted Jaja to move outside Bonny with many of his followers.

Again, Jaja's strategic nose had directed him to a location which commanded the route followed by the Bonny trading canoes on their journeys to and from the important markets of the Imo River to the extreme annoyance of the Manilla Pepple house. A bloody war broke out between the factions in which Jaja and his forces were beaten. He decided to secede from Bonny and its political instability to allow trade to develop.   In leaving Bonny, he retained the support of the other chiefs against the Manilla Pepple faction by agreeing to share all revenues levied on the European trading community including the 'comey', that is the agreed amount paid by them in return for the custom of the chiefs.

He then negotiated with the Andoni clan to legitimise his move into their territory and at the same time to promote their interests. He knew that if he could build a new settlement there, his control of the canoe traffic to and from the abundant palm oil markets would be absolute. He called the place Opubo after the chief of the canoe house who had taken him in as a slave, a name quickly and unknowingly corrupted to Opobo by European traders, missionaries and administrators and perpetuated by the cartographers.

Luck was with Jaja too.   He had made friends with two independent European traders who were finding it difficult to compete with the larger companies. They put forward the view that if he could find an outlet to the open sea navigable to ocean-going ships, it should be possible to attract the ships to transport the palm oil to the advantage of both parties. Soundings made by one of the traders showed that the bar was passable at high tide and a white flag was planted at an appropriate spot to inform ships' masters that Opobo was open for trading. And the ships started to arrive at Opobo in increasing numbers.

Intelligence, together with a strategic view and running with his luck, had helped Jaja to create victory out of defeat. In Bonny he had gone as far as he could go due to the opprobrium of his being an ex-slave. There was no such drawback in Opobo as he was the founder of the town. At just over fifty years of age Jaja had gone from slave to chief and from chief to king. His status was recognised in the agreement made between King Jaja and the British government in 1873 in which he received a guarantee that ships would not proceed further up the creek than Opobo town under pain of a heavy fine in rum puncheons. This ensured that the palm oil trade for the area had to be channelled through Opobo so ensuring that comey and other payments came to him.

CHAPTER 7

Jaja (2): The Effect of Economic Change

These changes which confronted King Jaja were taking place within a much wider context of change. Industrial innovations were being made in Britain with unprecedented speed and were beginning to spread to the near continent. The focus on mechanical engineering in Europe and the Americas brought forth new and improved products which needed palm oil, from the lubrication of axle boxes on railway rolling stock to its use as a flux in the manufacture of tinplate in the new steel mills themselves fuelled by the demand for new, steel-plated warships to maintain Britain's ocean superiority without which the Empire would break up.

Expanding populations in later Victorian times believed cleanliness was next to godliness and generated a demand for the mass market in soap for which palm oil was required in increasing quantities. The main fat used to make soap was tallow but in order to make a good lather it had to be blended with vegetable oil of which the best was palm oil. This in turn encouraged new competitors to enter the trade.

The development of steamship communication between Britain and the West African coast assisted this new competition. Steam transport was far quicker than sail and meant that traders could carry lower stocks on the coast and so reduce costs. Also, it speeded up the turnover. Consequently, palm oil could be changed into money much faster further reducing the amount of money needed to finance the business. Ships could be made bigger with a corresponding increase in carrying capacity and therefore promised a long-term reduction in freight rates. They would have an increased flexibility in that routes no longer needed to take account of the prevailing winds. This meant that other ports could be integrated into the export trade so reducing yet further long-run costs. With less money outstanding in credit at any one time, new competitors were arguably, demonstrably and increasingly able to enter the oil rivers trade as steam slowly took over from sail.

Another significant change was the move away from sending out ships which waited for the palm oil to come in from the sale of the goods they had brought out. These would sometimes wait for months until all the oil bought with the advances in goods was forthcoming. The ship's captains or other managers of the venture were replaced by permanent agents based on the hulks of old sailing ships made redundant by the advent of the steamships and the ships began to specialise in carriage of goods. The agents traded from these permanently moored vessels and supplemented the storage space with land rented on shore to store the casks of oil where a buffer stock could be maintained to facilitate a quicker loading and release of the vessel.

With the eventual arrival of the bigger, more expensive screw-propelled ships, owners realised that the high cost of the ship is best recovered by the number of journeys it can make and the speed with which it can be unloaded and loaded. Because of this, the use of trading hulks was to decline as the new land-based storage became the established mode. As specialist shipping companies became more and more important, the European traders acquired more and bigger 'beaches' or sites where the palm oil could be kept and shipped on the arrival of the steamer for transport to the markets, usually to the port of Liverpool which had a virtual monopoly of the West African trade. Company houses were set up on the beaches and the agent became shore-based.

Divorce of the ownership of the vessel from the trade in palm oil was complete. Among the new competitors who became part of the produce trading scene were other British companies and French, German and Dutch companies as well as Krio traders who were freed slaves or their descendants who had populated the coastal areas of Sierra Leone.

The traders introduced new practices as a result of the changes. The old method of charging comey according to a ship's tonnage or number of masts was replaced by a standard charge for a puncheon of oil. The gifts or dashes paid to the African middlemen and others also became standard charges as a direct result of the arrival of the steamship. Ships now carried oil for a variety of traders. Because of these changes, the chiefs felt they had less and less control over the way palm oil was distributed and paid for. Their autonomy was being circumscribed at many points.

Cash trading, pioneered by the German firm G.L. Gaiser, gave a lead to other firms. The oil trade came to rely on paper receipts which the African middleman would receive for his oil to redeem for goods at leisure. This made it possible to separate the sale of goods from the purchase of produce. It was part of an inexorable movement towards ending the trust system. If the trust system of credit relied on relationships, the deterioration of the relationships and the removal of the practices that sustained them put an end to it. It marked the end of distribution based on the kinds of relationships established in the days of the slave trade.

Traders of European origin were now less interested in making strong social relationships with Africans than interacting with other traders with whom they had a common interest. The development of factories and houses threw the European communities together. The future was one where practice based on local custom was giving way to one determined by the expatriate companies and by the British authorities who would gradually assume a greater say in the way in which the broader conduct of business was determined.

Innovations further to bring down costs were not possible within the existing political structure. Some European firms had tried to move inland with the idea of buying export crops more cheaply from the producers than from the coastal middlemen, only to be met with violence and destruction. This coincided with a period of depressed prices in the 1880s and a fall in value of local currencies like the manilla and the iron bar. It requires little imagination to see that rivalries between the various parties with interests in the trade would be likely to arise - between the tribes on the coast over areas of influence; between African traders on the coast and up-country suppliers who saw direct access to the European companies as a solution to the reduced prices; between the European companies and the African middlemen about the distribution of reduced profits; and between the middlemen and the small intermediaries and primary producers again on price.

This had the effect of sporadic interruptions of trade as minor wars broke out between tribes or strong coastal chiefs sought to suppress any attempt to short-circuit the purchase of palm oil by up-river entrepreneurs by punitive means. Allegations abounded of malpractice as the old trust arrangements foundered and adulteration of palm oil by some African middlemen and misrepresentation of the quality and specification of goods by some European traders proliferated.

The instability of the times was made worse by the phenomenon which induced the European powers to partition Africa among them. It was a development that was taking place on a worldwide scale but appeared to have been triggered by France seeking to expunge the memory of military defeat by Germany in 1870 by expanding its area of influence from its existing settlements in Algeria and Senegal. Germany, only recently united under Prince Bismarck, felt that the possession of colonies would help it economically to maintain parity with the other European powers already established in various parts of the world.

The chief exception was the basin of the Congo which, curiously enough, slipped through the hands of the principal imperial powers, Britain and France, and was secured by a royal speculator Leopold 11 of Belgium, masquerading as a philanthropic society, as Neal Ascherson tellingly describes in his masterly analysis *The King Incorporated*. Between 1880 and 1914 Belgium, Britain, France, Germany, Italy, Japan, the Netherlands and the USA all systematically attempted to translate economic and military supremacy into formal conquest, annexation and on-the-spot administration. But it was in Africa that the European powers competed most vigorously to carve out slices of the continent for themselves.

After the 1884-85 Berlin Conference called by Bismarck, the German Chancellor, to settle areas of colonial authority, there was a race to make treaties with local chiefs as the major players vied with each other to legitimate their claims supported in the cases of 'difficult' chiefs by military action where the chiefs did not accept the offer of protection. In the process it stimulated exploration of the lesser known parts of the continent. This of itself encouraged firms to extend their reach, particularly since there was now a back-up of military and naval force of a size and power that had not existed until this time. In the Niger Delta, European traders felt they could now appeal to the authority of the local consul with a greater likelihood of his support than in the past.

CHAPTER 8

Jaja (3): The Fight to Maintain Traditional Trading Practices

Against this background of dynamic change, King Jaja was busy consolidating the position he had achieved in the 1873 agreement. He demonstrated Opobo's power by holding regattas to show how each Opobo canoe house was prepared for war and punished individuals of other tribes who undertook activities opposed to his interests. There was one incident recorded in which he had the skin stripped from a recalcitrant prisoner of a minor tribe while he was still alive. By such means and by his earlier alliances with neighbouring tribes, he protected the hinterland on which Opobo's wealth relied.

He encouraged Europeans to come to Opobo for he knew they were central to the prosperity of his kingdom but discouraged them from influencing its traditions by requiring them to move away from the banks of the river opposite his settlement. Jaja fitted in well with the free trade spirit of the century - and the free use of military power that accompanied it. His militant entrepreneurship was encouraged by the fall in oil prices in the 1880s and the trade rivalries it created. Africans were hit at a time when they could not achieve economies in production and transportation. The European companies were hit at a time when their profit margins had already been reduced by increased competition.

Examples abounded of a new aggressiveness on the part of the companies and there was a further deterioration of relationships between them and the locals. Jaja was caught up in these commercial activities and associated political machinations. He opposed strongly the penetration of the hinterland by European traders stiffened in their resolve by the knowledge that the consul and the forces at his command could be called on to assist them as necessary. He believed that African as well as European interests should be served in any cooperative activity. By that he meant the interests of the chiefs which he would maintain was the interests of the people. When a trader called Watts set up on the Qua Eboe River over which Jaja had long assumed control, he organised a punitive expedition against the Ibenos who had provided Watts with the facilities. He destroyed their crops and took away 100 prisoners who were killed and exhibited at Opobo.

That Jaja had taken vengeance on the people rather than the new factory is an indication that he was only too aware that the latter action would have brought down on his head the wrath of the Royal Navy. He showed that he knew his people well enough to appreciate that the best way to stop foreigners trading in the markets of the hinterland was to frighten the local inhabitants and so dissuade them from entering into contracts with the European and Krio traders. The German philosopher Nietzsche admired the way the powerful could be ruthless, not because they enjoyed it but to preserve their commanding place at the forefront of affairs. Jaja was no different.

But Jaja reckoned without the prejudices of Consul Hewett, Her Britannic Majesty's representative in the Delta. Hewett had found Jaja a handful, perhaps because he realised the considerable intelligence of the man, but had to acknowledge him as king. He appeared to want to bring to a halt what he considered to be Jaja's disruptive influence in Opobo, namely his threatening to bypass the European traders and sell direct to the markets.

No doubt he was also influenced by the demand of some of the merchants for a more active policy. As early as 1883 he had recommended Jaja's deportation to the Foreign Office which quickly reminded him of Britain's obligation to Jaja under the treaty of 1873. However, the Berlin International Conference of 1885 which, among other matters, declared that the Niger and its tributaries would from then on be controlled by Britain as an international waterway giving free navigation to ships of all nations, took precedence over the 1873 agreement with Jaja. It did not rule on the right to free trade.

When Britain, following the conference, declared a protectorate over the area in 1885, the trading companies, encouraged by the acting consul, felt themselves at liberty to trade upstream. Jaja tried to repeat his earlier tactics of intimidation of the interior producers, but this time the odds were stacked against him. The matter was referred to the consul who declared the traders had the right to trade anywhere in Jaja's kingdom, freely interpreting the agreement made in Berlin. Harry Johnston, the vice-consul, in the absence of his master Hewett on leave, further undermined Jaja's position when he forbade European traders from doing business with him on pain of a fine of £500 until he agreed to the conditions earlier outlined by Hewett. This included Jaja's agreement to the cessation of the payment of comey. Jaja sought the assistance of the Foreign Office, but events moved too quickly for him.

Legally, it could have been put forward that Opobo was at the mouth of the Imo River and unconnected directly with the Niger river system which was the subject of international navigation rights. Johnston took it upon himself to set a trap to snatch Jaja, a course of action proposed by Hewett and later deplored by the British prime minister. Johnston sent Jaja a note requiring him to parley with him on his launch and assuring him that if he came he would be free to go when he had heard what he had to say.

Johnston's assurance was good enough for Jaja who knew about the word of an English gentleman. Contrary to his firm expectations he was taken prisoner and conveyed to the Gold Coast so that an enquiry could be heard. Despite the support of a number of European traders the enquiry became a trial and the court exiled Jaja to the West Indian island of St Vincent on a pension of £800 per year which, while substantial for a pension at the time, was as nothing compared to the £300,000 a year he was estimated to have received in *comey* payments. When he had spent four years there and his friends had continued their efforts to secure his return to his home, his release was authorised after he had given a written undertaking not to cause any trouble on his return to Opobo as a private citizen. He took ship for home but died in Santa Cruz in Tenerife in 1891. He was reported to have retained his dignity as a king to the end.

His death marked the end of the imperial era and heralded the beginning of the colonial one. The chiefs who had signed the model treaties putting themselves under the protection of Queen Victoria thought they were doing just that. They found in the event that they had signed away their birthright, not because of any duplicity on the part of the British government representatives (Harry Johnson's deception apart) but because of the external forces we have looked at. It would take two or three decades to undo the damage done by Johnson's action to the trust people had in the British administration in the area.

A tale similar to this could have been told in the Western Delta with somewhat different social organisation and commercial practices. The Itsekiri chief Nana Olomu took actions similar to those of Jaja. The chiefs of the area elected him *Gofine* or Governor of the Benin River not because of his inherited royal connections, but because of his success as a trader. This position was affirmed by the consul. The duty of the *Gofine* was to collect the *comey*. Like Jaja he attempted to exercise and defend his traditional authority and eventually suffered a similar fate at the instance of the same consular officials who had dealt with Jaja. He was exiled to the Gold Coast as the old order gave way to the new.

The old legitimacy within which traders had worked for well over 200 years was being eroded away and kings like Jaja and Nana found their authority undermined and eventually displaced.

CHAPTER 9

Mary Slessor: Christianity and the Economic and Political Changes

While in the early days of intrusion of foreign interests into West Africa it was true to say that the flag followed trade, it is also valid to claim that that order of precedence applied equally to the Cross as to trade. The advent of the missionaries to the area drained by the River Niger and surrounding areas had a political and economic effect just as the coming of the slavers and then the palm oil traders had. Political, economic and religious forces interacted to challenge or use the traditional authority structure of the people of the south of the country. The life of Mary Mitchell Slessor, a legend in her time, is a useful proxy for the influence of the missionaries in the period up to the First World War.

Mary Slessor worked in a textile mill in Dundee before being accepted to do missionary work in Calabar. Such was her faith and commitment in an era when Christianity was closely prescribed that she quickly established herself as a good learner, and by force of her personality became a fully fledged missionary in her own right. She entered an area where European traders did not dare to go. It was against this background that Mary Slessor worked on the Cross River and surroundings, often under conditions so arduous that most men would have buckled. All her travel was by water or on foot, indeed barefoot like the locals. Diseases were rife, superstition and inter-tribal war prevailed and human sacrifice was a commonplace.

Her work took her, a solitary white woman, into the lands of the Okoyong reputed to be the most westerly outpost of the Bantu tribes. They were openly addicted to witchcraft and animal and sometimes human sacrifice, usually on the death of a chief. They were utterly lawless and contemptuous of authority. They enslaved their Ibibio neighbours in incursions into their territory. Theft was common. To survive in the struggle of life a man needed to possess wives and children and slaves. If, through incompetence or misfortune he failed, he was regarded as lawful prey of the nearest chief.

Different groups fought each other and were only united in common enmity of other tribes. They hated the Calabar people because of their wealth and power arising from their favoured position near the coast for trading of produce directly with the European buyers and a state of chronic war existed between them. This underlined the desire of the people of the interior to have direct trading access to the coast for their palm products which were frustrated by the Efik chiefs on the coast who did everything in their power to maintain their monopoly of trade with the European houses established in Calabar. All efforts to bring them together in the interest of trade had been in vain. Messages from the Consul were ignored or treated with contempt.

Mary Slessor is particularly remembered for having saved the lives of twins who until her coming, were seen as the product of juju and were killed by being stuffed head-first into calabashes and abandoned while the mother was driven into the bush to die. 'May you have twins' was a curse too terrible for a woman to hear in the Efik country. She travelled quickly to any village where the birth of twins was rumoured to have occurred. Over her lifetime she saw, largely through her own efforts, the suppression of this practice. She saw that the mothers were cared for and the twins saved put into good homes in a village called Ikunetu. In the process she faced up to kings, mobs and natural hazards until she eventually won them over and gained a place in their hearts as *Ma Akamba* - the Great Mother.

But it would not do her justice to remember her only as the saviour of twins. She also campaigned against witchcraft practices. The tribes believed that all people died naturally through old age. Any sudden and premature death they ascribed to a juju put on the deceased, and possible offenders were required to take the ésére or Calabar bean to establish their innocence. The practice was known in the local pidgin as 'chopping nut'. This was taking a concoction of bean pounded and mixed with water which then became a lethal blend. The people believed it would kill the wrongdoers and establish the innocence of those who vomited it up. It was a refined version of another trial by ordeal - the custom of putting the hands of person suspected of having committed a crime (which had a flexible interpretation) into a pot of boiling palm oil. If the hands blistered the person was innocent. If not, a suitable punishment was meted out including not only the loss of the limb but sometimes even the head.

The only chance for the accused undergoing the ordeal of the bean lay in fixing the witch doctor so that the latter gave the person undergoing the ordeal an extra-heavy dose to produce the emetic effect that indicated innocence. Mary Slessor intervened in a number of cases where the bean was about to be administered. Such instances were to resurface temporarily in 1951 nearly 40 years after her death. When the death of a chief took place, slaves were sacrificed to the gods and this practice she opposed with all the strength of her being.

Eventually she was so successful in her missionary work that she prevailed on the Okoyong and the Ibibios to call a truce in their wars. This opened up the trade in palm oil to the Okoyong who now had access via the designated buyers of the coastal chiefs or the intermediaries who sold to them, to the Calabar beaches or 'factories' as they were sometimes called. (The name was adopted by the British from the Portuguese term *feitorias*, originally coastal enclaves leased to the Portuguese by local rulers, to which they were confined after being thwarted, in their bids to penetrate inland, by disease, the adverse climate and the skill of the Africans in deterring them).

The economic benefits were such that it was unlikely that they would be given up and a return made to the old ways of internecine warfare. It reinforced, as far as the European missionaries were concerned, the view that commerce, when allied to Christianity, assisted in the civilising of the local peoples whose callousness and cruelty as they saw it were unacceptable.

They found nothing that was attractive in native life and beliefs and countered it with the preaching of a Christianity in all its simplicity in the belief that nothing else would be effective. The opening up of trade also enabled the women she had saved from death to become self-supporting by participating in the process of preparing palm kernels for sale to a trader selling to intermediaries in touch with traders from the coast.

It became Mary Slessor's ambition to take her missionary zeal beyond the Ibibio country to the country of the Aro, an Ibo-speaking tribe although with lighter skins than was usual for the Ibo. She tried to persuade the Foreign Missions Committee of her church to do so. As funds were short she determined to press on herself without calling on the church to bear the cost. In 1891 she had been invited by the Governor to become a magistrate in the Native Court where her intimate knowledge of the language and the customs of the people would be invaluable. The people coming to court would have someone who knew their ways intimately and whom they trusted to give a fair judgment. For their part the District Commissioners would have a load removed from their shoulders. She accepted on condition she received £1 a year for herself, the remainder of the stipend to be used in the enhancement of her mission. Government officers, whose upbringing and traditions were so very different from her own, spoke of the joy of her naturalness and delightful sense of humour.

In fact, she never did achieve that ambition to work away from the Cross River area in the adjoining Ibo territory, to fight the abomination as she saw it, of the shrine of the Long Juju at Arochuku, situated in a well-guarded gorge and destroyed by government soldiers in 1901 before her plans could be implemented. The Long Juju was a shrine of the Aro people, famous throughout the Ibo lands and beyond, where supplicants came to ask for the juju's protection or for its assistance against their enemies and from which many did not return, to the awe of friends present who saw the colour of blood in the water and thought the supplicant had been devoured by the juju. In fact a colouring of animal blood or red camwood dye had been put into the water. The Aro enslavers sold their victims into slavery either locally or to Arab and other slavers from the North continuing to exercise their centuries-old trade after the cessation of the transatlantic traffic - the Tuareg, for example, who were herders who moved with their camels and their goats in search of pasture, had no word in their language for work, anything resembling labour being done by black slaves.

On special occasions such as the death of a juju priest, the Aro held cannibal feasts when hundreds were slaughtered. The victims were regarded as sacred and those who ate their flesh partook of the great god Chuku's power. The Long Juju had shown the Ibo at his worst and yet demonstrated that he was commercially acute and had cleverly developed two lines of activity, trade and religion, and made them serve each other. It is ironic that the Mary Slessor Memorial Home, a place where young women were trained for marriage with emphasis on African crafts, eventually found permanent quarters in Arochuku, home of the Ibo adopted god, for Chuku was said to have been originally an Ibibio god whom the Aro had taken for their own. A new area had been opened up for trade and law and order on the Cross River. It rose to a large extent on the foundations which the missionaries had laid over years of labour and sacrifice.

Mary Slessor continued with her work nearby setting up rest homes where exhausted missionaries could regain their strength, supporting her 'children' who had been rescued from almost certain infanticide, fighting for the dignity of women like the mothers of twins and widows who were subjected to intolerably harsh customs such as having to remain in their houses sometimes for years without washing, changing their clothes or combing their hair, dispensing justice and creating places of worship at minimum expense, participating herself in their erection.

When she was asked if she had ever had lessons in making cement she replied 'No, I just stir it like porridge; turn it out, smooth it with a stick, and all the time I keep praying "Lord, here's the cement; if to Thy glory, set it". and it has never once gone wrong'. She would receive latterday recognition of her worth by her compatriots in the issue of a commemorative ten pound note in the new millennium by the Clydesdale Bank. It would carry her likeness on the front of the note and on the back a map of the area around Itu which includes places mentioned in this book and an artist's representation of her work.

While Slessor's work was an outstanding example of fortitude sustained by an unswerving faith, love of her fellow humans and an iron constitution, it nevertheless typified the outlook of the missionaries who poured out to the coast of West Africa from the 1850s onwards. Her own organisation was started by Hope Waddell in Calabar under the aegis of what was to become the Church of Scotland. He negotiated the protection of its missionaries with the British government before setting foot in the country. Although that protection was more illusory than real given the circumstances of life in the bush at the time and the great distances administrative or other law enforcement officers had to travel, often on foot, it meant that administrators were required to look to the interests of the missionaries where their work or their persons were threatened.

The canons of their faith were at odds with the local religions and the spirit of the age did not permit compromise. They had a mission to Christianise and overcome unacceptable practices like the offering of sacrifices and the viewing of certain animals as sacred. As E A Ayandele points out in his treatise *The Missionary Impact on Modern Nigeria*, they tried to stop many traditional practices like polygamy which represented traditional wealth, and they fought vigorously to free slaves who were also a part of the wealth creating system. Not least, they undermined the authority of some chiefs by opposing many of their beliefs and by edicts in their teaching, which caused in certain cases anti-missionary feelings among the chiefs.

Where Christian missions had been long established, the government valued their efforts. It was the most Christian state of Egbe that was allowed to be independent up to the establishment of a single Colony and Protectorate of Nigeria in 1914 and it was only at the special request of the paramount chief that it was taken within the official administration at that time.

Where the locals had been Christianised, they were seen to be more amenable to the introduction of new ways. To that extent, the missionaries were the unconscious agents of British policy. Yet, as the administrative hierarchy was extended after the creation of a Protectorate of Northern Nigeria and a Protectorate and Colony of Southern Nigeria in 1900, and after the withdrawal of the Royal Charter from what had been the Royal Niger Company, to include districts under district commissioners, later designated district officers, the relationship between missions and administration became more and more strained. The values of the missionaries were not those of the administration and their moral and social programmes were sometimes perceived to undermine some of the work of the administration.

Yet both the peoples ministered to, and the administrators, in terms of developing the new Protectorate and Colony in the south of the territory, benefitted from the work of the missionaries. The Church Missionary Society, the overseas arm of the Church of England, was instrumental in the establishment and growth of a cotton-growing industry in the district around Abeokuta in the Yoruba south-west and had a ginnery built to separate the cottonseed from the seedcotton to provide the cotton lint and oilseed that could be exchanged for money in the commodity market. They brought in an expert from the British Cotton Growing Association to assist in the direction of its cultivation. In Calabar, the Hope Waddell Institution provided training in the trades that serviced the local industry in south-east Nigeria including that for clerks and messengers, mechanics, carpenters, bricklayers, blacksmiths, printers and tailors. Various skills to fit trainees for useful work were taught by the other denominations which arrived after the Presbyterian and the C of E missionaries.

The missionaries may have represented very different versions of the Christian faith but they had a great deal in common. They believed that the economic well-being of their own countries -

this was perhaps most evident among the British missionaries - stemmed from the faith of their countrymen. They firmly believed that economic development together with Christian principles and the civilising effect of these, would lead to a better life for their charges. All peoples, they believed together with the governing elite, moved along a continuum from barbarism to the present civilised condition of the European. They readily accepted the other side of the equation whereby the native peoples gave in return their labour and raw materials, or their surplus as the euphemism of the time had it. That was the exchange at the heart of imperial thinking.

It was the Christians who took the initiative in the cultivation of cash crops like cocoa, cotton and rubber and Christianity was associated with the wealth brought to the people as the farming of these crops increased and people prospered relatively to a degree unknown before this time. It was especially appropriate as these crops were beginning to be cultivated just when there was a depression in the palm oil trade. The missionaries had an important role in providing a foundation, together with traders and administrators, for the part that the commodities of cocoa, palm products, oil, cotton and rubber, plus groundnuts from the north, were to play in the later growth of the Nigerian economy.

CHAPTER 10

George Goldie (1): Developing the Niger's Resources

George Goldie insisted all his personal papers be destroyed and not made available to anyone. He therefore made it difficult for researchers or unasked biographers to do justice to the contribution he had made to the formation and development of Nigeria. His life characterises the determination of those who drove the companies that opened up the trade there. Born to money (his family made its fortune in smuggling goods into Ireland and England prior to the Isle of Man becoming an integral part of the United Kingdom) and to rank (his father was Speaker of the House of Keys in the Manx Parliament for all but two years of his time on the Niger), George Dashwood Goldie Taubman professed atheism, ran off with his governess whom he married in his thirtieth year after a life thus far noted for licentiousness and irresponsibility.

I shall refer to him from now on as Goldie for that was the name he assumed when he was knighted in 1887. His original surname of Taubman was German and the Goldie part that he elected to be known by, was a connection through his mother who came of a Dumfriesshire family in South-West Scotland. If he believed in anything it was that civilisation was a product of increasing prosperity. It was he who was to add the most populous of all the tropical African colonies to the British Empire and would lay the beginning of significant administrative policies in the colonies.

Through family finance and connections he took over a small firm, Holland Jacques and Company, that had been trading on the Niger without achieving an acceptable level of profit. His venture into the world of trade and politics in the Niger delta took place in 1875. Fired by the works of probably the greatest and certainly the most cerebral of the African explorers, Heinrich Barth, George Goldie read avidly the vast outpourings of that man's most inquiring mind.

A number of expeditions by men of experience on the rivers of West Africa, men like MacGregor Laird, Thomas Buxton and William Baikie failed to establish 'legitimate commerce' in those parts of the lower Niger where the river had not yet divided into its many mouths. This was due largely to the opposition of tribes allied to the Brassmen who had a vested interest in maintaining the monopoly of the coastal intermediaries. Goldie realised the problem confronting the company was too much competition and was of the private view that monopoly was the only cure. This in his opinion could only come about by amalgamation.

He formed a new company which bought the assets of Holland Jacques, gave itself power to amalgamate with other companies as necessary in their joint interest and amalgamated with two bigger and influential companies and smaller British companies under the name of the United African Company. Again the company bought all the assets of the member firms which received shares according to the proportion of the assets it had sold.

Their agreement prevented shareholders from operating on the Niger within a thousand miles of Akassa on the Nun River branch but allowed two substantial companies holding shares in the United African Company, Miller Brothers and James Pinnock, to operate their other activities in the oil rivers at Opobo and Benin by allowing them to trade independently outside a limit of 25 miles of any of the mouths of the Niger. In four years and at the early age of 33, Goldie, although a minor shareholder, took on the responsibility of running the amalgamated company, a move which was strongly supported by older and more experienced traders from the larger companies.

While these measures gave the new company a greater bargaining power with producers, particularly of palm oil, and established a new power balance on the river, Goldie's problems did not disappear. Just as his success seemed certain, a fresh challenge appeared from French interlopers. Unable to compete with British free trade, the French began to look to extend their existing colonies and establish strong economic bases in which they could set up tariffs against rivals and redeem the name of France after the ignominy of the defeat in the war of 1870 and the loss of Alsace Lorraine to which she would never be reconciled. Enterprising French traders began to appear on the lower Niger in competition with the recently formed United African Company. Goldie sensed an underlying political purpose behind their appearance when he linked this move to French activity near the source of the Niger.

The known French propensity for grandiose plans that connected scattered possessions on interior lines had convinced him that a latent threat existed. The French made a treaty with the Emir that gave them the right to trade freely among the Nupe. They followed this with the setting up of stations on the upper part of the lower Niger at Aboh and Onitsha and on the Benue. They even set up in the delta in competition with the United African Company. Prices paid to Africans for their palm oil went up by 25% and competition became cut-throat.

Goldie's response to this was to attempt to revive an old British solution that had been ousted by free trade - the monopoly arising from a Royal Charter which gave political and economic control to the chartered company as in the case of the East India Company well over a hundred years earlier. Legal advice suggested that charters were instruments of incorporation and that a company already incorporated under the Companies Act might not receive such a charter. Consequently, yet another new company was formed which purchased the assets of the old company. It made its balance sheet look sound by a 19th century form of creative accounting and it cultivated and appointed names of repute to the board to extend the influence of the company in high places. It was incorporated as the National African Company Limited.

The British administration did not want any more colonies with their necessarily expensive machinery of government. A protectorate would be established and control should continue to be asserted by the consul on his periodic visits with the assistance of vice-consuls. Any charge on imperial funds was out of the question. Goldie was able to take systematic advantage of the government's financial embarrassment and gradually attract to the National African Company an official status as agent of the British government. The chairman of the company, Lord Aberdare, a friend and ex-colleague of the prime minister and foreign secretary of the day, was invited to get the views of the traders on the issue of their paying tax to meet the costs of recurrent expenditure.

This played into Goldie's hands for Aberdare ignored the Liverpool interests in the Oil Rivers and consulted only Goldie and Hutton, both directors of the National African Company. The Liverpool interest was the African Association, a group of traders based in the coastal area based outside the area dominated with official sanction by the National African Company. Goldie realised that with finances to administer the Niger region, there would be little incentive for the government to transfer the administration to the company at a later date. If the charter was still the goal, then Goldie and his fellow directors had to ensure that the Foreign Office remained without funds. An earlier and repeated request to appoint David MacIntosh, the company chief agent, as a consul to assist in the struggle with the French was eventually conceded as a result of their refusal to recommend taxation of the traders.

By the end of two years since its formation, the National African Company had achieved much of the political power it had set out to obtain. The relationships between a chartered company that drew its authority from concessions from local leaders and the hands-off protection of the imperial power already existed in theory in every detail except the instrument itself conferring Royal Charter. At this point Goldie was confronted by another possible setback. This time it was the sudden and unexpected entry into Africa of Germany under Bismarck, motivated more by European politics than economics. The aim was to draw Britain more closely into the German system of alliances.

Germany had quickly established protectorates in the Cameroons, in South-West Africa and in Togo. It was Bismarck who had proposed the conference in Berlin to secure free navigation and define areas of interest among other items, on the Niger and the Oil Rivers. But it was the French ambitions for colonial expansion that spelt potential disaster for Goldie's plans. His hope of a monopoly on the river while the French traders were still there was clearly impossible. If Goldie could buy out the French traders before the conference then the British position would be transformed. With only the National African Company trading on the Niger, the British delegates could argue that a proposed plan for an international commission was totally irrelevant. Goldie lent his private fortune to the company to break the French by trading at a loss.

By June 1884 the two smaller French firms had had enough and sold out. Protracted negotiations continued with the largest French company, *Compagnie française de l'Afrique équatoriale.* A week before the conference Goldie was in a position to announce that the French company had capitulated. It agreed to amalgamate with the National African Company in a like way to that in which the original firms had formed the company in 1879. This enhanced Goldie's reputation and further enhanced the status of the company as quasi-official representative of the British government on the Niger.

The conference adopted a new Niger Navigation Act proposed by the British representatives which did not include an international commission. It was almost inevitable that the new British obligations would be fulfilled by granting Goldie's company a Royal Charter. It took more time to achieve this as there was resistance in the British cabinet to giving the company carte blanche to raise duties and taxes for revenue and profits. So much did the government prevaricate that Goldie proposed for consideration by the board, and leaked the information in official circles, that if there was no government action forthcoming, the company should be free to open negotiations with any foreign power with the object of placing itself under the flag of that country and transferring to it its treaties and the territory of which it was in effective occupation. After a time there was a compromise solution in which government had a certain control. The document, however, was drafted with such ambiguity that the company was really having a position legitimated that already existed.

The first regulations issued by the company on the day after the charter received its seal in 1886 and the company became known as the Royal Niger Company, were the tariff and licensing regulations. During the life of the company the only regulations ever made to which foreigners had to submit, apart from those setting out the framework for the administration, were commercial ones. Foreigners were any persons not born in the company's territories including Britons and Africans from the Oil Rivers or Lagos. These rules had the effect of establishing the greatest possible impediments to the trade of competitors according to Goldie's interpretation of the Berlin Act. Ships could only trade at listed ports of entry where import duties were exacted.

What stung the other European firms was not these rules but the duty of 100% of the landed value on spirits which were essential to the palm oil trade. If vessels were proceeding up-river beyond Lokoja they had to pay double duty. The company claimed property rights on all the land adjacent to the river and would not sell any for wharves or warehouses. It was therefore impossible to land, tie up, sell goods or set up shop without the company's assistance. The Lagos government which administered Lagos and Colony and whose authority extended in effect into the Yoruba lands of Western Nigeria and beyond were told from London to cease corresponding with the Nupe on the middle Niger as this was now regarded as the company's sphere. The company was also expected to engage France in the contest for the middle Niger. Goldie's vision now had a shape.

CHAPTER 11

George Goldie (2): From Economic to Political Power

Goldie's company upset a number of constituencies. The exclusion from the palm oil trade, as a result of the company's actions, of the Africans of the Oil Rivers Protectorate which was not within the territory of the company, provoked opposition on the part of the oil intermediaries in the area and the traders of the African Association, a group of Liverpool companies which bought the palm oil from the producers now restricted to the area immediately behind the coastal towns. The Liverpool traders were somewhat reluctant to complain over-loudly as they were aspiring to the same chartered status as was now held by the Royal Niger Company and felt they could not oppose the principle of chartered company administration. A rumoured amalgamation of the Royal Niger Company and the African Association alarmed the shipping companies who feared the monopoly power of such a large concentration of buying power. Goldie took advantage of the rumour and implied that if their opposition did not cease, the combined interests of the Royal Niger Company and the African Association would establish a new shipping line.

This opposition forced a real consideration by officials in London of the problem of responsibility and control. In 1889, a Major Claude Maxwell Macdonald was appointed to 'inquire into certain questions affecting Imperial and Colonial interests in the West Coast of Africa and into the position of the Royal Niger Company'. During his investigations the traders of Brass complained to him bitterly that they were now treated as foreigners and that their traditional trade among the tribes of the Delta under the Royal Niger Company's jurisdiction was thwarted by the company's regulations and enforcing mechanisms and that they had to resort to smuggling to win a living for themselves.

Macdonald's report found the company was operating within its rights in enforcing the regulations of which the Brassmen complained. Equally it found that these same regulations operated unfairly against the men of Brass. If Brass had been included within the Company's territory, there would have been little for the Brassmen to complain about. It was not in fact the fault of the company that Brass had not been included. Historians have little doubt, however, that the steps taken by the Company to consolidate its monopoly infringed the spirit of free trade it claimed to embrace.

As the years passed by and nothing was done to alleviate the condition of the Brassmen, so did the injustice start to fester. They were excluded from traditional markets and the government, although sounding as if it wanted to help, was doing nothing to arrest Brass's steady decline. In January 1895, some fifteen hundred warriors from Brass fell upon Akassa where the company's headquarters were and attacked its property which was destroyed or plundered. African staff of the company, Krios from Sierra Leone, were carried off and forty three of them were butchered and eaten. It is noteworthy that Christian chiefs of Brass and its allies refused to give up their prisoners or join in the cannibal feast.

The attack occasioned a punitive expedition which destroyed the town of Brass despite the handsome apology by King Koko for the attack on the company 'particularly in the killing and eating of parts of its employees… We now throw ourselves entirely at the mercy of the good old Queen, knowing her to be a most kind, tender-hearted and sympathetic old mother'. It is certain that the attack on the company's centre at Akassa was triggered by economic pressures. It was without doubt compounded psychologically by the strongly felt humbling of a once-proud city state, called indeed by one historian 'the Venice of the Niger Delta', that had been dominant in the palm oil trade.

At about the same time the company was involved in a struggle with the Fulani Emirs of Nupe and Ilorin in the middle of what is now Nigeria. These people raided for slaves even the villages along the banks of the Niger under the company's protection. All attempts to secure a peaceful solution having proved fruitless, Goldie decided to take action. A successful campaign was fought against both Emirs despite heroic opposition from their followers both mounted and on foot. The terms imposed on the Nupe and Ilorin included recognition of the suzerainty of the company. Goldie abolished the legal status of slavery within the company's territories. The proclamation had little practical effect as it simply meant that slavery was no longer recognised in the company courts which in any case did not exercise jurisdiction in the emirates. The political settlement with both Nupe and Ilorin was a lenient one. Goldie had continued to correspond with the Emirs from the first, convinced that the fault lay as much with the Lagos government as with Ilorin. This was to lay the foundation for a preference on the part of the Emirs for nominal British rather than direct French control of their affairs.

In the meantime the French, who had long been unhappy about the company's claimed authority over a wide area of the Middle Niger where its influence was negligible, and dismayed by the absorption of the French companies within what had become the Royal Niger Company in 1885, were seeking new territories to rule. The Company exercised an effective control over a very small proportion of the vast territory that was nominally under its government but maintained the image that it was in complete control. France was supreme on the Upper Niger. Among a group in France pressing for an extension of empire there was a hope that French influence might be expanded by treaty over those areas which lay on the ill-defined borders of the British Protectorate next to Dahomey in the area known as Borgu.

A Captain Decoeur left France in 1894 to obtain a treaty with the chief of Nikki to whom the chief of Bussa, a town in company territory, was vassal according to a French claim. Goldie heard of his departure and despatched Captain Frederick Lugard to forestall him which he did. A subsequent French expedition occupied Bussa which was open to navigation up the Niger from the sea and so threatened the company's monopoly. This followed an attempt by a Lieutenant Mizon with an armed party to sail up the Niger to make a treaty with a local emir.

Mizon was however discredited in France as a result of an over-zealous use of artillery in support of the emir against villages opposed to him. The French saw a growing willingness to use imperial funds to expand and defend British interests on the Niger as an attempt to frustrate their design for a compact block of North and West African territory. The Marchand expedition was already on its way to Fashoda to anticipate Kitchener's advance on the Upper Nile.

The Niger crisis was thus brought to the forefront of international politics. Goldie could not hope to maintain his existing position which focused entirely on the Niger. In spite of his earlier diplomatic triumphs, he could not expect to shape policies that had to take account of worldwide interests. When imperial troops duly made their appearance on the company's territories, Goldie's influence even on local issues was undermined. His claim to Bussa was legitimated by an eventual agreement between France and Britain that included issues across different territories in which there was some dispute concerning ownership or access.

The charter company had outlived its usefulness, a long time before this some would say. Goldie was able to negotiate a generous settlement for the takeover of his political commitments and the costs he had incurred in the British interest. He had made a major contribution to the building of Nigeria. Indeed he had done more than any other man, but the degree to which his talents and determination laid the country's foundation has never been fully acknowledged. Unlike Lugard, he left only the papers he was unable to destroy. Neither did he have the high profiling Lugard received from his admirer and later his wife, Flora Shaw, the colonial correspondent of *The Times* nor the influence with Joe Chamberlain, the Foreign Secretary, that she was able to exercise in Lugard's interest.

Goldie's genius had played a leading part not only in conceiving effective indirect rule in the Emirates, but also in laying down the policy which Lugard was instructed to follow. Lugard put the flesh on the bones of Goldie's ideas which were developed as early as 1886 based on the company's experience since 1879, albeit as justification of a budget totally inadequate for any form of direct administration. The idea was not new, having been introduced a century and a half earlier in parts of India, a fact that impressed Lugard. It was also a form of rule implemented by the Roman administration during the occupation of Celtic Britain and indeed conceived before that and applied in some provinces of the Roman Empire like Vasconia, the land of the oldest of the Europeans - the Basques. While establishing Roman law and direct administration in most territories of their empire, Roman leaders were able to distinguish where it was not politic to do this but to rule through the natural power holders. Even earlier, Alexander the Great ruled the conquered Persian Empire through 'satraps', the powerful rulers through whom even the Persians had administered their empire.

Goldie's light touch in relation to the Emirates convinced the Emirs that they indeed retained their authority whereas the French had shown a heavy-handedness that had not endeared them to these leaders. He had shaped not only the physical configuration and political direction of much of Nigeria but had laid the foundation of a mighty company that would be dominant for years in the West African produce and retail trade. The revocation of the Royal Niger Company's Charter removed the underlying grievances the Brassmen had but by this time the city state had gone into economic decline.

CHAPTER 12

George Goldie (3): The Rise in the Influence of Expatriate Companies and the Setting Up of the Marketing Boards

The period between the beginning of the century and the First World War and beyond reflected the influence of Goldie. It saw a revival of the fortunes of the expatriate companies as world prices moved back to a level which gave a good return after the down-turn in trade of the 1880s. They were able to move inland in the late 1890s, originally by the rivers, as the growing political influence of the consuls became more supportive together with their greater capacity to call on military power. Later they followed the railways.

The Niger Company, which lost its charter at the end of 1899 and so the 'Royal' part of its name, continued to trade on a large scale and was bought by William Lever in 1920. Another company, the African and Eastern Trading Company, itself formed from earlier amalgamations, eventually combined with the Lever organisation in 1929 to form the gigantic United Africa Company. Other companies were active throughout Nigeria in the export of produce, companies like G. B. Ollivant destined to be absorbed within the United Africa Company but retaining its old identity, John Holt and Company, a firm founded by a Liverpool merchant family, Paterson Zochonis which had Manchester connections, the French companies CFAO and SCOA and latterly A G Leventis, a brash new entrant to what was considered a protected association of companies.

These were all importing and exporting organisations. They were joined by the specialist exporting company Cadbury Brothers who later operated jointly with their competitor chocolate manufacturers Fry and Rowntree in both Nigeria and the Gold Coast to purchase cocoa for their factories in the United Kingdom which the Quaker families that owned them hoped would see chocolate take over from strong drink as a tipple for the masses. Early on, these companies, along with others in the trade, established a fairly tight control of the export trade in produce by what was tantamount to the sharing of markets.

These expatriate companies began to thrive on their protected produce markets. Bigger and better housing was built for company personnel. Improved living conditions and better public health resulted in an increasing number of wives going out to the coast, a development that was to be reflected also in the number of government officials whose wives began to accompany them, at least for a protracted stay, to the Coast. This was progressively to exert a change in social behaviour as the influence of the womenfolk made itself felt. Hard drinking was moderated, at least in the households where the wives were present. The taking of African mistresses by the menfolk was reduced and there was a general raising of the tone of daily living as a result of the presence of the women.

The Second World War threatened to cut off West Africa from the British market, at least in part, due to the lack of shipping and the continuing threat of enemy action. This could have resulted in the collapse of cocoa prices and a crisis among cocoa producers. After the collapse of vegetable oil and oilseed supplies from the Netherlands East Indies and Malaya as a consequence of Japanese occupation, there was a need to direct supplies of groundnuts and palm oil to Britain. Prices to producers were guaranteed through the West African Produce Control Board. To direct these products to specific destinations export licensing was established and a statutory monopoly in the handling of the principal exports was set up. This was to have a considerable effect on the post-war marketing of Nigerian exports. These controls remained in force until 1945 except for cocoa which was regulated until 1947.

Almost from their inception, these boards began to accumulate surpluses due to rising commodity prices. The merchants who had previously bought and shipped the cocoa became agents for the buying of the crop and shippers under the direction of the authorities. They would share the trade on a percentage quota based on past purchases and new entry into the trade was banned. According to P.T. Bauer in his classic work *West African Trade,* the quota system was unnecessary and harmful in that it froze the pattern of trade and hindered the growth of new firms. It impeded buying competition and reduced prices somewhat to producers which tends to reduce supplies.

The quota system was originated earlier in the century by the merchants as a confidential market-sharing agreement to restrict competition among themselves and to put up a barrier to new entrants to the trade through the agency of their Association of West African Merchants. It was given official sanction during World War 11 as a convenient means of the crops being bought by the wartime purchasing organisation, the Ministry of Food. Export quotas are easier to establish, to enforce and administer when there is only a single buyer, especially if that buyer is prepared to arrange a settlement between those who exceed their allotted shares and those who do not reach them. Thus the West African merchants were inclined to favour statutory export monopolies.

The system was imposed and ultimately managed by the Association of West African Merchants dominated by a handful of the larger firms. Many criticised the quota system, not least aspiring Nigerian nationals and others wanting to participate in it. It brought home to the merchants within the Association the advantages and profitability of market-sharing agreements. This greatly strengthened officials' determination to see a radical change in marketing methods. There had been criticism immediately before the war in successive reports but the war had put any action on them in abeyance.

A number of factors combined to bring about the establishment of the Produce Marketing Boards. Indigenous businessmen found that lack of capital inhibited their participation in the export trade and they brought political influence to bear on the decision makers to produce a system that made it easier for them to gain entry. There was a resentment directed against the larger and more successful expatriate firms. This stemmed largely from a profound ignorance on the part of many Nigerians of the working of an exchange and market economy. Accumulated wealth was thought to have been earned solely by the impoverishment of customers and competitors. It was a widespread article of faith that the wealth of mercantile firms had been extracted from the Africans and had in no way been created by the activities of the merchants themselves. Falls in prices on the terminal markets were likely to be seen as a deliberate attempt by expatriate companies to put them out of business. Any such fall in price was followed by assertions that the 'sons of the soil' were not getting their due returns. In the full knowledge that they had been excluded from the export trade during the period of quotas, they now reacted by demanding what they saw as a fair share of the trade by local businesses. They looked to government to assist in this. There were many officials who were only too willing to support such an argument.

There was also concern among officials about the ability of producers to survive the swings of the market prices and there was a strong lobby in favour of stabilising the payments to them. This was a course of action reflected in two important British parliamentary White Papers which dealt with arrangements for post-war marketing of West African cocoa. If surpluses could be accumulated when the world price is high, these could be used to support producers when the market price was low. There was also evidence in these papers of a distinct dislike of traders and intermediaries and this may have given an added impetus for urging drastic changes in marketing arrangements.

It was, however, the presence of the West African Produce Control Board at the end of the war that was a principal factor in the setting up of the marketing boards. Once a statutory monopoly has been in existence for some years, strong tendencies for self-perpetuation begin to appear. It causes intellectual and administrative vested interests. By and large it is easier to continue a system that is already established than to discard it. The proposals for cocoa were extended to the marketing of other West African agricultural exports. Legislation was enacted which set up the boards and defined their extensive duties. It is clear from the Nigeria Cocoa Marketing Ordinance of 1947 the wide extent of its authority. It is clear too that from their powers and organisation the boards were organs of government and not independent commercial organisations as had been officially claimed on their behalf. They could control and fix prices, prescribe quality, buy the total cocoa crop, appoint licensed buying agents to act on their behalf, grant or withhold licences and impose conditions under which they might or might not be renewed. Similar powers were given in respect of other products.

Among the advantages to indigenous businessmen of the establishment of the boards was the system of payment on declared, graded purchases which allowed them to receive payment subject to a monthly reconciliation against actual deliveries to Board stores at port. This enabled them to operate with a lower capital outlay as compared to the previous system. A separate government initiative set up a Cooperative Department responsible for the development of cooperative activities by these newly appointed buying agents whereby they achieved further economies of scale in transport, storage and administration reflected in the Association of Nigerian Cooperative Exporters. A Labour government in London was sympathetic to such monopoly practices by the Produce Marketing Boards. This reflected its own approach at the time to problems of production and marketing of many basic commodities at home and was a continuation of immediate post-war domestic arrangements.

Palm oil as an export commodity was originally used in the manufacture of soap and candles but, as production methods and hence its quality improved, it became increasingly used in the manufacture of margarine. It is an element in generic vegetable oil, a cooking medium, a covering description that enables the blenders who purchased it to alter the mix according to the price and availability of alternatives. Hydrogenated palm oil is used extensively in various food preparations including some 'ice creams'. Palm kernel oil, mostly extracted overseas, is used principally in the manufacture of margarine but is also used in the manufacture of soap. The combined market value of palm oil and kernels over the 1950s was approximately the same as that of cocoa, these two classes of produce leaving groundnuts as the only crop to come anywhere near them in money terms. In relation to weight there were more groundnuts shipped than cocoa indicating the much higher value of cocoa for a given weight.

Cocoa had not been a significant crop until after the First World War when it assumed a respectable share of Nigerian exports growing steadily in tonnage shipped right up to and through the 1950s. Groundnuts were not a commercially viable crop until the railway was completed to Kano in 1911 from which time exports increased spectacularly. It was not possible to gauge exactly how much was Nigerian production and how much came from the neighbouring French territories of Niger and Chad due to the cross-border trade. Of the marketing board products cotton had a relatively small production although important for the growers in the areas of its cultivation and for the incipient textile industry it served.

This growing importance of Nigerian produce was recognised by the British government in the mid-1920s and practical steps were taken to ensure that it was competitive with other suppliers by the establishment of the Produce Inspection Service within the Department of Agriculture. Produce inspection was also introduced about the same time in the Gold Coast and Zanzibar. All Nigerian commodity exports with the exception of minerals, hides and skins, timber and bananas were subject to compulsory official inspection.

On the establishment of the Marketing Boards, it was a reasonable organisational step to attach the Produce Inspection Service to it as it was a self-contained unit with its own administrative mechanisms. The system consisted of minimum export standards; only produce inspected and rated above the minimum could be exported. Compulsory grading was superimposed on the minimum standards and the differences between grades were spelt out in the standards laid down. There was in addition compulsory inspection of some produce not controlled by the marketing boards, notably rubber, ginger and chillies. I was now part of this system.

Part 3

On The Move

CHAPTER 13

Port Harcourt

I was posted to my first charge in Port Harcourt, the biggest port in Eastern Nigeria with a vast hinterland and a rail system completed in 1916 that facilitated evacuation of export commodities grown or extracted in the country it traversed from the closer producing areas around Enugu, Aba and Umuahia. It was eventually extended to join the line from Lagos to Kaduna and Kano which would be further extrended to Gusau and Nguru in the far north. This is where I would learn by doing. Named after a British colonial secretary of the time of its conception, Port Harcourt had special port and warehouse facilities built when the railway was extended there from Kaduna in 1916. It became a focal point for the transfer of goods from the interior to ocean-going ships and was connected to the south by water-borne transport in the creeks of the eastern side of the delta and the palmlands inland from the mangrove swamps.

I was accompanied by my steward Richard whom I had engaged in Lagos. The trip to Port Harcourt was our first extended one and was my first introduction to the long drives on corrugated, red laterite roads. The highlight for me was seeing a sign *Beware! Elephant Pass* somewhere between Ife and Benin. It appears elephants are creatures of habit and have a periodic circuit they do not deviate from. The trip was an opportunity to find out more - myself to get to know Richard and obtain from him as much information on the country and its customs as I could and Richard to get to know me better and to demonstrate the skills he possessed. His village, Obinze, was on the way. I tried to get him to talk.

Initially, Richard was unwilling to indulge in any conversation save to answer questions or carry out instructions.
'Tell me, Richard, I said,' what do you do in Obinze in the evenings when everybody finishes work for the day'?
'We talk, sah.'

'What things do you talk about?'

'All tings'.

'Tell me about them'.

'We talk. We tell story'.

'What kind of stories, Richard?

'Good stories, sah'

'Tell me one'

'No sah' Richard protested, 'I no fit tell Európean African story.'

'Pretend I am a black man.'

'You not be black man', Richard laughed in embarrassment at the impropriety of such a suggestion. 'Some tings dey for dis world' (some things are ordained on this earth of ours).

We spent the night in Onitsha and left refreshed in the morning. Richard could hardly contain himself. He was now in his home territory which he had not seen for two years.. His home village, Obinze in the Owerri province, was not far away and he grew more excited with each passing minute.

'How many miles to Obinze now, Richard?' I asked

'It nevah be far' Richard replied

'How many miles do you think?'

'I never see de stone mile.' This latter was a concrete post or milestone erected every so many miles with the intials of a destination and a number indicating the distance in miles. When eventually we reached Obinze there was no option but to let Richard spend some time with his family. We somehow made room for the bags of yams they quickly assembled for him and after this break we resumed the journey.

The posting to Port Harcourt was part of my training or learning-by-doing programme. I would have an area responsibility but a senior and a principal produce officer would be on hand in the station to keep an eye on me and provide advice should I need it. There was much to learn in a diverse region where the major production of palm produce took place and which took in the eastern side of the Niger Delta, involving extensive travel by car, launch and canoe. It also entailed visiting the best palm producing area in Nigeria in the lands just north of the delta.

On one of my first tours of inspection, I was cornered by market women in Mbawsi, in the heart of the palm producing region, who complained in the strongest possible terms that they were not being paid the full price for their palm kernels at the local buying station. This was not strictly within my remit but I talked to them as best I could and wrote out a form of words they could incorporate in a letter to the appropriate authority. It appeared to assuage them somewhat. When I recounted this to Bill Holland, the Senior District Officer, he told me I was lucky to get away with my clothes on - no doubt one of these statements meant to signify the exercise of extreme caution in such circumstances, I thought. His coded caution went back to how the Ibo women, when they believed a rumour they were going to have to pay a head tax just at the time of the Great Depression of 1929-31 that caused prices to plummet and virtually wiped out demand for palm oil and kernels, eventually gathered together in their thousands to give voice to their complaints. This was as a result, it is believed, of deliberations in secret societies which they were known to have.

Such was the scale and force of the protest that it became known as the 'Ibo Women's War' although there were some Ibibio women involved too. The women of Mbawsi had been to the fore in what for a time was a situation that the administration could not handle. The women had brushed aside police rushed to confront them and had injured many including Europeans. Some of the older women among them protesting at the price the produce buyers were paying them could well have been among the 'soldiers' of the Women's War, less than 25 years before. A similar group had destroyed the commercial and administrative buildings in Aba and Opobo. The feminine militancy collapsed only when a British officer, presumably interpreting an administrative instruction, ordered Hausa troops to open fire on a gathering of them which had got out of hand. Well over 50 women died in the shooting and subsequent panic and many more were injured.

This happened during my lifetime for goodness' sake. It was only ten years after the Amritsar massacre in India when Ghurka soldiers opened fire on Hindu demonstrators on the command of a British general. Yet the shooting of the women was neither nationalist fervour nor an emotional response to the murder of Europeans as in Amritsar. It was women who believed they had a legitimate complaint about commercial matters that was not being addressed by the authorities and who had taken violent but not life-threatening action in an effort to seek redress. Yet it is difficult, if not impossible, to find any account in the histories of the time. It is not even mentioned in the *History of Nigeria* written by a former Acting Governor Sir Alan Burns, originally published in the year of the Ibo Women's War and updated in 1947 some four years before I read it prior to going out to West Africa.

Neither does it appear in the major imperial histories, presumably because it was not a turning point like Amritsar in the fortunes of the emerging Nigerian political opposition. It is nevertheless surprising that the issue has not been aired more widely considering the number and sex of those who died, the nature of their protest and its underlying cause. There is an enlightening study of the women's revolt, *The Road to Aba,* by an American researcher H A Gailey.

The root cause of the tragedy was neither the depression nor the rumoured tax on the women but the failure of the system of indirect rule which had worked successfully in Northern Nigeria and which had been introduced by decree into the south of the country. It depended for its efficacy on the authority of the traditional chiefs through whom the system was given effect. In the Yoruba West the chiefs were established and by and large their authority was still recognised, albeit reluctantly by some. Among the Ibo and Ibibio people in the East, traditionally organised in family groups in their villages in what was a fairly complex social structure, the appointment of warrant chiefs unrelated to the traditional system was a complete disaster (*pace* Lord Lugard, military adventurer, mercenary, serial adulterer, colonial theorist and administrator and member of the League of Nations Mandates Commission, who has been credited - with only limited justification - with the initiation of this policy which was adopted in the North and extended later to Western and Eastern Nigeria and widely implemented in other colonies).

The rioting convinced the British authorities that they could no longer continue to impose this system on the Ibo people and others in the predominantly Ibo East. As a result, they had to revert to direct rule and eventually to a system which, if not through the traditional authority, was a reasonable compromise between traditional and modern colonial forms of administration producing decentralised local government agencies. A similar system was introduced in the Yoruba west anticipating the fact that an educated elite was beginning to challenge the authority of the traditional chiefs there.

Indirect rule was seen for what it was, a flawed idea which might be put to use successfully in certain places but was anything but a universal concept in the governing of subject peoples despite the advocacy of Lugard, prompted and supported by his intellectually equal and politically astute wife Flora. Recent British imperial histories mention indirect rule and the influence of Lugard in introducing its general use in Nigeria and its adoption in other colonies, but fail to point out that it was in certain instances an abject failure, leaving the impression it was the one tried and applicable orthodoxy. It was dependent on the continuing power of the traditional rulers where hierarchy prevailed and presented a bulwark against educated nationalists and other radicals.

Touring in the creeks of the delta was dependent on water-borne transport and presented difficulties from an unexpected quarter. The Department of Marketing and Exports was looked on by some of the Nigeria Marine, it transpired, as an upstart department usurping some of its functions. Marine Department officers were reluctant to make a touring launch available claiming that the department should use its own launches. Since the Marketing and Exports launches were designed for harbour work only, they hadn't a strong argument. I still had to resort to talking about the Produce Inspection Service rather than the department to which I was attached, for they had made launches available to it willingly when the service was attached to the Agricultural Department and that designation did not evoke the same astringent response. It was as if there was no common purpose underlying the work of the departments. I found it hard to credit that so petty a subject as allocation of resources, even scarce ones, could be subject to such childish animosities. The last verse of the Lanark Grammar School song came to mind:

We may be four yet four in one,
One team with but one race to run,
One motto o'er all other flies
That all our strength in union lies.

A D Robertson, rector of the school and author of the words of the song would have been appalled as I was.

In Port Harcourt I again came across the Nigerian press as a raw force in politics. The *Nigerian Eastern Guardian* was a vigorous promoter of the Ibo cause and of Nigerian autonomy in the manner envisaged by Dr Azikiwe without the unrelenting editorial venom of that leader's *West African Pilot*. It appeared to have a policy of finding stories to the discredit of Europeans and particularly civil service and business expatriates. When my turn came it was to inform me through its columns without any specific detail, that all was not well in my office and it was time I found out about it. If there was any truth in it, it did not surface again. If there was something - and I checked everything that I could think of - it could well have had a useful effect. Despite it's sniping, as it might have been called from the standpoint of the authorities, the local news sheet struck a note of optimism for the future of Nigeria. That optimism was widely felt and was reflected in things like the name of the local bus company *The Hope Rising Society.*

It was also, I think, the *Nigerian Eastern Guardian* that gave me an early example of the use of euphemism having no place in the written language as indeed it most certainly had not in the spoken one, and in which the particular and the detailed are given emphasis at the expense of the general and the conceptual. A young man and woman, having engaged in the sexual act, could not get uncoupled. Hearing their cries, neighbours had entered the house they were in, lifted the unity on to a hand-cart, covered it with a sheet and wheeled it to hospital. The paper's report of the incident described it as a series of actions in the order in which it happened, drawing on the accounts of eye-witnesses at each stage. At no time was reference made to the broader physiological and psychological aspects of the unusual but not unique occurrence.

Inevitably, because of the continuous delivery of produce to, and evacuation of produce from, its warehouses and wharves, the port had to have regular supervision. It was here I first came across phantom shipments when non-existing palm kernels were tallied out of the warehouse and into a ship. It was only shortly after that I came across the tallying into port storage of produce that never was. The first was only discovered on receipt by the buyer (produce tended to be sold in the terminal markets while on the high seas or in overseas warehouses) and often meant carelessness or collusion between the ship's tallyman and Board's tallyman or the diverting of the attention of the Board's tallyman while the deed was done; it was without exception carried out when the warehouses were full as the accurate checking of stocks was nearly impossible in these circumstances. The second was more handlable and provable.

Also associated with the port was the BOP or Bulk Oil Plant where drums and casks were emptied and pumped into tanks awaiting bulk shipment - one more development in reducing the costs of handling and distributing palm oil. The BOP was a place where I learnt much about the adulteration of palm oil by the process of adding chemicals that gave a distorted positive reading when standard tests were made before the drums were decanted.

CHAPTER 14

Onyecha

The Port Harcourt area took in much of the Ibo country and had a principally Ibo population with a fair scattering of other tribal groups concentrated in the delta of the Niger. The Ibo are found in the forests of south-east Nigeria where the population densities are high and the soil debased as a result of intensive working without the luxury of being able to leave plots fallow on a regular basis to allow them to recover their original fertility. They cleared the forest and put it to work in the cultivation of their crops which they husbanded as a subsistence economy. They lived in 'village democracies', that is, they lived in a society without hierarchy where the extended family was the basic social unit. It could comprise twenty families or more. Sometimes it took on a more complex form which embraced all the descendants of a particular ancestor who occupied the same territory or village. The eldest living male was head of this social unit. Some villages might consist of several of these patrilineal groups, one of whom was recognised as senior and he was the figurehead in whose name a village council took its decisions.

There was no hierarchy and this seemed to promote an outward-looking attitude. It was reflected in competition among villages to build schools and carry out other community projects. The Ibo are a hard-working, thrifty people who have gained the reputation of being good traders, good technicians and administrators. Their lack of hierarchy meant that that they were never inhibited in making known their point of view and some people found them difficult to work with.

Some officers whose work had previously been confined to the North where there was a more hierarchic social structure and where people when given an instruction would normally comply without demur, found the Ibo hard to adjust to and longed to be posted back to the North for which they claimed a superior mode of living by which they meant a more gentlemanly tenour of life. That was certainly the case as far as the climate was concerned;
86

the dry heat of the north being much more tolerable than the sweatbox of the oil palm belt. We saw it as the soft option. The Ibo women shared the tendency of their men to put their views forward with the utmost cogency as I had found among the women of the Ngwa clan in Mbawsi. Sometimes people from other ethnic groups found the Ibo arrogant, aggressive and grasping and regarded with disfavour the noisy exhibitionism and the brash disregard for humility of some when they had become successful. I was to come to realise that once an Ibo trusted you, you had a friend for life.

The pressure of population had created an Ibo diaspora with many of their number seeking work with government or commercial organisations outside Ibo territory. The special areas designated for those not of the faith outside cities of the Muslim north were largely populated by the Ibo and a smaller Yoruba minority who were indispensable to the running of the administration there. Many of them had embraced Christianity as a consequence of the activities of missions of different denominations from the second half of the nineteenth century and had achieved under the tutelage of the missions a standard of education that left all other tribes behind in the acquisition of the skills needed for advancement in a colonial or any other situation requiring clerical and intellectual skills.

A significant number of the population were not Christian but animists who attributed soul - spirit is probably a more appropriate word - to natural objects and phenomena. They had a close relationship with the natural world, with the world of spirits, of the arts, and the ancestors. Such people were previously called by the more negative name of pagans. They believed that everything in the universe was a manifestation of deity and therefore sacred, that the world of the spirits is a deep source of wisdom, healing and inspiration.

Many of those who had embraced the Christian religions, particularly in the remoter regions, still propitiated the spirits with suitable offerings which acted in effect as a kind of double indemnity. They had many gods but there was a boss-god in charge, Chuku, to whom the other gods were subservient. They appeared to have had little difficulty in embracing the Christian God as Number One in the hierarchy as long as they were not forced to abandon the worship of their own spirits. The Ibo is noted for his ability to adjust his behaviour to circumstances.

My steward Richard was an Ibo, so I always had an interpreter to translate the culture and the language for me. This made life a lot easier than it would otherwise have been. Soon I got to know some of the customs that I would almost certainly have had trouble with in the beginning. When we entered a new place and someone raised a clenched fist, that was not a threat but a greeting. It was almost invariably accompanied by *Onyecha* meaning 'white man'. Without Richard's mediation the whole atmosphere could have seemed menacing and unfriendly except that the smiles were never all that far away. *Onyoji* ('black man') was an acceptable response but had to be accompanied by a smile.

Later, when we would move to other parts where other languages were spoken or people were itinerant like the Hausa traders, there would be different customs but always 'white man' whether *oyibo* in Yoruba, *baturi* in Hausa or *mbakara* in Efik. There is a Jamaican slang word '*backra*' meaning 'a white man' which suggests to me that the Efik and Ibibio country (the two tribes shared the same language) was the source of many of the slaves shipped to the West Indies in the 17th and 18th centuries. I began to realise that wherever we went in the bush, we were the cinema, the jugglers and the passing show all rolled into one. If people crowded round it was out of interest and curiosity rather than bad manners which is very much a concept that is value-laden and varies from country to country and indeed from region to region.

On one occasion when I was in a part of the country that had, as I later found out, been providing a slight political problem as far as the administration was concerned, my car broke down. As I was lying under it trying to find out what was wrong, a crowd of villagers offered to help on behalf of the mechanics among their number - almost half the men in Nigeria, it seemed, claimed to be mechanics - a gesture much appreciated but in the event unnecessary in this case as it was a familiar problem. Shortly afterwards, a police lorry rolled up and a squad of policemen got down fitted out in full riot gear and wielding their *kobokos*. Never was there a greater incongruity between my perception of the gesture that had just been made to me and the impression given of the people by the police action. When I recounted this to the Resident, he admonished me for not keeping him informed of my movements so that I could have been warned of a possible explosive situation. Thereafter I made sure he received a copy of my proposed itinerary but reserved my judgment about the 'explosiveness' of the situation I had witnessed which was presumptuous of me, I suppose, but a natural reaction or so I tell myself.

Richard had a habit of making his own judgments about the actions of drivers and cyclists, particularly where in his judgment they had erred. If he perceived a very bad breach of his traffic code, he would push his head out of the window and call 'You bloody fool'. This trait led me to wonder where it was that he had heard this expression and it did not take me long to hazard a guess. It connoted in his book severe displeasure on the part of the utterer and one wondered whether there had been a former employer whose fuse was too short for long survival in the tropics.

If the person to whom Richard's comment was directed showed the least inclination to challenge what he had said - and his fellow Ibos were unlikely to take such a comment without a vociferous reply - he would immediately extend his arm out of the window turning the open palm of his hand towards the person concerned who would be behind us by this time, in a final gesture of contemptuous dismissal. This was, I established early on in our relationship, the ultimate curse. Richard was on safe ground so to speak, conveying his malediction to the recipient from the safety of a moving vehicle. Another of his salient characteristics, which he shared with many of his countrymen, was to indicate direction with his lips - never with a finger. If he was pointing out someone who had contravened his code, this was done with an exaggerated action. He would open his lips and nod vigorously in the direction of the person saying '*Dat man dere*', indicating the direction with rounded lips and a final nod on the last syllable.

CHAPTER 15

The Mammy Water

The Niger Delta covers some fourteen thousand square miles and contains many hundreds of creeks. It has been called the biggest swamp in the world. The Port Harcourt area took in nearly a half of the delta. Some of these creeks are broad and easily navigable while others are narrow and have to be squeezed through. The narrow ones are best approached by small launch or canoe and that by persons well versed in the unique geography of the delta. In my time there, these were inevitably local people who had been brought up in the area. Sometimes they ran a ferry service providing regular contact between the inhabited islands and the main centres of population; Chief Tom Big Harry ran a ferry from Port Harcourt to places like Bakana and Buguma that was an indispensable service, especially for itinerant traders and workers in Port Harcourt returning to the magnet of family, as well as for distibution of goods through the hands of a plethora of middlemen.

The most dramatic as well as the biggest of the ferries was the sternwheeler 'Delta Queen' which towered out of the water and took us back I would guess, at least two generations. I have an abiding mental picture of the corrugated iron cladding on the lofty superstructure glinting in the sun as she steamed away from the wharf churning up the water behind her into a froth as she moved out into mid-river, sending out sound-waves as well as making bow-waves. Sometimes the experts on river navigation were fishermen who wrested a precarious living from the crocodile infested waters.

Other experts were members of the Nigeria Marine who were trained to negotiate the bends and snags and natural hazards to facilitate the travel of government officers going about their daily business. There was also a team of very competent Dutchmen from a firm called NEDECO involved in clearing snags to guarantee the safe access of sea-going vessels to the ports of the delta as well as the many ships carrying traffic on the main branches of the Niger and on its major tributary the Benue. It was fascinating to see how some of them nosed their launches into the bank, went astern on full tiller for a short distance then with the tiller on the opposite hand would ease forward again. Gradually by this process they negotiated the tightest of bends.

Staff of the Nigeria Marine, probably working under instruction, stuck to the main waterways as far as their duties allowed. Touring launches like the 'Edith' were big investments. Demands on their services were high and this usage merited looking after them well. This was my commonest form of transport in the creeks unless I was going short distances when I would use a canoe, or to Strongface Creek which was approached from Opobo by Marine gig with two uniformed pullers. I was always intrigued in a guarded kind of way by the watchful insouciance of the crocodiles as the wake of the launch washed the bank. They would half-open their yellow eyes and peer over the tips of their snouts as if recording the scene. In contrast to the lethargy of the crocodiles, African Grey parrots would once in a while flit from tree to tree, occasionally essaying a dart across the creek and providing a welcome flash of colour as the red of their tail feathers fleetingly stood out against the more sombre background of the surrounding browns and greens.

It was hard to imagine that the remote and small community of Opobo, now accessible by road from Port Harcourt, was the domain of the same King Jaja who signed an accord with Britain, had been awarded a sword of honour by Queen Victoria for sending some fifty men to fight in the Ashanti wars in the Gold Coast, and who had died far from his home for defending traditional values as well as his own commercial interests. He was apprehended for trial by means viewed by many as unacceptable and un-British. His fame and admiration among his own people is evident from the statue erected to him by public subscription in Opobo Town in the early 1900s and still an object of respect and pride when I was there on tour as was witnessed by the eagerness of locals to point him out.

The vegetation of the area varies. There is the mangrove which somehow manages to survive the swamps exposing daylight through the twisted roots that rise above the level of the brackish water rather like dancers on stilts, with the occasional fisherman's hut in the foliage and his canoe pulled up into the mud. Then there is the oil palm, the *Eleias Guineensis*, which thrives on the more solid ground to provide a living for many of the river people. The mystery of the oil palm to the uninitiated is that despite its name indicating a local origin in the area washed by the Gulf of Guinea, it is not to be found in primary forest, certainly not in Nigerian forests, giving rise to the claim by some that it was not indigenous to Nigeria. This was erroneous and the explanation is relatively simple. It needs plenty of light which is not available in the forest covering of high trees but grows in abundance when the forest has been cleared. The area of the southern part of Ibo country is well suited to the growing and harvesting of palm fruits as they give a better yield and quality there than in any other part.

The oil palm grows, at the crown of the tree, large stems known as *bangas* which sprout spiky bunches of fruits. These are harvested by specialist collectors. The collector shins up the trees with the assistance of a stout rope of plaited lianas which he passes round the trunk of the tree and round his back. Pushing his back against the rope and his feet against the trunk, he moves up the tree step by step. As he levers himself up with all the power of his legs thrust his feet against the tree, he whips the rope further up the tree, and repeats the action until he reaches the crown of the tree where three or four bangas are clumped together. From this position he cuts the stalks with a short, sharp cutting tool and drops the bangas to the ground.

If he has time and energy - some trees are more easily climbed than others - he will lower it to the ground on another rope, an action that prevents the bruising of the fruits which raises the free fatty acid content and reduces the quality of the oil produced. Some palm oil collectors make variations on this theme depending on the size and configuration of the tree and the availability of useful appurtenances like small car tyres tied to the tree and used to support the feet when cutting the fruits, illustrating once more the ability of the Nigerian to improvise with what is available locally. He performs his specialist task for a fee, likely as not in kind, as not all farmers are as strong, skilled and fit as he is. As a result he is often a self-employed itinerant worker within a limited area.

The fruits so harvested have a thick, purplish-orange pericarp or skin with a kernel inside contained in a hard shell. Between the colourful wall of the fruit and the nut is a rich, reddish-orange oil which is used to cook locally and is exported for the manufacture of margarine and, in the case of oil with a high free fatty acid content, as additives for paints and as a lubricant. It is traditionally extracted by first of all removing the fruit from the spikes, boiling them in water to soften the pericarp, pounding the them in a tall, narrow mortar or trampling them in clay-lined pits or in dugout canoes to loosen the pericarp and fibres from the nuts. These are stirred in hot water and the fibres picked out and pressed by hand to remove the oil. Where the fibres are small, I have seen them taken out by hand and strained through a sieve and the remaining oil squeezed out by hand pressure. When the fibres have been removed and dried they make good firelighters. The oil made by this method was known as 'hard oil' that had a relatively high content of free fatty acids and was less valuable than 'soft oil' produced cold and more likely to provide oil of edible quality.

Palm oil was also used locally to provide a naked flame from a round 50-cigarette tin with a whole punched in the lid to take a wick that goes down into the oil. It gives enough light to make out figures and products on stalls in night markets and can be compared to a candle in terms of its effect. Goldsmiths used it in their brass lamps. The oil I also saw being used by women in the process of grooming their own or their children's hair into criss-cross patterns. It was produced by local peasants in small quantities. To get to market it passed through a number of hands, each time increasing the quantity until finally it was of sufficient size to justify a purchase by a trader who sold it on to licensed buying agents.

The kernel, once its shell has been cracked, yields a high quality edible oil, also used in the making of soap when pressed out but this cannot always be done locally as it requires high investment crushing plant, although Unilever did have a factory for the manufacture of margarine with the *'Blue Band'* label and the making of soap. Kernels are sometimes also used when processed as an additive to gin. The residue after the oil has been extracted is used for cattle cake, which is good for the milk yield of cattle in temperate climates in winter when there is no grass. As a result of such activities there was a small export industry based on this by-product of palm oil production.

The palm oil and kernels were produced by local farmers unless they were the output of a small local oil-mill to which the fruits could be taken to be sold for cash. These were called 'pioneer oil mills' and they were financed by the Eastern Regional Production Development Board for more economic production and distribution. Some 50 of these had been established by the Eastern Region Production Development Board with money allocated by the Oil Palm Produce Marketing Board and many more were projected. These were purpose-built plants which increased the extraction rate of palm oil from just over 50% by treading under foot and 65% by wooden hand press to 85% in their processes. Only an affiliate of the United Africa Company had the right to lease land for the setting up of a plantation within Nigeria and that was so that best practice could be observed and incorporated where possible in the pioneer oil mills.

Kernels produced by a family unit were traditionally left to accumulate until a quiet time when the family could take them to the cracking machine available in many villages. The heaps that grew up outside the houses were sometimes referred to as 'the poor man's bank'. Ibos in particular had the patience and determination to perform the tiresome task of cracking the nuts, 90% of Nigerian palm kernels coming from Ibo areas while only just over 50% of the palm oil originated there, probably due in part to the demand for oil to feed the highly concentrated population but also because the Ibos were more assiduous in gathering and cracking the nuts.

In some communities palm kernels became the perquisites of the women who were often responsible for the cracking. In the more remote areas they were often cracked by the women with stones. This provided a welcome addition to the family income. The kernels had then to be transported to a middleman or an official buying station, either by a family member or carrier who expected payment for his services or who took possession of the kernels as an intermediary. While they were normally bought by weight, they were bought by measure in Opobo perpetuating a custom going back more than a century. They were then inspected for quality and that they were free from undue amounts of shell by weight, fibre or other impurities, were not damaged by insects or contained kernels that were rotten. They were then bagged to the requisite 185 pounds and sealed for export.

Local economies were often dependent on the contribution of the womenfolk. They laboured together in the cultivation and harvesting of crops. In remoter areas where they worked the land communally, they would go to work singing. Stories abounded of their durability - of how they worked until a child was on the point of being born and returned to their work shortly after the birth, retrieving the child from older family minders to feed and comfort it, or even carry the child tied to her back while she worked. The nursing service and the medical services of the missions encouraged them to come to see them at important times in pregnancy and after the birth. So appalling was the infant mortality rate that in some places it was not customary to give a name to a child until it was about a year old.

Mothers were encouraged to seek help immediately after the birth to ensure there was no possibility of umbilical hernia which manifested itself in the umbilicus developing into an unsightly and uncomfortable protuberance in the growing child. That they paid attention to the advice given that the cord should be examined and cut as soon as possible after the birth at the centre for medical care, was illustrated by the story told me by one of the nursing sisters. On one occasion, the mother of a new-born child had walked miles through the bush to the centre carrying her baby with the umbilical cord still attached. It was as well that the people of the Ibo lands and of the delta region had reasonable nourishment considering the rigour of their lives. The oil and fish diet which were the staples of the river people was, it has been claimed by Pip Powell, the man who coached (voluntarily) the Nigerian national athletics team in the 1950s, the basis of the exceptionally high performance of athletes from that part of Nigeria. Peter Esiri, one of my staff stationed in the Delta, was the Nigerian triple jump champion and competed internationally.

Lest I have given the impression that everyone was in his or her small corner doing what he or she was good at or was forced to do as part of a social group, let me correct that idea. One facet of the Nigerian is that he, and perhaps even more so, she, is a natural trader. Almost everybody had another interest of some kind that brought in money. In the creeks trading was the general practice, if only part time. The people regard it as part of existence itself, not necessarily a distinct occupation. In consequence, they are good at it. While some women traders might turn over thousands in a year, trading took place too at a level accessible to the poorest.

Enterprisers would buy a packet of sugar cubes and sell them in lots of ten or whatever number corresponded to the lowest denomination of coin. While the market women might buy scent by the case, their customers would buy a bottle and sell by the drop. Even schoolchildren were involved. They would sell four or five dabs of scent for a penny. Professional people like doctors and lawyers often had trading interests and wives did business with husbands. At one time there was even a report of a wife suing her husband for a commercial debt.

This tradition of involvement in trade stems from the proliferation of intermediaries in internal trade and in the community at large. The large number and variety of intermediaries were often criticised by official and unofficial observers. In fact, these traders substituted semi-skilled or unskilled labour for capital which was in short supply. Their trading methods were economic in that they used resources that were redundant and economised in the use of capital and supervisory staff for which there was a keen demand and for which there were more valuable uses. It was a way of matching segments of supply and demand that met conditions in the local environment. Many traders, especially importers, were often less than meticulous in honouring commercial contracts. Often their failure to meet obligations stemmed not from dishonesty or even irresponsible risk-taking, but from a mixture of shortage of capital, wide price fluctuations and a tendency to overtrade, sometimes encouraged by European exporters.

Into this background enter Sam Bleasby who was a legend in his time. He was reputed to have worked for the United Africa Company as its agent in Opobo. He left the company to become a licensed buying agent of the Nigeria Palm Produce Marketing Board in an abandoned plot, it was said, of the United Africa Company. The land had to be rented as Europeans were not permitted by law to own land. In the clubs of the delta his name was a byword, usually for the eccentricity of living like a hermit or for having 'gone native'. The local people knew him as a friend. He knew their customs better than anyone in the expatriate community and respected their way of life.

Sam was a very private man who would not join in the social activities of the expatriate community. He would never be so ungracious as to turn down an invitation of the Queen's representative the Governor, but these occasions came round at very infrequent intervals. I met him only once and was invited to his house - a most unusual occurrence I was assured by my principal produce officer. I may have been honoured but he possibly saw in me an innocence of my new world and that there was hope for me to escape the kind of life which he shunned. I saw a gentle, spare, frail, old-looking man with a tunic that reached well down past his waist and was buttoned across his neck in Chinese fashion.

It was not at all what I expected of a former successful UAC agent whom you expected to be tough and positive in his talk and actions and to dress in the more accepted fashion. He extended an old world courtesy to me and his quiet dignity held me and at the same time kept me at a distance. He was reputed to have prepared a will leaving all his worldly goods including his business to his servants. The locals were also mystified and intrigued by his way of life. They knew that every Sunday he disappeared for the day in his launch down the creeks which he was said to know like the back of his hand. When asked what he did there, one of these river people smiled and said 'Maybe he get *Mami Wata* for dat place'

The *Mami Wata* or mammy water, was the pidgin name they gave in these parts to the manatee which is the sea-cow, the aquatic mammal that most closely resembles the fabled mermaid and whose perception on the rivers as a nymph with special powers could well stem from the figureheads on the prows of early sailing ships that visited the Coast. She could appear in different places simultaneously. The manatee is found mostly in brackish water, its infrequent sightings adding to the myth that has grown up round it. The water spirit or goddess who, they say, resides in it, is reputed to influence the happiness or unhappiness of the individual. She is characterised as a beautiful and seductive creature with long flowing hair and a light skin. Sometimes her followers are rumoured to have a sexual relationship with her in the spirit world.

The term *Mami Wata* is also used generally for extraordinarily beautiful women who are believed to embody the qualities of the goddess. Likenesses of her can be seen in a few locations around the coast. She is usually characterised as looking in all directions by the expedient of repeating the fashioned figure of the goddess a number of times in an outward-facing circle. In the slaving days someone delegated by a ship's master would not infrequently take a whip called a 'manatea', made from the skin of a manatee, to slaves and sometimes to crew members themselves of the ships conveying them to distant lands far from their homes. Maybe old Sam knew something the rest of us were unaware of.   Or maybe it was just that he was never less idle than when unoccupied, nor less alone than when without company.

CHAPTER 16

The Palm Oil Barons

My principal in Port Harcourt, John Brown, was as well known for his silences as were his native Lammermuir Hills; in fact some of his contemporaries called him 'Noisy' Brown. That sobriquet was not deserved, I always felt, but the fact remains that John did not say anything unless it was worth saying. So when he started to tell me about things that went on when he came to Nigeria in the late 1920's in that compelling, quiet voice of his, I listened. He told stories of how he had seen bottles of human blood for sale in Aba market, of when he was made a special constable on the spot to help contain a local inter-tribal war, of when there was a plague of locusts that left not a single blade of grass on Lagos racecourse and how on one occasion he was in a bush rest house when stationed in Yandev when it was struck by lightning. He was accompanied in the last instance by his wife May who had been a missionary, knew the country and was no mean exponent herself of the art of bush living. He felt a shock in his arm and found he couldn't move it. Not wanting to worry his wife he lay quietly for an hour or so until he felt the feeling begin to come back into his arm and he went back to sleep and told his wife about it in the morning. After all this he let out that in a corner of the rest house had been a drum of petrol which he had brought in for security reasons from his kitcar.

John would tell his tale as he saw it with the beginning of a smile at the corner of his mouth and in his eyes which occasionally culminated in a full smile that transformed his features and reminded me of Gary Cooper as did his rangy gait. He preferred to tell his tale over a whisky. He had completed his Associateship of the Imperial College of Tropical Agriculture in Trinidad, a far step from his native hills. He took his whisky with Angostura bitters which he had come to enjoy while he was there, that aromatic accompaniment to drinks derived from the bark of certain trees found along the Orinoco River in Venezuela. I have never met anyone else with that particular predilection. Bitters are usually taken with gin and constitute the pink element of a pink gin.

Of the tales I listened to avidly, none were more fascinating than how some of our countrymen involved in various commercial activities behaved. John suspected all entrepreneurs, certainly expatriate ones, of dishonest or at best self-serving motives and I have no doubt of his sincerity in what he related. He considered himself an expert by experience or at second hand (he had been too late for their heyday) of the Palm Oil Barons as they came to be referred to by many. He preferred the term 'palm oil ruffians' believing them to be completely undeserving of capital letters equated at this time with God and Bank Rate. I think he viewed them as remittance men or men finding escape from the long arm of the law or who had done something they were ashamed of with good reason. As far as he was concerned they were moral *castrati*. 'Chancers' was a word that sprang easily to his lips when talking about them. They had little, he maintained, to contribute to the benefit of Nigeria.

The palm oil ruffians were men who came to the coast to work with companies that had been set up to buy produce in demand in Europe and to sell what was in demand locally, European technology having largely snuffed out local manufacture by traditional methods and established a market for European exports as a result. The original companies were merchant adventurers motivated by a consuming desire to make a good living in a place where they saw opportunity. One of the companies still referred to its individual operations on the Coast as 'ventures' each of which had to create its own profitability - 'every tub on its own bottom' as the business slang of the day had it. They operated at a time when men of action were needed and long before control was exercised by accountants. These men were called 'agents' and were paid on commission related to the profits generated by the venture. Some of these agents were no doubt highly principled. Many, according to John, were crooks, very different from the well educated and professional managers of today. Government officers had to be circumspect, in the view of John and his departmental contemporaries, in the friends they made in trade, particularly those whose work brought them into contact with the traders.

John recalled being told of one of these men who was responsible for the purchase of large amounts of palm oil that had been poled down the river. The oil was contained in large casks bound together with sticks from the calamas palm or bamboos and lashed with lianas to form large rafts and brought down from Lake Oguta to the delta buying stations at least two weeks away. The crews erected temporary dwellings on the rafts and roofed them with a thatch of palm fronds, a practice that was still being followed but was slowly being phased out with the replacement of casks with steel drums and the development of road transport. The wives cooked and performed household chores while the men did the poling and steering.

When they arrived at the beach and had agreed a price to be paid for the palm oil, their casks of palm oil were winched one by one on to the landing. This particular individual in John's tale would never leave his desk. He refused to let his winch be oiled. His control was to write down £5 every time it creaked to indicate that another cask had been hove-to. That was alleged to be his own cut of the proceeds, no doubt a form of insurance against the contingency of a poverty-stricken old age. To be fair, the man might just have been keeping a running total of his commission or perhaps he was bored with a very limited existence and was whiling away the time.

One governor pointed out to the Foreign Office in London just before the First World War that the practice of paying agents by commission on profits resulted in these men never looking beyond the short term and, indeed, that they were likely to oppose any measures in the future that might impose a temporary handicap on trade. The 'palm oil ruffians' about whom Mary Kingsley, the intrepid traveller, had been warned prior to her journeys in West Africa in the late 1890's, were warmly praised by her as the true servants of their country. At a time when the British saw themselves as having a civilising mission in Africa and as being privileged in this duty, Kingsley saw it as pure commerce which would aid imperial expansion. These traders had, she maintained, a vested interest in the country far beyond that of any colonial officials. She despised missionaries with an equal fervour - an account of her meeting with Mary Slessor would have been interesting but no unbiased fly on the wall has recorded what actually passed between them when they met.

It has to be said, however, that Mary Kingsley, apart from defending polygamy for which a strong argument could be produced, also defended the use of slaves which had cogent economic arguments in support but no moral ones. She went close to condoning ritual murder, voicing the arguments of those chiefs who saw their positions and traditions threatened by the missionaries as well as their economic well-being. But she had her point. These men chose to work in conditions where they were often alone, exposed to disease, were required to undertake long hours of work, enjoyed little recreation save that which they could themselves make, and lived in the knowledge that some of their countrymen saw them as a lesser breed. What Mary Kingsley did not do was to bring to the light of day the failure of some of these people to act in a way that reflected the higher moral spirit ascribed to these times.

The common view of the Bight of Benin as a place not to go at that time was mirrored in the words of the shipping agents for West Africa who cheerfully informed prospective travellers that they did not issue return tickets. This view was compounded by reports that it was not unusual to see a flag flying at half-mast over the 'factories' where the palm oil was bought as another palm oil ruffian succumbed to yellow fever or other disease, to be buried almost immediately in the most basic of graves to prevent the cadaver from putrefying and further hazarding the health of the afflicted community.

These men were good traders. They had competitors who were equally astute. They were not averse to doing each other in the eye if a particular advantage was to be gained. In the evenings they would meet over drinks and a meal and exhibit all the characteristics of bonhomie. If their world was in any way threatened they would band together in mutual defence. It was said in Port Harcourt when I was there that in Abonnema on the New Calabar River (Abonnema had at one time been called 'New Calabar') a trading town just across the watery divide form the government station of Degema, there was a headstone erected in memory of one of these men which bore his name and carried the simple inscription *Friends have done their worst.* I was intrigued and had meant to search for it on the only occasion I went there but I had to change my plans as a result of hearing of the death of King George the Sixth early in the morning of the 6th of February 1952, the twenty-seventh anniversary of my birth. I was informed by the clerk of the native authority in Degema that a 'public holiday has been declared' subsequent to the demise of the king in the night. I grieved all the way back to Port Harcourt as the crew of the launch proceeded there with all speed to enjoy what little remained of the day.

The stress on traders who had built up the palm oil export trade in that period, particularly on those who could not bear their own company for very long, was considerable. It was one of the reasons Mary Kingsley admired them so much. One tale of the trading assistants, the apprentices to the palm oil trade, comes from Opobo. The trading beaches lay near the mouth of the Imo River in south-east Nigeria and were close to the spot where Jaja built a township and set himself up as king. It was a place from which the produce of the area was shipped but had a sandbar which made access to the sea difficult and the channel had to be dredged on a regular basis. Ships' masters talked about 'bouncing' their vessels across the bar. In my day it was dying as a port due not so much to the silting up of the bar as the development of a road to Port Harcourt that made Opobo less attractive commercially as a place to trade from, if not redundant. Yet at one time it had a reputation and notoriety that matched its considerable commercial importance.

I have been long addicted to the scanning of gravestones as stimulants to the imagination and aids to the history of a place. I was motivated to visit the graveyard in Opobo as a result of yet another tale told me by the same John Brown whose memories of such matters went back as far as 1929. What is incontestable is that there are gravestones of three very young European men whose deaths all occurred within a period of a few days. Their story sheds light on the harshness and loneliness of life for the traders of the day.

To tell it requires a look at the background against which it all happened. The 'beaches' on which the produce of the countryside was bought and stored until it was shipped, were owned by companies with names above the factories like MacIvor's and Miller's, but in reality part of the Niger Company empire and the African and Eastern Trading Company, both shortly to be amalgamated within the United Africa Company. There was also a Cooperative Wholesale Society factory and one belonging to one of the French companies less than a half hour's trip by water from these beaches and possibly a few others I am unable to recall. Each beach was overlooked by a house owned by the company in which lived all its expatriate employees. Typically it was built on stilts and the accommodation was characteristically divided into two. One half was occupied by the manager or 'agent'. The other half was shared by up to three or four assistants. Work went on in all the daylight hours from Monday to Friday by which time everybody was ready to do something different.

While abstemiousness was enforced on the assistants through the week by a rationing of strong drink and lengthy hours of work, weekends tended to develop into drinking sessions which began on Friday evenings and ended after lunch on Sunday when the effects of a palm oil stew on top of a skinful of schnapps combined to see the actors in this tale sleep until sober. It was considered improper to turn up for work on a Monday morning showing signs of the weekend's excesses, not for any moral reason but because of the possible adverse effect on profits. The agent, whose income depended on these profits, had the power to ensure anyone not meeting this norm might not return from leave.

Towards the end of one such weekend, an assistant in one of these houses challenged another to a game of Russian roulette.

The challenge was accepted and the acceptor blew his brains out. The man who had made the challenge was so overcome with remorse when he came to that he took his own life. A third man, travelling by motor cycle to the funeral of the second, hit a pothole just short of his destination and broke his neck. No doubt their relatives thousands of miles away were informed of a tragic accident to their dear ones. There were other gravestones in Opobo where people had died within a short time of each other but that was usually the effect of an epidemic like yellow fever that did not discriminate by age or sex.

The agent who had the other half of the house on stilts collected brass objects similar in appearance to widened horse shoes in shape, and called manillas. People used them as money in the south-east of the country. The name appears to derive from the Portuguese word for 'bracelet'. Their origin is the source of speculation but the favoured theory is that they were copied from the metal rings and bracelets used as a currency by Phoenician sailors reputed to have explored the coast of West Africa in the 5th century BC. They had acquired value in the intervening years. In the many years of Portuguese dominance of the West African trade they were worn by Portuguese as anklets and often exchanged for slaves. They appear on a Nigerian stamp of the early 1950's. They had a currency just as cowrie shells had in other places like the neighbouring Western Delta, and like all money, varied in value; they were worth more in the height of the palm oil season than in the off-season. If the value of the manilla was low, the agent would buy them at the going rate and store them in sealed casks under his house until they rose in value when they would be released on to the market for sale. This was a kind of extra-mural activity possibly intended as a further insurance to supplement the retirement pension in Akeld, Dollar, Falmouth, Maiden Bradley or wherever. The manilla was abolished as a currency in 1949.

What would John have thought of the dealers in the City today and the financiers who shift their money around the world to extract the maximum gain from changes in the exchange rate or interest rates?   A difference of kind or a difference of degree from the palm oil ruffians?

CHAPTER 17

On Tour

'On tour' has a ring to it that suggests ease and freedom except for people who tread the boards. Nothing could be further from the reality in its Nigerian context. The touring officer had to go on his inspections at regular intervals irrespective of the prevailing season and on all kinds of roads and tracks and waterways. How he decided his particular choice of stations to visit was up to him. Because he had to give details of his visits in regular reports, failure to visit certain stations for reason of bad roads or unfavourable conditions would be picked up by his seniors.

It was not all that difficult to get used to the corrugations and potholes on the laterite roads. The vibration was initially upsetting but eventually you found the speed it was most comfortable to drive at - in the case of my car around 45 miles per hour. There were two critical speeds at which the vibrations got bad before you reached the most comfortable speed. Apparently the optimum speed varied with the length of the wheel-base of the vehicle you were driving. A certain vibration was transmitted to the person even at optimum speed. I wondered how this compared with vibro-massage offered in the barber shops of my youth which I had never experienced. However it might have contrasted with barber shop invigoration, the vibration could loosen nuts in the engine. Hence the need for numerous looks under the bonnet at convenient spots to identify any loose nuts or wires. I recalled an old hand saying that you could feel a pound note flying out of the window with every mile covered.

When you got into savannah country you got away from the everlasting palm trees that put a dark-green cover over all the countryside and could see much further. The character of the houses changed too. Instead of the rectangular houses in the compounds of the forest belt, people lived in open country in round mud huts thickly thatched with grass with no windows and low doors. It was possible to identify an oncoming vehicle from afar by the cloud of dust that heralded its approach. Dust went with the job. When you arrived at a destination your shirt was covered with it across the shoulders where it combined with sweat to provide an outer coral-coloured crust when it dried. It has been said in polite society that 'horses sweat, gentlemen perspire and ladies glow'. Very nearly everyone gives off litres of perspiration in the southern parts of Nigeria where the heat and the high humidity smother you in a clammy embrace; the least exertion makes you sweat like a sheltie pony necessitating frequent baths and changes of clothing. What starts as a small dark patch under the armpit just grows and grows. Those who cannot sweat have a rough time as it is part of the cooling process. Indeed there were stories told of people who had to return home for that reason. I did wonder, perhaps unkindly, whether it was psychosomatic and that it was the very English antipathy to sweaty smells that unconsciously affected whatever controls the sweat glands.

One of the chores of touring in the dry season was clearing away the insects which splattered the windscreen which they hit continuously. We all kept a bottle of water and rubber scraper for the explicit purpose of clearing the driver's vision. Ultimately the problem was mitigated by the appearance on the market of a plastic deflector which was fixed at the front of the bonnet. This in theory sent the insects over the top of the car and cured the problem. In practice, some still contrived to stick to the glass and it wasn't until the advent of the windscreen washer that it was most effectively resolved. This was anticipated by many drivers who kept water in a plastic bottle - a recent innovation - and squirted it on the windscreen by the simple expedient of winding down the window, putting the right arm out of the vehicle and squeezing the water over the glass simultaneously operating the windscreen wipers. It was only a matter of time before the car manufacturers would incorporate the feature in a more elegant way. Elegance and good design go together.

I always made a point of keeping a full tank of petrol where possible as it was not readily available in the bush. All petrol was moved in 44 gallon drums, often lashed together in rafts to the side of a river steamer. I don't remember ever having seen a petrol tanker in Nigeria with the sole exception of the bowser at Ikeja airport. Up-country, the sellers dispensed the petrol straight from the drum. A portable pump was inserted into the bung-hole of the drum. It had a glass bottle which held exactly one gallon. The attendant would pump the handle until the bottle was full. When he had released it into the tank of the car he would produce a pebble from his pocket and place it on the drum. Then he would repeat the process. The number of pebbles was his and your way of checking that the appropriate volume was delivered and paid for.

The south of Nigeria was criss-crossed by rivers that slowed down progress between any areas separated by them. Ferries provided the necessary continuity. The big ones like the one that plied across the Niger from Asaba to Onitsha and the Jamieson River at Sapele had their own excitements. When a lorry driver at Asaba found his front wheels had slipped from the metal ramps, it was treated as a matter of course that a rope would be fed through to the rear axle and tied to it. The other end of the rope was taken under the front of the lorry and up and over the crossbar of the ferry and tied securely. The driver then went into reverse gear and eased back slowly. As the rope tightened and the front of the vehicle came up, volunteers pushed the front end of the lorry until the wheels were again above the guides. The driver put his gear shift into neutral or moved forward fractionally and lo the lorry was ready again to drive on to the ferry. On another occasion the driver might be one of the volunteers helping another driver to get safely on board the ferry. Onlookers from Asaba town would willingly lend a hand and would applaud when the lorry was righted.

The smaller ferries were pontoons built on canoes and usually took one vehicle only. Paddlers conveyed the contraption to the other side. They needed skills in proportion to the strength of the current. At the Mfum ferry on the Upper Cross River, the river was sometimes too fast and too high to cross because of heavy rains in the mountains of the Cameroons where the river had its source. We would drive out to the ferry from the rest house at Ikom only to find that the levels were still too high. The produce inspectors in Ikom must have wondered what he had done to deserve such a close examination of their work. Once we had to wait as much as two days to go on to the Cameroons on the road which was officially only a trace as far as Mamfe. And you travelled it at your own risk. Not having yet been officially adopted, there was no guarantee you would be recovered if you broke down. Recovery vehicles were kept by the Public Works Department only. On one occasion we arrived at the ferry to meet a disconsolate lorry driver who apparently had been standing speaking with others on the far side when his lorry had moved forward, tippled into the water and disappeared. It was at a spot where the onrushing water had gouged out a deep channel on the bend of the river and had completely swallowed the wagon. When I asked how it had happened the driver said 'My brakes done disappoint me'.

When the ferry was operational again I drove my car on to the pontoon which was then hauled upstream by hand using lianas fixed to trees. The canoemen cast off and then piled on to the one side of the pontoon and paddled like fury to the other side of the river where they braked by reverse paddling and others held on to ropes to keep the pontoon fast. It was then possible to drive off with two wheels on dry land and two in the water. Skill and coordinated man-power combined to get people and transport safely across. I felt a satisfaction in interacting with the men responsible for getting us across such barriers.

A touring officer needs a chop box, not least in the very extensive areas where you could be away from your station for up to three weeks at a time. At least in Richard's view it was an indispensable adjunct to travel. Rather than have him cast as the servant of an impecunious or mean small master without the nous, wherewithal or importance to get the necessary accompaniments to comfortable movement in the bush, I lashed out on the services of a carpenter who received detailed

112

instructions from Richard for the construction of such an item. The result was a substantial box with hinged lid and hasp and staple which would allow it to be padlocked. It was reinforced with cross-pieces and dovetailed to guard against its coming asunder. Much smaller than I had anticipated, it was more like a small safe than a container.

When Richard took on cooking duties, the box was kept in a prominent position in the kitchen. From time to time I would see it open and empty for the purpose of giving it a good scrubbing. Richard was a keen learner and his previous employment with the Deputy Director of Medical Services had obviously provided him with lessons in hygiene. It also helped to define standards for me for whom Richard had ambitions. We must have been compatible for, despite occasional differences, we retained a respect for each other. He would make individual requests for items to be carried in the box. Never did he give me a list.

So I was forced, cajoled, and shamed over time into buying a mustard spoon and then a salt spoon. After that it had to be a silver salver (which he called 'slaver'). This was to pass me any letters or messages that might be received. The salver I bought was of stainless steel which seemed, to my relief, to meet the case. Richard even took it with him on tour. Then there was the teapot which figured large in daily use. I had no preferences in this regard and suggested he buy one he thought would be suitable. What he came up with was a large one with splotches of pink and gold that seemed to fill any room he produced it in. These items along with the necessary eating irons and glasses were somehow packed into the box. All this in addition to the flour and oils needed for cooking.

There was no need to take meat as it didn't keep even in an insulated coolbag with ice in it. If we couldn't get it locally we took with us a live chicken duly hobbled which fed the inner man on tour of the outstations or we managed to buy a scratcher locally. The markets were every five to eight days and such was the number of stations we had to visit that it was impossible to arrange our visit to coincide with market day. If we did happen to arrive when it was market day, I enjoyed a local steak which even in these latter days had to be sold showing the hide to ensure it was not human flesh. As Richard said, 'It be to make sure de meat nevah be from peson.'

Alone the chop box was insufficient for survival. The touring stove had to accompany us. Then we had to have a potable liquid. So we had to take beer along too. There were few occasions when I didn't have a cold beer. We'd be in some remote place and the beer would still be cold.

'How do you manage to make the beer cold?' I asked.

'I get broda (brother) for dis place' he replied, 'he make space for his master's fridge'. In the bush, and in many stations, the kerosene-fuelled refrigerator was the only means of preserving food and keeping drinks cool. Electrolux made a model that was convertible from kerosene to electricity and vice-versa. I was to have such a model in my quarters in Warri which was just as well since the local power station was a wood-burning one and shut down for whatever reason from time to time.

When we moved on to yet another station and again cold beer would appear, I would ask again how the beer came to be so acceptably cool.

'I get broda for dis place'

'Your father and mother, Richard, they must have plenty sons?' The question had been nagging at the back of my mind for a long time.

'No sah' he laughed, 'they no fit have plenty plenty son. Dis broda have same fada, different moda, but live for de same compound'.

The extended family is strong. A brother does not necessarily mean a male sibling. If it does, an Ibo will always add 'Same father, same mother', which in a polygamous society is essential for understanding. 'Brother' may mean just a man from the same compound or village. Even without brothers he would produce beer which, if not exactly cold, was not warm either. If we had been travelling by launch or canoe to some remote rest house, his solution to the problem of cold beer was to put it in a canvas

114

bucket which was trailed in the water behind the canoe or launch. His was the perfect example to demonstrate that the connection between education and intelligence is a tenuous one at best.

Where creative solutions were not necessary, he made sure that whatever had to be done was carried out with the same care. Drinking water as in gin and water and water for cooking had to be boiled and filtered. The candles of the filter he usually scrubbed regularly himself to ensure effective operation. He would explain the need for this to David who would take due note. Not once did I see the job delegated completely to him. If David did the cleaning, Richard was on hand to make sure it he did it properly. He took it upon himself to be responsible for my health.

You could not eat your dinner without a light to see it. The pressure lamp was another indispensable item of equipment on tour and on station. Together we mastered the intricacies and the vagaries of our Tilley lamp. We had to remember always to carry methylated spirit needed to get it going. Experience taught us to carry a spare vaporiser as the contingency of one wearing out could be trying even if it happened only rarely. I never did get round to an Aladdin lamp or its de luxe version the bi-Aladdin which gave a softer light than the Tilley. The lamp was put away from the table when I ate and placed in a basin of water when I retired to my camp bed. That was because the moths and ants were attracted to it and fluttered round it in their hundreds. When I reached out of my mosquito net to turn it out, the basin would be full of their dead bodies. What didn't go into the basin went on the table it stood on or fell on the floor where the lizards had a midnight feast. They left the transparent wings, evident in the mornings, which the ants had shed when they vibrated round the lamp, but had consumed all the bodies.

No meal could be made on tour without water and the sources were unreliable. I had a folding canvas bath I took everywhere as it was a necessity after a day's work and before a meal. I had resisted the temptation to buy a zinc hip bath, wicker-covered, as advised prior to my departure from the United Kingdom and bought the folding one from a Canadian, Clair Gosnell, who was returning to his native land after a short and unsatisfactory spell as an assistant district officer. In one rest house there was a place to suspend a bucket which had holes in it to make a very acceptable makeshift shower. I did wonder whose initiative this had been. Richard or David were not so keen on it as it required their presence to keep it filled whereas the sit-in bath could be prepared beforehand.

It was good to remember that the servants needed time to themselves. On tour they did this by a kind of unspoken negotiation whereby in return for preparing all my needs in advance, they could have time off for their own purposes like seeing their brothers, making necessary purchases and accepting hospitality. In relation to the last mentioned, they were aware that there is a generosity in receiving which is not an innate European concept. Hospitality, especially from 'brodas' was of a most generous kind. The bath water was always improved by the addition of some Dettol disinfectant, carried in a gallon tin, to mix in the bath water to counter any bugs that might be there and also conceal any smell.

The chop box symbolises for me the difference between a collective society where every aspect of life is interrelated and a society that puts emphasis on the separation of events, people and responsibilities and the linearity of time. There is a common thread that unites people and distinguishes them from a society which specialises and then has to be coordinated, usually with difficulty. It is all encapsulated for me in the recalled destination board of a Lagos bus 'Lagos All Roads'.

CHAPTER 18

Calabar

Transfer to Calabar from Eastern Region Headquarters gave me the opportunity to work on my own without anybody looking over my shoulder when I was in the office. My office in Port Harcourt during my training stint had been next door to that of the senior produce officer. My new area included the Calabar province, and as far north as Ogoja and the southern part of what was the British Cameroons administered by the Nigerian Government. I visited variously by plane and Land Rover, launch, canoe and car. To get anywhere by road, we had to take the ferry to Oron down the Calabar River and over the Cross River, a journey of an hour and a half or so. To get to the Upper Cross River stations involved a long circuitous journey by way of Afikpo and Abakaliki.

There was a submarine cable that followed the same route as the ferry and carried telephone communications from Port Harcourt to Calabar. During my term there the cable broke and there was no direct line from Port Harcourt and Lagos. This meant that there was no one from Port Harcourt or Lagos requesting immediate information or explanation, everything having to come by post, sometimes a lengthy process. It also meant that my superiors arrived unannounced - or thought they did. My Chief Clerk had a connection in the shipping office who had access to the passenger list on arrival and he dispatched a runner to the office if anyone of importance was on it. The local mafia operated well. It does in a collective society.

My office incidentally was reputed to have been occupied by Sir Roger Casement, Irish (Protestant) patriot or British traitor (later to be hanged) depending on your point of view or, perhaps more accurately, the accident of your birth. He acted for a short time before the First World War as British Consul in Calabar. The first Consul on the coast of the Oil Rivers was appointed in Calabar in 1851, partly to abolish the trade in slaves, nine years before the occupation of Lagos, and partly to assist the development of trade in the area.

I was quartered in a bungalow of what had been the old barracks. There was a magnificent purple bougainvillea bush just outside my compound which was said to have been planted by Lord Trenchard when he was a subaltern in the Nigeria Regiment. This regiment distinguished itself with the 81st (West African) Division in Burma (Max my cook served in it). Max said the troops were told they were going to Sierra Leone and ended up in India prior to being moved to the war zone where the British 14th Army was fighting the Japanese. As I recall, Lord Trenchard went on to become a Marshal of the Royal Air Force and ultimately first Chancellor of the University of Ibadan and Chairman of the United Africa Company.

No more living in temporary accommodation. Now I had my own house with verandah on two sides where it was possible to have breakfast in the morning which was the coolest time of day, where my steward, Richard, could get on with his work in his own way. Richard had a wife always referred to as Mrs Richard and a daughter Onyerije, and he was as pleased as I was to have permanent accommodation with privacy and relative space.

What an improvement on the makeshift accommodation in which I had spent my nights in Port Harcourt when not on tour and Richard in quarters he was not happy with. There was a wall outside the servants' quarters built of blocks which had a regular pattern of holes, not to be seen in the United Kingdom until they appeared in garden centres and the yards of builders' merchants a couple of decades later. Through this wall grew a leafy plant with fruits that looked like cucumbers. In fact it was the loofah plant. Strip away the skin and there was the loofah. It would have been ready to use in the bath when dried if it had been possible to get all the seeds out. It had colourful yellow flowers before fruiting and somehow added a kind of dignity to what was often a miserable outlook from the servants' quarters.

Richard took charge of the cultivation of yams, a Nigerian staple, and kept an eye on the part time garden boy who attended to the compound. Yam cakes appeared with dinner on many occasions. I had avocados growing which were unvaryingly spoken of as 'English pears' and they were sometimes served as a starter before the main course at dinner. There were mango and pawpaw trees in the compound too and the pawpaw became a favourite breakfast fruit. There was also a cashew tree that harboured a colony of caterpillars which were in the process of stripping bare the leaves. In the silence of the night you could hear the communal crunching as they continued their defoliation. Of the decorative trees there was a hibiscus, the said bougainvillea which looked to be part of the compound, and a frangipanni. Just beyond the compound, but looking part of it from the window looking out to the rear of the house, was a palm tree which weaver birds took over shortly after I arrived there. They proceeded to strip the leaves, building their nests with the bits of frond at the extremity of the bare stems with an abandon and apparent randomness so different from the studied and relentless efficiency of the caterpillars on the cashew tree.

Like myself, Richard was now able to entertain. On such occasions David would be on duty. 'Did you have a good time last night?' I asked Richard the morning after one such occasion..
'Yes,sah', he said, 'it was fine fine'.
'What did you do?'
'We take some kola.' The chewing of kola nut was widespread. This is the fruit of a tree found in the rainforest and grows as star-shaped clusters of woody pods. A pod contains a handful of plum-sized seeds wrongly described as nuts. It is habit-forming and acts as a stimulant. Its role may be likened to the combined functions of a cigarette, a cup of coffee and a piece of chewing gum. It also has high nutritive value and can provide instant energy like a Mars bar. It is easy to tell when people have taken it for their lips and gums are red for a time afterwards.
'Did you have something to drink?'
'We drink *tombo* (palm wine)',he replied.
'Do you ever get drunk?'

'No, sah', he laughed in a strangulated way. His reply was in a tone that implied hurt that I should harbour such thoughts, 'I tink massa too vex if I do dat. Good steward never drink too much'.

After administering this gentle rebuke from the moral high ground, Richard signalled he would like to return to his work. 'I tink massa never need me now'.

'Off you go, Richard'. And he returned to the kitchen where he would not be asked damned silly questions.

Calabar was paradise. A full social life both on station and on tour, good friends - I remember particularly Joe Widdell who was an administrative officer brought up in Huddersfield. Little did I think that I would set up my first home in the UK in the town he was brought up in. While in Calabar, I heard on my not inappropriately named Bush radio, of the loss in the Irish Sea of the Princess Victoria out of Stranraer. I was not to know that my future father-in-law had been booked on that very ferry and had later cancelled his booking.

Spanish officials from Fernando Po where indentured labourers from Calabar found employment, visited us. We had a range of sporting and social activities. It was a new and enjoyable experience for me. I never did manage to get on a return visit to Santa Ysabel not always being available as a touring officer, but through that place I was introduced to products sold under the name 'Pedro Domecq' and especially did I like the Spanish brandy which was probably smuggled at five bob a bottle. That compared with eleven and sixpence for a bottle of whisky. Tennis and cricket were the main sports. We occasionally had a few rubbers of bridge but for the most part the evenings were given over to conversation. At parties we would all do our party pieces. This varied from my own one-man rendering of the duet 'Give Me thy hand, O Fairest' from *Don Giovanni* to a recital of the first chapter of Genesis in pidgin English by an old hand on the coast. Occasionally one of the rugby songs clique would sing *The A.D.O. Bende.* An A.D.O. was an assistant district officer.

I started as A.D.O. Bende
I was nervous and shy to begin
So I got me a young Ibo virgin
For the price of a bottle of gin

and so on through postings to Yola, Warri and Lagos in the progressive education of a young administrative officer on the ways of women, his problems finally being resolved when he wrote to the Chief Secretary and was directed by him to Secret Circular 'B'. When on tour from Port Harcourt, I had visited Bende and the mud-built house thatched with palm fronds of the then Assistant District Officer there. The verses made me think of Robert Louis Stevenson and his battles with the intransigent donkey Modestine which were to mirror his struggles to understand the female of any species.

I met a number of my countrymen in Calabar. The Hope Waddell Institution was set up by Scottish missionaries and provided schooling at secondary level and training in artisanal skills as well as pastoral care. The official name of the church was the Presbyterian Church of Eastern Nigeria and the Bight of Biafra. I enjoyed the service on a Sunday evening and extended my circle of friends and acquaintances as a result. It was the place where Mary Slessor made her name. I duly visited her grave in the cemetery in Duke Town. Where I lived in the Old Barracks was within a stone's throw of where in 1914 she was honoured guest of an 'At Home' attended by all kinds of important people prior to her receiving the insignia of the Order of the Hospital of St John of Jerusalem in England of which the King was Sovereign Head.

CHAPTER 19

Kamerun

In the club in Calabar hung a photograph of the Calabar Volunteers who had joined the colours at the outbreak of the Great War, had been trained locally and had then been sent off to fight the Kaiser's forces in the nearby German Kamerun or Cameroons where some were attached to the Nigeria Regiment which was sent to fight there and later in East Africa. Many of their servants volunteered to join the forces and often served in the same units as their masters.

The Cameroons had been annexed in 1884 by Germany, at the instigation of the imperial German Chancellor, Prince Bismarck, during what has been described as 'the scramble for Africa'. After the First World War, the territory was mandated to Britain by the League of Nations and made a British trusteeship territory in 1947 by the United Nations. Since 1924 it had been administered under the government of Nigeria. The German influence persisted even after all these years. The Portuguese originally discovered it and they left their own legacy in the name of the country which comes from the Portuguese word for shrimps, presumably as a result of there being an abundance of them off the coast and in the Rio del Rey (the King's River), a delta rich in waterborne resources.

The flight from Calabar to Tiko in the Cameroons was originally served by two-engined De Havilland Dove 12-seater aircraft and these were succeeded by the Handley Page Marathon with four relatively low powered engines. The pilot would open a door behind him and address the passengers to give them information as the situation required. The workhorse was the Bristol Freighter which was introduced to the route during my time there. Among its duties was to take pilgrims on the Haj to Mecca. This was a workaday plane with the working of the control wires for the tailplane and ailerons open to the view of the passengers seated by the windows on very basic seats. Stewards were introduced about this time. On one occasion, one of them gave his little talk before take-off, pointing out the usual facilities. 'The lavatory' he said 'is at the rear. To open the door, turn the handle to the right and push. '

There is always an awkward passenger and the inevitable one posed his inevitable question 'What happens if you pull the door?'.

'It comes off' the steward replied.

When you landed by air in Tiko, you were hurried past well-drilled rows of banana trees as the plane touched down on the runway. The plantations were neatly laid out and connected to the centre of operations by a light gauge railway. The system was one left by the Germans after the Second World War. The company that had originally built it bought it back from the Nigerian government in 1923 and ran it until 1939. The plantations were bought by the Nigerian government in 1946 from the Custodier of Enemy Property. It set up an independent body called the Cameroons Development Corporation to run them 'for the use and common benefit of the inhabitants of the territory'.

In the proximity of the plantations at certain times of the year were protected herds of elephant which had an annual circuit from which they deviated little. They could do untold damage to banana trees if they came crashing through the undergrowth. After years of observation people realised that if there was anything that switched on an elephant it was sweet potatoes. They would overcome any difficulty to get at them and could sense them from a distance. People said that wise managers gave locals incentives to plant their sweet potatoes well away from the plantations and the track of the annual elephant circuit. That said, there was probably more damage done to banana plantations by freak storms. Over two million trees were blown down by a tornado in a few hours in 1951 which must have disrupted the regular schedule of a shipload of bananas every five days or so.

Victoria, the principal town near the coast, manifested the German connection in the magnificent botanic gardens there.

When I last visited Victoria, I spent some time in the gardens and admired the now somewhat wild shrubs, trees and plants still bearing their nameplates in German and Latin with a separate plate in English - one I recognised but did not know the Latin name of was the *hibiscus sinensis double red* which grew in my compound in Calabar. The rocky coast provided challenges on water, giving members of Outward Bound type courses, usually but not exclusively government employees, an opportunity to find out about themselves in heaving seas in Man o' War Bay. This bay was named after the anchorage for British warships which lay in wait there for the outlawed slave trader ships after the abolition of slavery in Britain and the law forbidding the carriage of slaves in British ships in the early 1800s. By 1824, slaving had become a capital offence in Britain. Under an earlier ruling of the Court of Session in Scotland, any slave setting foot in Scotland was immediately a free man, in effect abolishing slavery some 30 years before it was done away with under English Law.

The department Land Rover was available for travel in the Cameroons and I used it when I flew to Tiko. It incorporated a feature that appealed initially. That was the panel that ran the width of the car under the windscreen and could be opened to admit air. This had a very cooling effect and I kept it open all the time on the first occasion I used it. The upshot was that I caught my first, and hope last, cold in the eyes which oozed matter for days and left the eyes bloodshot and my general appearance debauched-looking, which was not the image I liked to think people had of me. Thereafter I opened the panel for short periods only.

In Buea, the Commissioner for the Cameroons had his office in what was a more than passing likeness of a German Schloss built on the side of a hill and looking for all the world like one of the castles on the Rhine. It was built in 1899 by the German governor of Kamerun and reputed nephew of Bismarck, Herr von Puttkamer. The story goes that he built it for his mistress, a Berlin opera singer, out of a fund allocated for the building of roads. After all that she refused to come. He filled the house with her photographs and flowers and ordered an extra place always to be laid at table. Below the Schloss stands a wrought-iron gate with two entwined P's - presumed to be Pauline and Puttkamer.

Buea has more than its fair share of rain, and nearby Mount Cameroon which rises to nearly 14,000 feet (4,000 metres) has probably the heaviest precipitation in Africa, over 400 inches of rain (10 metres) in a year. Even in these days Civil Service training programmes had a strong outdoor bias with ascent of the Cameroon mountain a required activity. The clouds seemed to be lower here than in any other part of Africa I have visited, and I have an abiding memory of them swirling past the windows of the houses as you looked out, rather like the view from an aeroplane as it strains for the clear blue sky after take-off.

Further north is Kumba where cocoa is grown, surprisingly, in the surrounding area of lower ground. Growers had to arrange for roofs on wheels to keep the fermenting cocoa beans dry when the rain threatened. The sophistication of the cover was quite novel in my experience and a very big investment for the smallholders. The bulk of the Nigerian crop, including the output of the Cameroons, was produced by a hard-working, independent peasantry just like the palm oil with the exception of that produced in the pioneer oil mills. Typically the crop was worked by a family unlike some of the production in the Ivory Coast where vast plantations were established at the cost of traditional social organisation.

The Cameroons Development Corporation had an ongoing experimental programme in the growing of coffee, arabica in the mountains and robusta at lower levels. I always think that an analogy can be drawn with whisky. Arabica corresponds to the single malt and robusta to grain whisky. Most commercial offerings are a combination of the two. If you could afford it you would always drink the single malt whisky and the arabica coffee, all things being equal which they rarely are. There is more low ground available to grow robusta coffee than high ground for the superior arabica. The man in charge of the experimental farm I visited was Dutch. He had just commissioned a coffee mill as the experiments were sufficiently advanced to justify that investment. The indigenous languages spanned the borders long before English and French became established official languages or indeed before the border was arbitrarily drawn some sixty years before.

The road north from Kumba winds up an escarpment eventually to meet the road from the West near Mamfe. It was open for up-traffic on Mondays, Wednesdays and Friday and for down-traffic on Tuesdays, Thursdays and Saturdays. It was closed on Sundays, not for reasons of Sunday observance but because the necessary maintenance of the road had to be carried out then. It continues to Bamenda on a road built originally by German engineers. This stretch traverses such a difficult terrain for road builders that it bears comparison with much larger construction projects round the world in its vision and execution. The road rises to 6,000 feet at Bamenda itself. Bamenda has a climate exceedingly pleasant for Europeans and can produce potatoes and salad vegetables. You can have fresh meat and milk on a regular basis and you can get a good sleep at night without sweating into the pillow.

Bamenda was distinguished by a type of fort not usually seen in British administered territories in Africa. With its walls and crenellations it seemed an appropriate location to make a film of the French Foreign Legion with legionnaires in their képis occasionally appearing in the vision of the viewer from outside as they passed the crenellations in the wall from which the garrison could observe and be seen. It was now the administrative centre for the region. Hard by, I found the inescapable cemetery and the pointers to a troubled past. Colonial powers had inevitably to have garrisons of troops in strategic locations. Like so many, the soldiers were unaccustomed to the diseases that seemed to thrive locally and had little immunity to them. There were graves where soldiers lay who had died *'ges.'* (tombstone German for *gestorben)* probably in some place remote from the fort where the exposure to disease was higher, or who had been killed in battle *gef.* (tombstone for *gefallen*) in some bloody local encounter probably unrecorded. One wondered what the driving force had been and whether it had been worth the cost. Did Kaporal Moeller who fell in some battle or other, have time to contemplate his past or have the last rites administered? Did the people back home have any knowledge of what was going on in their name? The scenario of 'All Quiet on the Western Front' was immediate and local compared to forces in distant Kamerun in times of war or not. *Es gibt ein Stück eines fremden Feldes das immer Deutschland ist* (with apologies to Rupert Brooke's 'There is a piece of a foreign field…'). In retrospect I am reminded that, after the Falklands war, the Argentinian writer Jorge Luis Borgès likened the conflict to two bald men arguing over a comb. Objective reality disappears, if indeed it exists at all, when perception takes over as a basis for doing things.

Does this development regularise my undiscovered crime that, contrary to Colonial Regulations, I crossed the border into the French Cameroons without the permission of the Governor, to visit a friend at Nkongsamba where my car broke down? Had it not been for a French motor mechanic who worked the whole weekend on it to get it going again, I might have had to return to a hot reception and disciplinary action. Despite the fact that such unendorsed cross-border trips took place regularly, the crime was being caught. It was fun to talk in French. It was the first time I had heard black people speaking the language and it seemed odd and I presumed there was pidgin French spoken here. It seemed bizarre, too, to see a local authority vehicle with 'Ville de Douala' painted on its side. Maybe it was part of the continuing process of deconstructing the Anglocentric viewpoint with which those of us born and bred in Britain were unknowingly imbued, a process less evident today as the concept of Britain and Britishness recedes with the weakening of the nation state or 'internal decolonisation' as it has been colourfully described.

CHAPTER 20

On Tour Again

The rainy season gave a nice contrast to the heat and dust of the dry season. The rain came as a welcome relief and people celebrated it by going out and revelling in it. For the government official, or anyone else whose work took them round the countryside, the relief was short lived. The touring officer found himself developing new capabilities to cope with the changed weather conditions. Just driving normally on the roads required the acquisition of new competences. Driving in mud and in snow have much in common. In order to exercise control you quickly learn the golden rule that you should drive at the lowest possible speed in the highest possible gear. That is only a starting point for it still requires the judgment of the individual in a given situation. The Land Rover in the Cameroons overcame many of the problems associated with mud. The four-wheel drive was a bonus, not a necessity. Outside the trusteeship territory we had to soldier on, but didn't see it as much of a drawback, with rear wheel drive; and inside the territory too when we arrived by car from Eastern Nigeria.

Another drawback to the rainy season was the tendency for windscreens to mist up. The blowing of hot air had not arrived and occasionally I applied a demisting stick to them of the kind used inside gas masks. The rain often came down like stair rods and that precluded the winding down of windows. This in turn made it warm inside the car, for the humidity was high in such circumstances and with two or three bodies in addition to give off heat, it created an uncomfortable physical atmosphere reminiscent of the smell of wet humanity on the old Glasgow subway. We were always relieved to get to our destination. We could while away the time in the car with conversation in a way that was not possible when we toured by launch when Richard would share the crew's quarters much of the time.

'What you do in the evening in your village, Richard, apart from telling stories?'

'What we do for evening time, sah?'

'Yes, when you are not telling stories'.

'We do plenty ting'.

'Like what?'

'We wrastle.'

'Are you a good wrestler?'

Richard laughed in a self-deprecatory way. 'I de try'.

'Who is the best wrestler in Iboland?'

'Ikolo, sah'.

'Is he another of your brothers, Richard?'

At this Richard convulsed with laughter, his whole body seeming to crease as he did so. 'No, he be fine fine wrestler for Ibo story.'

'What did he do?'

'He fight de spirit. He win him and break his head for a rock. Den he fight one with two heads, den four heads and he win them all. And den he lose for de spirits tink eight time wit eight heads and dey break Ikolo head for a rock. Den juju man from his village put stuff from de bush for his eyes and he get better.'

'Is that the whole story?'

'No sah. Den de spirits follow. Just before Ikolo reach his compound from de spirit country, dey cut him for back with matchet'.

'Did he die?'

'No. But dat is why every peson get line for his back.'

Even in the rainy season there could be bright and sunny days. On one such occasion we put up at the rest house at Bansara. There the local John Holt agent, Jimmy Pryde, didn't get many visitors and insisted on having a celebration. This not only included roasting a goat on a spit but also arranging a musical accompaniment to the alfresco meal - provided by the local brass band to which his predecessor had sold the instruments. As most of the members had not played until the last year or so, the notes that emerged were far from what the composer of the music intended. Nevertheless, it was played and listened to in a good spirit.

I gave Richard a couple of cartridges earlier for the 12 bore and he came back with three guinea fowl and one unspent cartridge. He was very responsible with a shotgun and always carried it broken as I had instructed him. I gave a brace to our host as a token of my appreciation of his hospitality. Richard was right royally entertained by our host's servants and I think they polished off the remaining *dinda bird*. The savannah country was good growing land for cassava and you just had to walk into it and the guinea fowl rose up in front of you. You had to be careful how you walked in the cassava as it was a preferred haunt of snakes. If you gave them warning by beating the bush they would slither away. It was only if they felt under attack that they would bite.

When we returned from tour in the rains, the car would be caked brown with mud more than half way up the side and was an indication to those who were in station that I had done a good many miles on that trip, the implication being that if I had done a lot of miles, then I would be collecting substantial mileage allowance. There was a myth that at one time a touring officer could live on his allowances and bank his salary. Such was the view of some of those who did not have to leave the station. Would that that had been so but, sadly, what it did was to increase concern about the state of the car and the cost of repairs.

I am reminded of something I later saw on the staff notice board in the UTC garage in Ibadan. It was a letter signed by a man calling himself Lawyer Koofrey whose suspension had parted company with his car in the bush after it had been serviced there. He was threatening all sorts of dire actions if it was not put right immediately at no cost to him and in such a way that he could have faith in his garage in future. There are certain things that can't be proved or disproved and that is where the costs arise. In fact my car broke down seriously only two or three times in all the time I was in Nigeria. Once was the incident in the Cameroons. Another time was also very far from home when I got a broken differential through fitting town and country tyres for the rains. Of the minor irritations, the worst was punctures of which I must have had 30 or 40 in my years in Nigeria. We therefore had to take tyre levers and patches for inner tubes which were a necessary part of the loads on any tour of inspection as well as a footpump, a tyre gauge and the like.

This problem of punctures was perhaps compounded by the custom of running the tyres until the canvas showed, there being no law at that time which said you could not and the economics of maintenance dictated the custom. The safety equation did not enter into it in the dry season as a smooth tyre had more contact with the road surface and provided good road-holding and braking.

Breakdowns in Nigeria were never without their attendant experts. On every occasion of a breakdown there was no shortage of willing hands who claimed to be mechanics. They would be seen beside broken down lorries where the fault could be a major one like a big end having gone. I was never quite sure whether they were chancing their luck in the hope of a reward or whether they really believed they could resolve any mechanical difficulty given time and patience. From time to time you would see a lorry with its bonnet up and parts laid out in a line on the sandy road in the order in which they had been removed. This was to assist in the reassembly of what had been dismantled by putting the parts back in reverse order. If in the process a broken part was identified, the driver would send a runner to the nearest town with the broken part for identification and supply.

If a breakdown took place in an area of population, no matter how small or scattered, a variety of onlookers, not only self-designated experts in the workings of the internal combustion engine, would gather round from nowhere. Local women would set up makeshift wayside stalls and start cooking items like baked yams, pepper soup and palm oil fritters for the temporarily marooned travellers who accompanied any load carrying vehicle as paying passengers, abandoning whatever activity they had been engaged upon.

Other enterprisers, often women too, would emanate from nowhere with their own productions for sale like lemonade and home-made beer while boys materialised from the bush peddling cigarettes and palm wine to create a social event out of a minor crisis. Younger males would hawk betel nut and gum. The news of the gathering would percolate to the children who would come to play around their mothers and fathers and brothers and sisters and duck and jump under and over the incapacitated vehicle. The witch doctor purveying his amulets, feathers and bat wings might also arrive to promise cure for any ailment or curse, protection from a juju or revenge for a perceived wrong.

Animated conversations would ensue even if nothing was sold giving the impression that the meeting and talking were more important than the sale. Laugher, banter and argument pierced the humid silence of the day. Passing lorries might stop to take advantage of the victuals on sale or participate in the activities, further increasing the number of bodies and sounds and colourful movements. A breakdown, like any other unusual circumstance, had become a community heaving with life itself.

Hold-ups were not only caused by mechanical failure. Progress could be halted by the terrain and the weather. Fortunately, the human species displays the capacity to adapt to all manner of circumstances. This was exemplified in Nigeria by the way products for one purpose were used for another or have a secondary use, whether by organisations or by individuals.

One such product was expanded metal sheet, sometimes referred to as expamet or XPM which were favoured initials of a partly illiterate society that liked to shorten a description of a few words into a combination of easily recognised and familiar symbols. Its original function was for security to prevent unauthorised access to property and to protect windows vulnerable to penetration by thieves. It was linked together in large sheets to make landings possible on grass runways during the rainy season. More familiarly, it was used to make a cage, with doors that could be padlocked, on the back of kit cars. These were pick-up trucks, often but not exclusively of American origin, which allowed loads to be carried in safety to wherever they were being transported and which were usually capable of negotiating potholed and muddy tracks.

A use not always appreciated was as a means of recovering your vehicle when it was trapped in mud which was not an unusual occurrence in the Calabar area in the wet season. To achieve this it was necessary first of all to wire a number of two foot by one foot pieces (600mm x 300mm) together and fold them back on themselves in a kind of accordion for handy storage. When the contingency called for action, all you had to do was unfold the XPM under the drive wheels and it was odds on you would get clear. A poor alternative was to lay out under the wheels a number of gunny bags which would otherwise have been used for holding kernels or cocoa, a sometimes messy and uncertain alternative.

I made one epic journey to the Cameroons in convoy with Josie Bull who worked for the Department of Rural Science in Bamenda. It was the rainy season and if I stuck at the top of a hill Josie stuck half way up. We ended up with her car being so bogged down it could only be released by specialist equipment. The XPM had to give best on this occasion. Together we drove to Mamfe in my trusty Vanguard with its 16 inch wheels and the same engine as used in the Ferguson tractor. We arrived late in the evening. The District Officer called out the manager of the Catering Rest House who had the staff cook us a meal. When the roads improved, Josie's car was brought back to Mamfe by the PWD recovery lorry and she resumed her journey to Bamenda. I didn't see her again.

I remember her telegraphic address was 'Bull Farmstead Bamenda'. There was a woman who acted in the best traditions of colonial service. She was aptly named. She had all the characteristics normally attributed to John Bull by the Scottish writer who created him and the traits he embodied. When the mud eventually dried and fell off my oil sump, I found it had cracked, presumably on some stone embedded in the mire of the rainy season, and had to be replaced.

It is a similar story with the humble four gallon kerosene can. Kerosene not 'kerosine' as spelt today and not paraffin because it was imported from the USA where the word paraffin is unknown. These tins were of square section and could be transported cheaply since they fitted snugly against each other. It is interesting to note that the supplying companies tried to replace them with cylindrical cans as these cost less to buy from their suppliers. The market in West Africa deemed otherwise and it was not long before the traditional tins were reinstated. They were after all cheaper to transport, easier to store, took up less room and, perhaps most importantly, they had a resale value after the kerosene had been used.

This resale value was demonstrated in the use to which they were put. In the first place, if you removed the top with a tin opener and nailed a round piece of wood, cut to size, across it, there you had an effective implement for shovelling cocoa beans into a riddle or 'shiftah' which a second person shook vigorously from side to side and round and round to get rid of unwanted trash before emptying the beans remaining into a bag, or to fill bags of groundnuts or palm kernels.

It could be used too by a very special kind of transporter. That was the man with a bicycle who had a carrier over the back wheel on which kerosene tins of palm oil half to three quarters full were placed two on top of two for conveying along forest tracks to the nearest buying point. Hardier men or men with a shorter distance to cover, could be seen in the oil palm lands from time to time with another two tins hanging from the handlebars. When you consider that water weighs ten pounds to the gallon and palm oil is denser, you get an idea of the weight of liquid being transported. Nobody knew better than the palm oil carrier, who was often the erstwhile owner of the oil, which make of bicycle was the best buy. Not even those who used them as single passenger taxis experienced the same wear and tear. You bought your bicycle from an assembler who imported it in kit form or 'completely knocked down' as the export jargon had it, so attracting the Commonwealth preferential import duty. Then you took it to a repairer who tightened the spokes and ensured it was in good order and left the brown paper on the mudguards as a status symbol if that was your wish.

In the oil palm belt the straining figure of the palm oil carrier was a regular feature, his often frail frame fighting to keep the bicycle on an even keel under his heavy load of kerosene tins, a kenspeckle scene on the bush paths and roads of south-east Nigeria. His bicycle was the equivalent of the canoe in the creeks. Individual farmers sold their production to a bicycle carrier who took the output of a number of farmers and sold it on to a bigger trader who might be motorised and so on until the oil passed in commercial quantities to the ultimate buyer in the local representative of one of the Licensed Buying Agents of the Board. These were the many palm oil traders in the distribution chain of export produce and were the mirror image of the multiplicity of intermediaries in the Nigerian import trade.

Kerosene tins and expanded metal combined to serve a useful purpose when an officer was visiting his outstations. He generated his own supply of tins as a user of paraffin to light the Tilley or Aladdin lamps or provide the heat for irons (Tilley irons were the subject of horrific tales of alarm and destruction arising from their unreliability). His servants would take two kerosene tins and cut round three quarters of the top of each. They then placed these side by side about 18 inches apart and the three-quarters-cut top formed a lid with a hinge. Across this was placed a sheet of expanded metal which, when faggots of wood cut from the bush was placed under it and between the tins and set alight, provided the range on which pans could be boiled for the bath or the tea. When the lids were brought down, there were two ovens ready complete with doors, to receive the prepared food and cook the *plat du jour*.

While Richard was so engaged, David, if he came with us, would take some embers from the fire for the charcoal iron that was a necessity on tour according to Richard. This was unquestionably true when we were away for ten or twelve days at a time. David would blow on the embers to keep the heat going and proceed with the ironing.

CHAPTER 21

Warri

If Port Harcourt was on the left flank of the mouths of the Niger delta and Calabar a bit further away to the left, Warri was at its heart and took in the right flank. I was now going to be responsible after leave and transfer from Calabar for the quality of export produce in that other part of the Niger Delta to the west of the area I had worked in when I was in Port Harcourt. I was to become, almost involuntarily, extremely knowledgable about the produce of the whole Delta area and the way it was marketed.

My first few days in Warri were spent in the Catering Rest House there while my predecessor and myself went through the handing-over process. There I met someone who would give me further insights into the workings of the local markets as far as imports were concerned. Bill Hayes owned a company called Hayes, Green and Bryden. I had seen his premises in Lagos some years before. He was an enthusiastic and charismatic man of 68 years who continued to work in Nigeria when others of his age and generation were enjoying a gentle game of golf in places like Crieff or Hastings or had died. Presumably, the other partners in the company had either retired or had gone to the great godown in the sky and Bill had managed to find the finance to buy out their stakes and run it on his own. He enjoyed conversation and was as gracious to relative newcomers to the Coast as to the Resident's lady.

Bill didn't tender direct advice as did some the old hands I had met. He preferred to quote examples of how certain situations had been handled and questioned their usefulness if he did not agree with them. This appealed to me in that it brought my own views into the discussion. His philosophy was to enjoy the country to the full and to do this he implied that you needed to know a whole lot more about it. He had come out to Nigeria as a young man before the first world war. He had fallen heir to photographs of men much older than himself whose recollections must have gone back to the 1870s, and appeared to carry them around with him, perhaps to remind him of what he was trying to do if he felt the weight of his years. He had so much respect for their staying power and their ability to adapt to their environment even if their clothing of plaid or worsted in what was patently a West African scene suggested Hexham or Harestanes in deep mid-winter. In some ways he resembled them, particularly in their durability. I suspect he drew inspiration from them.

He travelled all over by plane and kitcar (not the self-assembly, sporty machine but the sturdy, open backed pick-up with wooden canopy and expanded metal grills at the sides and doors of similar material at the back secured by a stout padlock). Kitcars had the high ground clearance necessary for negotiating the muddy terrain in the wet season and the heavy springing needed to cope with the uneven and bumpy road surfaces. He was in the textile business which had a long history of trade in West Africa and drew particularly on Indian designs which had the most striking colours and were greatly favoured at one time. Manufacturers in Manchester had copied Indian ideas, and incidentally put many of the Indian mills out of business, and had become more and more important in trade with the Guinea Coast. This could be profitable in those latter days for those who knew their markets. Bigger firms Bill could not compete with unless he knew something more about the market than they did, such were the economies of scale they could create.

There was also the growing competition from local companies supplied by Japanese producers whose cloths were cheaper than those from the United Kingdom. I noticed that the khaki cloth from Japan was lighter in weight and poorer in quality by my lights. It was only much later I was to realise that 'fitness for purpose' was to become the classic definition of quality. When I was in Lagos it was not unusual to see Japanese ships with names like *Asama Maru* arrive in Lagos laden to the Plimsoll line, and leave in ballast making me wonder if the Japanese would ever become buyers of things Nigerian. Among the cargoes were thousands of bales of cloth.

In all this Bill remained true to his suppliers and his origins. Once a year he would make the journey to London and go on to Manchester to view the latest textile designs and feed the designers with ideas from his own experience. He would collect samples of all the cloths he felt might be of interest and would return with them to Nigeria. Perhaps one of the reasons for his remarkable survival at his age was the fact that he returned to a temperate climate every year when most others were there for a tour of up to 24 months or much more in the case of the clergy. I am more inclined to think it was because he was at ease in the country and consequently was not affected by stress which can afflict the toughest physically in an alien environment.

Anyway, Bill returned to Nigeria and proceeded to take his samples down into the Niger delta. It was to the country of the Itsekiri people he went, going from town to village and showing his wares to the womenfolk. We were now in the heart of that country. He had absorbed the lesson that conversation is good and produces information. He knew from experience that the Itsekiri women, from a minority tribe, were leaders of fashion in the country. If he could find out what their preferences were, then he could go ahead and order in quantity the cloths they liked best. He knew that what the Itsekiri women wear today, the vast majority of women in the highly populated - some would say over-populated - Ibo lands will wear tomorrow. Given his knowledge of this, he was in a position to steal a march over his bigger rivals and place the rolls of cloth he handled in the markets that mattered - in Onitsha and Aba and the entrepot of Lagos where the market women knew their wares and their customers. And the customers knew what they wanted.

I didn't see him again. When I was to return to Lagos some five years after from my sojourns in Port Harcourt, Calabar, Warri and Ibadan, the firm of Hayes, Green and Bryden would no longer exist, but I would think of him later when I read about social and market research techniques. How he would have lifted back his head and laughed his characteristic, infectious laugh if anyone had suggested to him that he administer a questionnaire, conduct a structured interview, establish a test market or facilitate a focus group research among potential customers. But that's what he was doing in effect. I liked his philosophy and enjoyed his company.

My first nights in my own quarters in Warri were during the rains when four inches (10cm) could fall in a night. You quickly became accustomed to the rain beating on the corrugated iron roof like a quartet of tambourines and you eventually fell asleep to its regular pulsation, occasionally changing into a higher key as a particulary heavy deluge swept across. It was more difficult to get accustomed to the noise of the bullfrogs that persisted during the hours of darkness. First a single frog would lead off and then the others would take up the chorus. There was no rhythm or soporific drumming to it. It was as if there was a cheer leader whom the others willingly followed in irregular and unpredictable din. The frogs were most appreciated by the snakes which found them tasty morsels. On one of my first evenings in my house I sat at the top of the steps leading up to my house and watched a snake mesmerise its victim and then snatch it with a lightning strike from the position it had frozen in. It then digested the frog over a period and it was possible to see the bulge where the frog lay inside the snake.

Warri was a river port rather like Calabar was but without the same docking space. Like other rivers along the delta coast giving access to ports, where the mouth breaks the white strip that marks the coastline, a solid green wall is all that is seen from approaching ships. Local knowledge was indispensable in moving ships up the Forcados River into the creeks of the delta and getting them berthed in a narrow channel. It required the services of the Nigeria Marine pilot as they approached the port. At one point in the channel up the Forcados River there was a spot where a great letter V was cut into the bush. This was on a bend of the river which was difficult to negotiate and masters chose to ease the vessel into the mangrove and let the tow of the current bring the boat round until the bow was aligned with the new direction when 'Slow ahead' would be signalled.

Ships were mostly Palm Line and Elder Dempster Lines operating out of Liverpool and specialising in West African cargo. Elder Dempster subsumed the British and African Steam Navigation Company, set up to exploit the Glasgow interest in palm oil. The shipping business to West Africa at that period was conducted by a good old-fashioned cartel known as the West African Conference. The exports of the region were principally palm kernels and palm oil, the latter being bulk-handled and shipped. There were also groundnuts evacuated from up-river when the water was high which was during the months of August to October. Activity was frenetic to evacuate all the stocks before the dry season and fall in water levels prevented the river steamers from plying the upper reaches of the river as payment to the companies was finalised on delivery to the ship. As much as 35 feet between high and low water has been recorded although the average is just over 20 feet.

There was a grandly named laboratory for which I was responsible where a laboratory assistant tested the oil content of the groundnuts. If by any chance the previous year's crop had not been fully evacuated during the high water season, the nuts would lose a significant percentage of their oil content and lose value on the market. Some of the palm oil was still bought in wooden puncheons of 50 to 70 gallons although these were being fast superseded by 44 gallon metal drums. Both could be lashed together and either rafted downstream up to ten days or more to a buying point or were secured to the sides of a river boat where the water was wide enough to take it to an appropriate place of purchase and inspection.

The gradual elimination of the wooden casks meant also the end of the road for the men who made them. The coopers who fashioned the staves and shrank on the hoops had been important people in the development of the palm oil trade. There were expatriate artisans needed in the early days to make the casks and carry out repairs on ships, and indeed to build boats and instruct Nigerian apprentices in the secrets of their trade. The development of the skills needed for making the casks were among the earlier trades taught at the Hope Waddell Institution in

Calabar. It was similar in nearby Sapele, approached from the sea by the Benin River. It was another important river port which I had to visit regularly. From here bales of ribbed, smoked rubber sheet from the Benin area and timber in log form but more often as sawn billets or as plywood were shipped in addition to palm kernels.

The timber-processing industry surrounded itself with associated trades and brought in saw-doctors and specialists in the production and processing of the wood. They too had skills to pass on to willing learners. It was just as well they did so as a matter of policy as the cry for Africanisation or Nigerianisation became more strident as the 1950's wore on. 'Indigenisation' was the word eventually adopted and used as the expression to mobilise support around measures to eliminate competition from established foreigners like the very hard-working and successful businessmen of Greek-Cypriot, Asian and Syrian/Lebanese origin.

Names like Raccah in the groundnut export trade, Thomopoulos in rubber exports, Armel, Khalil and Zarpas in transport, and Chelleram, Leventis and Mandillas in retail services, contributed in no small measure to the development of trade in the country. In Benin, a Lebanese entrepreneur started to make crepe for use in the manufacture of shoes and sandals from cup lump rubber. This was rubber from latex that had hardened in the cup before collection from trees that had been tapped. Prior to this, there was no industry associated with cup lump and no value-added activities in the country. It was considered unexportable in unprocessed form.

Palm oil was stored at bulk oil plants at Burutu down-river from Warri, and Koko down-river from Sapele and pumped from them by a pipe to the ships. From time to time there was trouble caused by adulteration of the oil either by adding an adulterant to casks which could be interfered with more easily than drums as the tinplates used to seal them were not particularly secure. All kinds of vegetable matter from oranges to fibre could be found from time to time in these to make the casks weigh heavier. Proof of adulteration was hard to get. A more subtle means of adding apparent value in the adulterer's view was to put an alkaline solution, usually lime, in the oil to reduce the apparent free fatty acid (FFA) content when the oil was inspected; the lower the recorded FFA within the different grades established, the higher was the premium paid.

At Burutu on one occasion this form of adulteration, which results in the oil turning into soap, caused the stocks to bubble out of the flumes leading from the storage tanks in a froth that spread everywhere. As a consequence, the company operating the BOP as a bulk oil plant is known, incurred high cleaning-up costs which had to be met by the Board for which it acted as agent.

Water was also used as an adulterant to increase the weight for which an unprincipled seller hoped to be paid. It was detected by the use of a steel sectional 'try-rod' which permitted an employee of Licensed Buying Agents to sample the drum at a number of levels under the supervision of a produce inspector, and scraped the bottom of the drum where water or other adulterants lay. The try-rod had a slide which was withdrawn before the taking of the sample and when the open rod was drawn across the drum it was closed before it was taken out and discharged into a try-pan. By heating the sample put in the copper 'try-pan' and holding it up to let the oil run down, you could see evidence of water adulteration as any water bubbles ran down ahead of the oil. This would be confirmed by subsequent laboratory test.

The UAC general manager in Warri showed me a photograph, from the time of the Royal Niger Company around the 1890s, of the testing of palm oil using similar try-rods, beautifully manufactured, which were being utilised even then. New testing kits were now available to produce inspection staff to measure the amount of free fatty acid content and used a solution of NaoH for testing and grading the oil in the field. The try-pans were magnificent copper pans with concave sides much coveted by Europeans with a view to their use in UK kitchens.

The 'trying' of oil was the expression used by the traders to the west coast of Africa 200 years ago; they obviously had similar problems. When several of the perpetrators of the Burutu adulteration were eventually caught, the local magistrate made an example of them which made our work much easier as news of such punitive judgments was soon picked up by the grapevine and acted as a deterrent to some of the would-be miscreants. On one occasion when trying to identify the people responsible for this I was travelling up the Assay Creek when I met my African Assistant Produce Officer on the way down. He had three pullers for the canoe carrying him and a fourth man who held an umbrella over his head to protect him from the sun. He had all the trappings of a panjandrum and was deferred to appropriately. Mr Olowofuyeku (not his real name for it escapes me) was a power in his own land. Woe betide the oil adulterer if he found out.

Warri was a small station with a good club and a pleasant atmosphere. People of various tribes worked side by side in the town and communicated with each other in pidgin English. There was a nice balance between government officers and businessmen. A mutual dependence fostered a good spirit with the Resident and the UAC General Manager setting the tone. Once in a while there would be a weekend when the entire expatriate population of Burutu, employees and families of an affiliate firm of the United Africa Company responsible for the operation of the bulk oil plant there, would come by the *Gongola*, a stern-wheeler that would not have looked out of place on the Mississippi of the 1900s and looked as if it was a working museum exhibit kept by the company for such away-days, or so the landlubbers of the Warri station believed.

The visitors would be accommodated by their hosts and usually a cricket match and a special Sunday lunch would be laid on before they returned to the *Gongola* and their duties in Burutu. We openly cheated - it was in the unwritten rules - to incapacitate or otherwise reduce the effectiveness of the opposition by plying them with pink gins and a surfeit of curry. Tennis was also a popular means of relaxation and the time available for it always

144

seemed to be foreshortened by the rain which started to fall at about the same time every day. It wasn't unusual for an oil bean pod on the surrounding trees to split open and disgorge its contents on to the court which could disconcert the players if any should land on their heads.

My office in Warri had a picture of Her Majesty the Queen on the wall behind my desk, a reminder of the hopes for a new Elizabethan age on her accession. I was conditioned by upbringing to be a good Queen's man. I had responded to the loyal toast on a number of occasions, had positively glowed with a British pride when she came to Moor Plantation just outside Ibadan during the 1956 royal visit to witness what was being done to improve export crops that were important for the economy and duly noted she had good legs. With many others I had deplored the coverage of it by the British tabloid press which diminished the United Kingdom, Herself and those of us who identified with Nigerian pride and aspirations, by its cavalier treatment of a hospitable people, appealing to the 'superior' instincts of its readers.

My loyalty was stretched to near breaking point, I think, when a colleague in Warri showed me the original text of the national anthem, the first verse of which I had sung the bass of so lustily and for which I had stood still to attention, saluted or doffed my cap. This last verse, thankfully now omitted for obvious reasons, enjoins the Almighty to assist Marshal Wade in crushing rebellious Scots. Something I treasured died in me at that moment

CHAPTER 22

Tom Lycett Lies Here

In the Warri area there is an island in the middle of one of the branches of the mighty River Niger as it fans out to make its lazy way through the delta. It is reached by canoe from the lush green banks at the river's edge and is insignificant in relation to the brooding forest just inland on either bank. There is an endless swell lapping lightly on its shoreline. It is an undistinguished place. When I visited it for the first time, a somewhat rusty shed of corrugated iron where produce was bought and graded, some scrub and some bits of old metal were all that met the casual eye. The island was uninhabited except for the clerk in charge of the buying station and two labourers who paddled a canoe across to it each morning. Other than the men and women who brought their palm oil and kernels there by canoe to sell them, only the UAC manager responsible for operations on that part of the river for shipment to ocean vessel and Produce Inspection staff visited the place. But look further. These bits of metal lying around reveal, with assistance from the imagination, the outline of a ship with the boss at the end of a drive shaft sticking out on either side where paddles had once driven the vessel through the waves of the ocean on its voyage out from Britain to carry cargoes up and down the river and along its many creeks.

It was in the 1870s to the 1890s that the paddle steamer had its heyday on the river. Steam-driven vessels had slowly been taking over from sailing ships. But paddles were cumbersome in some of the creeks and these boats were succeeded by sternwheelers or screw-driven ships which were more manoeuvrable in the snagged waters and more suited to towing barges, most easily accomplished in the creeks of the Niger delta by lashing them to the side of the vessel. When it came time to retire this particular paddle steamer, someone in authority thought it would be a good idea to drive it on to a sandbank where it caught the silt as it came downriver in the rainy season and gradually built up into an island which the locals called Gana

Gana. It was a one-off variation of the hulks which littered the Delta and which were marked on the ordnance survey maps of the day. Gana Gana provided an outlet to palm oil and kernel traders who would otherwise have had to go much further to sell their produce and it was a convenient spot to load bags of kernels and drums of palm oil on to boats going to Warri and Burutu.

Originally the sailing ships were ships that arrived on the coast with a cargo of general merchandise from Europe. The captain, who was probably a shareholder in the venture and a trader himself, or a nominated commercial manager or 'supercargo', bartered its contents for palm oil, returning to his home port when all the merchandise had been disposed of and the cargo of palm oil for which the goods were exchanged was all loaded. This was acceptable as long as profits were high but the advent of competition from other companies both British and foreign, with the establishment of the Niger as an international waterway, showed this activity to be ineffective in cost terms.

The hulks were these obsolescent old sailing ships or equally out-of-date relics from the early era of steam which had had their day and were put to work in their new identities of trading posts. The trading companies placed agents on the hulks which doubled as house and warehouse. In this capacity they brought the benefits of basic tools which rendered locally made tools redundant, gunpowder, gin and cloth to the locals, and acted as a store for crocodile skins, castor seed and elephant tusks as well as vegetable ivory - the fruit of the raffia palm much in demand in the latter part of the 19th century for making into shirt buttons. Larger items for sale and purchase like brass neptunes (large basins used mostly in the production of palm oil) and casks of palm oil were kept in premises leased on shore and enabled ships coming out from the United Kingdom to be unloaded of their imports and loaded with their exports, usually palm oil, without having to wait for all the goods they had brought to be sold. The hulks were easily distinguished from ships visiting the coast by the roofs erected on them made of palm fronds or grass, to give protection from the sun. The ships taking imports up the Niger, bringing down the produce from the upper reaches of the river and from the Benue, also carried passengers as the waterways were the easiest and sometimes the only form of transportation, probably to and from the ancient port of Forcados, a natural anchorage near the mouth of the delta and serving the upper reaches of the Niger and the Benue. Forcados remained the principal port until the bar at Lagos was dredged just before the First World War when Forcados went into decline as the fortunes of Lagos took off.

It was in a small corner of the small island I came across it. A simple stone bearing the inscription *Tom Lycett, L.G.R. lies here. Died 23rd May 1911*

From the companionship and community of a small Dorset town, for that was the only place I had had previous contact with the name, Gana Gana seemed an awful place to lie buried. Alone in an expanse of water fringed by oil palms whose fronds reached up into a sky in which a blazing sun stoked up an already humid air. Dead, the unbeliever might say, with no people from his own place to exchange the time of day with or argue the toss about some long gone happening not susceptible of proof. Dead with nothing but the letters L.G.R. to tell us something about him. What manner of man had he been, this fellow human being I presumed to have been a West Countryman, whose bones would have been stripped of their flesh by alien grubs and had been left here in this distant land to moulder and never to be grieved over by friends or family?

L.G.R. stood for Lagos Government Railway. Nigerian Railways had not yet been established for the very good reason that in 1911 there was as yet no Nigeria. That was to happen three years later when the Protectorate of Northern Nigeria and the Protectorate and Colony of Southern Nigeria would be joined. The name was coined and the unification urged by Flora Shaw, the journalist and colonial correspondent on *The Times* who was eventually to marry Sir Frederick, later Lord Lugard, the adventurer turned colonial administrator. The Lagos government built the railway with a view to developing the interior of the country and establishing the ascendancy of the new port with its recently dredged bar and its deep-water facilities. This official entrepreneurship stemmed from the knowledge that in such a recently acquired colony there were too many contentious issues associated with land rights and labour problems to leave the building of the railway to private contractors. Tribal rights in rural land were, and still are, often so complex that land was an unsatisfactory security for loans.

Indeed, private investors were not exactly rushing to invest in West African projects nor were contractors rushing to build railways there when they could see wider and more substantial opportunities in South America, Russia and Asia. The colonial government therefore built them with public capital which would require a return on its investment from the benefits conferred by the much improved infrastructure. That return was necessary to pay for the administration of the territory as the government in London was not at that time prepared or able to subsidise its overseas possessions and had dealt a blow to public finances by forbidding the import of 'trade spirits' (cheap gin and rum from Germany and Holland used for barter by the trading companies) into Nigeria, the duty on which had provided a large part of the government's revenue.

The British government was eventually to have a change of heart and would provide substantial subsidies on an *ad hoc* basis from the 1920s when loans and outright grants were made to the colonies. This was extended to a regular annual commitment of millions by the passing of the Colonial Development and Welfare Act in 1946. A year later the Colonial Development Corporation came into being, publicly funded and given the responsibility for the creation of public utilities in the colonies.

Before these subsidies were given effect, the Northern part of what is now Nigeria was the only region of the colony unable to finance its own administration. Without an outlet to the sea for its produce, principally groundnuts, it would be struggling to survive economically. It was for this reason that the railway was built first to Kaduna and then on to Kano. It was later extended from Kano to Nguru and to Gusau and beyond with spurs along the way to places like Jos. Not only would this give a fillip to the production of produce, it would also stimulate a greater demand for imports on which custom duties could be exacted to pay for the normal expenses of government. The terrain it had to cross, especially in the south of the country, meant it had to qualify as one of the great feats of engineering construction when you consider earth was moved by headpan before the days of the bulldozer in country where workers were exposed to all kinds of tropical illnesses which were often terminal.

It is unlikely Tom was a high official. Latter day managers even in Tom's time would have received a proper burial in the cemetery of the nearest town where a decent send-off could be guaranteed to join others of like background who had died at an early age. He was probably a skilled worker who had learnt his trade with one of the British railway companies. Here he was, even in death, separated from others by a class distinction then at the height of its observance. He was probably helping to build the railway and was presumably returning downriver from his labours suffering from some disease. Had he caught malaria through the attentions of that awful variety of mosquito, the anopheles, which carried the disease, the parasitic infestation it carries and recycles producing such life-threatening consequences as congestion of blood cells in the brain or kidney collapse? Or maybe it was yellow fever or blackwater fever that had done for him and had induced his fellow travellers to leave him here. Perhaps he hadn't been suited to the life and had found solace in alcohol, an excess of which can kill off the liver. Or perhaps it was something more violent. It is odds-on he died on board a river steamer. It would have needed a three puncheon canoe and a couple of pullers to move such an awkward cargo decently from the ship on to the island shore.

Did the captain of the ship read the funeral service? What kind of message did the railway send to his mother or next of kin? Did he lie in a wooden coffin or was his winding sheet a piece of canvas stitched up by some old man of the river? Presumably, because he was in a place which was a Niger Company trading station (a forerunner of the United Africa Company and given the benefit of the doubt to do the decent thing in such circumstances), he would have avoided the ultimate indignity that befell many an honest artisan as well as palm oil ruffians. This was to have a 'gun case and top hat funeral' where empty wooden cases that had contained dane guns were used as coffins and if the deceased was too tall, the end of the case was removed so that his head could stick out and be covered by a top hat nailed to the ends before the body was lowered into his final resting place. Will Tom ever know the results of his labours - of how the railway some forty-odd years later was able to move upwards of 800,000 tons of groundnuts in a year on the single track from furthest Kano nearly 800 miles to the north to the ports of Lagos and Port Harcourt, thanks to his efforts and those of unsung workers like him? What in the name of God induced him to come to this far country?

Poor Tom's a-cold. Is there a world of ghosts for him to move among and feel himself the shadow of a dream?

CHAPTER 23

The Emotan Tree

Some tales persist. One that did so without being committed to historical record to my knowledge was that of the Emotan tree told to me in Benin City when on an inspection from Warri. It told of an Inspector of Works in Benin City who had the tree cut down to assist some technical project and created a furore he could not have foreseen. The Oba, the traditional ruler of Benin, was rumoured to have demanded six European heads in compensation.

Emotan was a market woman who dared to stand on the side of truth and justice some centuries ago when it was neither safe nor fashionable to do so. Because of what she did and what she did not do, a usurper king lost his life and his throne while the legitimate king, who had lived in exile in the forest, regained his rightful place in the palace. Some Binis claimed she incorporated the soul of Benin. Associated with her memory was this tree which grew to be revered rather like an important national monument but which in terms of progress held up the accomplishment of scheduled public works. The *fait accompli* represented by its unheralded felling by the aforesaid inspector of works sparked off riots by the affronted Binis and it was then that the Oba was alleged to have voiced his demands.

That such tales circulate feeds on the history of Benin itself. Half a century earlier Benin was incorporated in a greater Southern Nigeria by force of arms contrary to the more general practice there of negotiating an accord with local chiefs, often it must be said, with standard forms of agreement which many did not understand but felt was a small price to pay for the protection of Queen Victoria. The situation in Benin arose, as an immediate response, from the massacre of the acting Consul General and unarmed officials on an announced visit to the Oba and, with less immediacy, as the result of reports which had percolated through over a period of atrocities committed against slaves and their own people.

When troops of the punitive expedition entered the city of Benin in 1897 they found unbelievable horrors. Streams of dried human blood, pits filled with bodies, crucifixions on trees, women slaves gagged and pegged to the ground on their backs, the abdominal wall cut in the form of a cross and the uninjured gut hanging out as they waited to die in the sun. Fresh blood dripped off big bronze heads with huge ivory tusks fixed in them in the middle of the Oba's compound. The infiltration of Christianity through Portuguese missionaries over a long period of time, then their withdrawal because of the high death rate of priests due to the unrelenting climate, resulted in its adherents falling back into fetishism. The sign of the cross cut on the bodies, the crucifixions and a bronze head of Jesus Christ were all that was left of the symbols of Christianity brought with the best of intentions by the Portuguese priests and the Binis who went to Lisbon for instruction and returned to continue the work of the departed Europeans in the 17th century.

The worship of inanimate things in West Africa and their associated rituals stems, it has been claimed, from the ways the cultures have prevented the creation of mental images outside the confines of everyday things, a state of affairs addressed in the later consideration of Nigerian pidgin. This in turn has resulted, so the argument goes, in people being unable to distinguish between animate and inanimate objects, giving rise to the idea that everything has a soul. A worshipper of an object could obtain from its owner, in return for a fee or reciprocal favour, the services of the spirit lodged within it, whether for benign purposes or otherwise; whether for protection or revenge for a perceived wrong. The word *fetish* comes from the Portuguese name given to the West African gods and has a similarity to their own relics of saints; it normally means 'magic'. Interestingly, the French referred to it as *juju* from the French word for toy and the same word is also used in English, putting emphasis on the object rather than its supernatural or spiritual qualities and perhaps demonstrating that the Portuguese were closer to understanding the African mind than the French and British traders who were much later visitors to these shores.

Human eyeballs, particularly of white men, were apparently in demand as a charm. It was with good reason Benin was called 'the City of Blood'. It was not difficult to find Nigerians who believed that terrible things still happened in Benin, a view reinforced by the known fact that the then current Oba's father had twice been accused of sacrificing a wife but was acquitted on each occasion. I was surprised to realise that some of the older Binis I saw could have been party or witness to some of these happenings. When I asked an assistant produce officer during a conversation what his father had done, he replied that he had been a warrior.

This picture of Benin contrasts vividly with the image formed on arrival at Benin by the traveller in the mid-1950s. A walk around the city would elicit smiles of acknowledgement and welcome - with the exception of some of the politically aware and active, a far cry from the welcome one would have received half a century earlier. It was no longer isolated. It had an airport with connections to other parts of Nigeria. On departure you were informed that, when three bells were rung, your aircraft had been sighted. Six bells were the signal for passengers to go forward for embarkation on the aircraft. On flights out of Benin it was possible to get an overall picture of the extent of the tree cover in the region, the dark green carpet below formed by the trees relieved only by the occasional glimpse of red laterite roads that looked pencil thin against the vast area of forest. The flight to Port Harcourt showed just how much the forest was intersected by waterways and why the river-borne means of transport were the preferred mode of travel in the early days and the only viable one in the delta in many cases to this day.

There was a catering rest house in the town where officers on tour and members of the travelling public could put up. These were nominally under the control of the local administrative officer. There you would meet others like Forest Officers and Agricultural Officers and company managers overseeing their domains. Here it was possible to exchange information about local conditions and connections. It was quite a surprise to meet two men from Lagos who introduced themselves as ladies' hairdressers, but I was impressed by their enterprise and energy. When I later transferred back to Lagos I came across them again in their secondary capacity of Messrs Strutt and Williams, makers of fine lampshades of unique design.

Benin was a striking-off point for a visit to Siluko which I decided to inspect during a break in the rains. It had not been visited by the man I took over from and perhaps I was about to find out the reason. To get to Siluko from Benin you had to cross a trestle bridge built over a shallow gorge laid with two strips of planks only at a width between them that would accommodate the wheels of lorries which, to avoid an exceptionally long detour, had to pass that way when evacuating produce. It was almost too wide for the wheels of my car and my Assistant Produce Officer, Oye Sode, agreed to guide me across. I was worried in case he fell over as he walked backwards indicating to me whether I should move the wheel a fraction this way or that. He was worried lest I should go over with the car. I suspect we lost a few pounds between us. When we got to Siluko we knew we had to come back across the trestle but somehow having done it once it was not such a problem.

Walking along the main street of Siluko, I observed the chalk board of the local alternative medicine specialist offering traditional treatment for *moon madness and unpowerful penis* pre-empting by some forty five years the putting of the drug 'Viagra' on the market and the openness of discussion on the subject of male impotence. As ever, the local expression is so much more descriptive and real. 'Erectile dysfunction' as the qualified practitioners call it, seems dry and impersonal by comparison. Its conceptualisation eliminates all feeling for what must be a distressing human condition. I write later about the Nigerian use of expressive and non-conceptual language and this is yet another example.

Before I ever found out about many of the things I have described above, I felt much more uncomfortable in Benin than any other station I have known and at work had more trouble there than elsewhere. Was there a malign spirit at work? Did that same spirit make the Ighuoriaki ferry move forward as I was driving on? Even at the club, after what had been an enjoyable evening, I was pushing my car backwards on to a slope to start it (somehow my battery was always flat) and tried to close the door before engaging gear when it caught on a pillar and forced the door right back leaving a seriously crumpled wing so differentiating my car from all others. Not that I believed any of that juju stuff, I kept on telling myself.

CHAPTER 24

On Tour One More Time

It was always interesting to see how colleagues adapted to the demands of touring. I never ceased to be amazed how people reacted differently to similar situations. A load-carrying estate car or a pick-up truck with expanded metal cage on the back was normal. When Charles Simpson arrived at Ibadan on his way back to his station from leave, he turned up at Jim Brown's house while I was there complete with a Rolls Royce hearse he had 'bought for a song' in the United Kingdom. When we inquired if he was anticipating a funeral, he claimed nothing was further from his mind. It still had its rollers which he asserted would be of considerable assistance in stowing his touring loads. 'Handy too for loading the crates of beer' he added with relish.

Not all touring officers had that same eye for an application other than its intended function. Others like myself concentrated on the detail of ensuring we got there - and back - by attention to more mundane detail. A prized possession was the long-handled touring axe that was honed to a sharpness to meet most contingencies. If there had been a heavy squall, the wind could reach quite high speed and the tops of the oil palms in particular looked as if they had moved through ninety degrees. It occasionally blew trees across the road. Sometimes they had to be cut with the axe to allow passage. The best situations were when there were lorries in front of us and others would cut away the obstruction. I think Richard was secretly pleased when I let him use it for the first time. In the course of our travels we used it to construct small bridges on a couple of occasions when the rains had washed away the road or to fill in with brushwood and logs a ditch that had appeared overnight. If we had a hold-up, Richard would sometimes ask questions about the UK.

'You get garage for your compound in Scotland?' The fact that this was my first full-time job apart from my stint in the Royal Navy, and that I had been in various digs or staying with my parents was the truth of the matter.

'No, Richard, I used my father's car but not very often as he needed it for his work. I hired a car once or twice.'

'What you do for go work?' The idea that I had had no transport of my own was something to deplore. That I might have gone to work on a bicycle or by bus or, say it quietly, on foot, was too awful for him to contemplate. He would lose face among his peers if it got out.

'When I was in London for a short time I went to work by train' I volunteered.

'Na true, sah?'

'Na true', Richard. Trains run like buses in Lagos to take you from one street to another. I go by the underground'.

'Underground sah?'

'In London the trains run under the ground and take millions of people to work each day.'

Richard laughed. 'Massa make joke. Train never go for under de ground'.

'Na so'.

'How you go down?'

'You go by stair that moves. You don't need to walk until you get to the bottom where the trains are.'

Richard doubled up. This was hilarious. Trains that went under the ground, stairs that moved. I would be telling him next that you could sometimes go down in a cage that moved when you pressed a button.

'I tink you make we laugh too much' he said.

The exertions of building small bridges were kept to a minimum in the Warri area as a result of the provincial engineer Jim Brown constructing floating bridges made of empty oil drums lashed together with planks laid along them for vehicle or bicycle access across shallow water liable to flooding in the rainy season. It was no mean feat where access is difficult, funds are limited and materials not always available. This was the kind of improvisation that contributed to the development of the local infrastructure and general welfare of rural areas and was also the kind of activity that went unrecognised, largely, I suppose, because it was the big projects that caught the eye. Jim's improvising abilities were reflected in the way that he harnessed his interest in being a radio ham with a daily communication link to his wife and daughter in Cardiff when they were not with him in Nigeria. His ability to turn his hand to anything rebounded on him on one occasion when a home-made burglar alarm went off in the middle of the night when the electricity supply failed to his, and his wife Anna Maria's, consternation.

Difficulties in progression are not confined to the roads. The many branches of the Niger delta and the estuaries of other rivers are all linked by a network of creeks that provide navigable channels of smooth water from west to east. These open out from time to time into wide lagoons that make canoeing relatively easy. It is possible by these waterways to go by canoe from Calabar in the east to Badagri in the west and indeed beyond to Porto Novo in Dahomey (now Benin). A colleague, Charles Pridmore, recounted the story of the chief in Okitipupa who used to send a canoe the 150 miles by creek and lagoon to Lagos to collect his tins of Barney's tobacco. Presumably there were also other commissions to be carried out and other requirements to be met. Charles, who was intrigued by the trouble taken to get supplies of his favourite tobacco, wrote to Barney's with this snippet of information and received a pound tin of tobacco by way of acknowledgement of yet another genuine appreciation of their product.

Sometimes a creek, if it was slow-flowing, got blocked by sudd or lettuce weed that grew right across the waterway. You could from time to time see small birds running or hopping across it and small frogs hopping from leaf to leaf. While travelling by launch on one of these creeks, somewhere on the Siluko River I think, clearing a channel of water in the green carpet as we went, we attracted a woman paddling her canoe like fury to keep up with us while there was still a good wake and clear water, her breasts or 'bobis' (reflecting the influence of an English regional expression?) as they were referred to in pidgin, swaying rhythmically in time with the movement of her paddle. When she changed hands to push the paddle into the water from the other side to make any corrections of direction, they made a kind of circular motion before taking their cue from the new movement.

She appeared to be enjoying it but eventually it was an unequal struggle and she ceased her exertions, her top or *buba* which had worked its way up to her neck as a result of her exertions, falling back down to its normal position. Even launches could get snarled up in the weed if the roots were long and became entangled with the propeller and the snag had to be cleared from the propeller by hand which meant someone going over the side to do so. This became an increasing problem as outboard motors became more available and facilitated travel on water for a growing number of people.

When on tour in the remoter parts of my area, life would be more like it was before the coming of the white man. Women wore only the lappa and it was an eye-opener to me to see how the configuration of their breasts changed with age from the high carried bosoms of the young women and the rounded fullness of young motherhood which I was aware of, to the ample bosoms of the mature women and the cracked pepper pots of the old grandmothers. I was flabbergasted on one occasion early on in my trips to the bush when a matronly woman with big breasts laid down on her back with her head on her hands and they just flopped under her armpits That reality had not been captured by the classic paintings I had glimpsed in galleries or in the more libidinous photographs in the *Men Only* of my youth. From that moment the American mammary culture has not impressed me. Since then, ample bosoms in brassieres suggest to me a conflict between an unstoppable force backed by the laws of gravity and an unyielding restraint.

In far Ogoja and the Cameroons, young girls just reaching puberty would walk past unselfconsciously and with a natural dignity. They would have firm, well-rounded breasts and a string of beads covering but barely concealing their pudenda.

'What do you think of that girl, Richard?' I asked on one occasion,' nodding in the direction of one of the nearly nude young girls with a slender neck, perfect figure and an easy, graceful walk.

'They be bush people, sah' Richard replied in his more superior tone, 'they nevah go learn for dis place'.

'Do you fancy that young girl?' I pursued my original question.

'I no de heah' said Richard

I restructured my question 'You like to take her home for second wife?'

'No sah' said Richard in his scandalised voice.

'Why not?'

'They no be Ibo people'.

'Why do you say they are bush people?'

'They never weah cloth'.

The remoter parts of my area also afforded us the opportunity to observe the local wildlife. 'De cutting grass be too fine chop' Richard would say every time we saw the large rodent-like creature resembling an outsize rat which has been used as food *in extremis* by Europeans and is greatly in demand among poorer Africans. The dead ones I saw all had yellow teeth and I wondered if they had been born with that characteristic or whether it was part of the maturing process.

'How do you cook this cutting grass?' I enquired.

'We cook am with coco yam. It make fine fine chop.' In fact, I did taste it subsequently and found it quite acceptable.

The land in the Warri area provided countless opportunities to see it. Any animal that was not domesticated was considered 'bush meat' and fair game if you could get it. On one occasion when I was just outside Benin in a place called Ekiadolor, a small deer jumped the fence into a 'beach' and stumbled in panic over hundreds of drums of palm oil. Workers in the yard immediately dropped tools and ran from all corners to surround it and eventually cornered it, held it by its antlers, and after a time cut its throat and let it bleed to death. I was given to understand the subsequent steaks were shared out amidst great argument. There were of course the bigger animals which could only be shot with a high-powered rifle. There was the bush cow, a formidable African form of bison reputed to be the most dangerous animal in the country. It differs from other big game in that when it is wounded, it waits for you and charges when it thinks it has an opportunity to get you. It will only give up when dead. The leopard was still a menace but was rapidly being shot out of existence.

I met a fellow Scot I could not stomach whose obsession was the shooting of bush cow and elephant. I always felt the shooting of elephant was a pointless exercise and hard to conceive of as a sport. No doubt it requires a steady hand and nerve. I much preferred the actions of a departmental colleague, Ken Masters, who found a Nigerian lion cub somewhere near Abuja, long before that place would become a new capital built out of oil money. He gave it to Regent's Park Zoo in London and saw it placed next to one that had been donated by Winston Churchill. It must have been an odd feeling, and perhaps one of pride (no pun intended), that he experienced when he saw the brass plate that bore his name as the donor next to that bearing the name of Churchill.

The most prevalent weapon among local hunters was the dane gun, a long-barrelled, muzzle-loading piece of some antiquity the provision of which a Birmingham arms manufacturers had perpetuated over the years for the lucrative West African market. They were used to despatch the less aggressive animals. It formed a significant part of the range of goods used by the trading companies to barter for palm oil in the second half of the nineteenth century. Hunters could be incredibly casual in the pursuit of their prey.

From time to time the press recorded unbelievable accidents associated with these guns. One was about the trial of a hunter accused of shooting someone. His excuse was that he had had a juju put on him. Another, on a similar charge, claimed he thought it was a monkey he was shooting at in the dark of the forest at night. I did in fact witness a monkey being shot and only winged and its screams of pain scar my memory to this day. It is one thing to shoot a guinea fowl for the pot at 25 yards with a 12 bore and No. 6 shot with a near certainty of executing the action cleanly. It is something else to aim for a deer or larger animal at a much greater distance and be certain of an outright kill. 'The equaliser' is an American expression for the Winchester rifle. To me the rifle is 'the diminisher', certainly for those who are not particularly good shots. The only true 'equaliser' is the human spirit and the mental strength it can engender.

But touring was not all difficulty and frustration enlivened by banter. There were pleasures that left a warm afterglow. To happen by chance on a group of Urhobo stilt dancers as they move to the steady rhythms of the drums and the repetitive note sequences getting imperceptibly faster and faster, was a memorable sight if slightly embarrassing for me at that time in mixed company as it moved to a climax symbolising the culmination of the sexual act. To be invited to judge the entries of cocoa farmers at the Ilaro show was a relaxation and an indication of the high quality of cocoa on presentation. Here was a centre of the cocoa-growing industry where awareness of best practice was at its highest and competition was an occasion for fun.

You met some of the most interesting people on tour like Cy and Phoebe Ottenberg, anthropologists from North Western University, Chicago, I think, doing some research, I seem to recall, on the social implications of the yam festival. I enjoyed a swim with Phoebe in a cool, uninhabited pool (certainly by undesirable creatures) on a hillside by their house in Afikpo. Not least, you met locals of character who were the source of unusual information and the best of company like Ma Ayolu whose palm oil fritters, bean cakes and repartee were unsurpassed. You were confronted by puzzles like how did a British sailor come to be killed in action and be buried in a cemetery in Abakaliki, so far from the sea, as recently as 1924? Am I in danger of breaking my own principle that only fools make judgments according to their latterday values on issues that would have been adjudged differently when they happened?

CHAPTER 25

Ibadan

The Macpherson constitution which was introduced just before my arrival in Nigeria proved difficult to operate in practice. Dr Azikiwe's exclusion from the House of Representatives, noted below, tended to weaken the support his party gave to the new constitution. A convention of his party, the NCNC, instructed its ministers to resign. Most of them refused to do so and started a new party, the National Independence Party, which tried to carry on as a minority government in the East and a constitutional deadlock ensued. The Northern Peoples' Congress objected to a motion put forward by an Action Group (Western Region, Yoruba dominated) member demanding the acceptance of 'self-government by 1956' because it feared southern domination. The political impasse was due largely to the regional basis of the parties which meant that no one party could command a clear majority in the House of Representatives. The upshot was a decision to provide for greater devolution of authority and the removal of powers of intervention by the Centre in matters which could, without detriment to other regions, be placed entirely within regional competence.

In December 1954 a new constitution was introduced which effectively created a federal structure which gave much greater control to the regions while retaining matters like defence and external relations at the centre. The Marketing Boards were to be regionalised. The political decision was in due course reflected in a reorganisation of the department. The produce inspection function became a regional matter. I was invited to join the Western Region where I was already serving. I was in the fullness of time transferred from Warri to Ibadan headquarters where my job was more administrative than technical. On an earlier visit to Ibadan, my Assistant Director had told me informally I was being promoted to Senior Produce Officer and that I would shortly receive the Secretary of State's confirmation of this through the Civil Service Commission. The world was informed of such developments through the Nigeria Gazette, now to be regionalised as far as we were concerned as the Western Nigeria Gazette.

Your salary and your previous history were available to all and sundry through the Staff List which was updated at regular intervals. Some officers, a small minority, referred to the Staff List as the 'Stud Book' whether in self-affirmation of their pedigree or their sexual prowess I wasn't always quite sure. While I might now make tours of inspection to the areas, these would not bring me in touch so much with people on the ground as in the past, certainly in the very often small, even remote, stations. Touring of the kind that took me into the real bush was finished. Now I was between a Ministry of Trade and Industry and the men who ran the areas and often had to interpret the requirements of the ministry to the latter and occasionally explaining the needs of the area officers to the Permanent Secretary's staff. I was involved in the early stages of the reorganisation of the Produce Inspection Service in the region into circles to meet the new political conditions. An anomalous situation was the position of Senior Produce Officer, Lagos where we had a strong Western Region presence in federal territory, largely because there was a considerable amount of produce emanating from Western Nigeria as it was now to be called. Municipal Lagos was now declared federal territory.

It was at this time I came to know Caywood Brown Harry, a senior produce officer like myself who had been originally in what was referred to as the Junior Service, or lower posts filled by Africans. Both European and African staff agreed that it was by sheer ability and personality that he had been promoted to the senior ranks and now found himself in charge of the Lagos Port Area. I was junior to him in seniority as a Senior Produce Officer and was surprised when I was appointed Acting Deputy Chief Produce Officer in Ibadan for a period of a few months which was in due course published in the Western Nigeria Gazette. The reason given for the preference being given to me was that I was *in situ* in Ibadan and that the appointment was limited in duration. I wondered if 'C B', as he was widely known, would be upset by this but he saw it as a rational decision made in the interest of continuity. I was later to succeed him in the Lagos post while he moved to Ibadan.

C B was brought up in a village community in the eastern Niger delta, son of a much respected chief and transport entrepreneur. Because he did not belong to one of the major ethnic groups and did not have the hubris that seemed to stem from a long period of domination as a member of a majority tribe, he combined humility with a the natural authority of a chief's son. Since the organisation of his people was based on a very restricted hierarchy he was much more open to external influences and read widely. He was a big man who laughed a great deal. Even when not actually laughing, his eyes were. CB gave me much to think about in discussions we had of the future.

He was a strong believer in one Nigeria and accepted the new arrangements without demur. He believed that tribalism was the enemy of such a consummation. To such an extent did he hold this view that he condemned any action that set one ethnic group against another. The responsibility rested in the first instance with those people fortunate enough to have insights into the possibilities of a federal system whether through education or experience and intelligence. In pursuit of this ideal, people must learn the different ways of others and be tolerant in their judgments.

He had believed in the one Nigeria ideal of Dr Nnamdi Azikiwe's National Council for Nigeria and the Cameroons and felt that Azikiwe, an Easterner, had betrayed his pan-Nigerian vision when, after being elected to the Western House of Assembly in 1951 and been unsuccessful in getting getting nominated to the federal House of a Representatives as a result of a ploy by the ruling Action Group, he refused to be leader of the opposition and resigned to return to the east. CB saw in Zik's action the tribalisation of politics and the obliteration of a dream. He would have liked to serve in the North before regionalisation. Not a single native southern Nigerian had been stationed as a senior officer there, presumably because of the backlash that

166

might call forth among the local Hausa/Fulani. He would have relished the challenge.

CB's views on how people should work across the cultural and linguistic divide also extended to how people within their ethnic groups tended to promote the interests of any member of that group irrespective of the claims of others. This was another form of tribalism that operated against the interests of the country in that it advanced someone of the 'in-group' or tribe at the expense of merit. I wondered how valid this view was.

'Caywood,'I said, 'don't you think that within a federal system it doesn't matter if a bit of nepotism is exercised? After all, people speak the same language, share the same kind of beliefs in what is good and what is bad'.

'That may be all very well in a country like England where everybody does speak the same language and by and large share the same culture. Assume I, from the minority Kalabari people, was working in one of the regions. Do you think I would become the Chief Produce Officer under an independent government? I'm sufficiently conceited to think that I have got where I am through merit. That was under a fair system instituted by your countrymen. Without a system that encourages the recognition of ability the mediocre come to the top.'

'How do you guarantee that merit will be rewarded then?' I asked.

CB hesitated and then gave a measured answer. 'Institutions won't resolve it. If the country's interest is to be served, we need politicians who are not self-serving. I can point out current politicians whose actions belie their words. What we need is politicians who have a selfless commitment and an electorate that is able to think.'

'You're just the man to fill that political bill' I thought to myself.

CB appeared to have that capacity to put the interest of others first. He had a wide reputation for integrity, possessed an easy charm, a persuasive tongue, an innate sense of fairness and fun and an analytical mind which seemed to me the embodiment of the very qualities he was advocating. Of all the Africans I met, he was the one who encapsulated for me the inherent invalidity of any residual post-imperial beliefs of white superiority with which I was unknowingly imbued on my arrival in Nigeria despite my course in social anthropology at university.

It was in discussions such as these and observations of developments that showed pressure on the administration to fix a date for independence that I concluded that the future in Nigeria was with people like CB and the younger generation whose education and background took them beyond ethnicity. There were signs that the pressures for self-determination were mounting like the appointment of officers on contract and then the appointment of indigenous officers only except where expatriates brought skills not available locally.

When I was Senior Produce Officer at Regional Headquarters in Ibadan we talked of the need for a wider induction for new entrants but no funds were available for the extra training. At no time to my knowledge was any consideration given to the training of Nigerian staff for eventual assumption of top posts. Firms like the United Africa Company were already training Africans for senior appointments and in talking to members of the UAC hierarchy, it was obvious that they were considering pulling out of the produce business and considering alternatives within an expected autonomous Nigeria. As far as the Produce Inspection Service was concerned a hiatus could be left if the expatriates were to leave within a relatively short period. The writing was well and truly on the wall as far as the European was concerned. Their days in the country were numbered, I would have said. In future, the government policies would be made according to ground rules worked out by the local people according to their view of the needs of the situation as they had done before the traditional authorities were displaced or influenced by economic and political events more than 50 years earlier. Only this time the rules would not evolve according to the unfolding situations within the sovereignty of kings but would be made by elected representatives working in the name of a parliamentary system in which individual ministers could exercise much power. It was people like C B Harry who gave you a sense of hope for this future.

CHAPTER 26

Musings from a Sickbed

'Where do you hail from?' the Medical Officer in charge at the hospital in Ibadan asked when I was conveyed into his care after having been driven over three hundred miles.

'Lanark' I said.

The Medical Officer smiled. 'I'm a Lanark man too.'

It transpired that he was Leslie Banks, a Lanarkian and elder brother of Dr Tommy Banks in my home town, and both sons of old Dr Banks who practised in the town well into his eighties and did his rounds on a bicycle.

This got me thinking about how many Lanarkians were in Nigeria. There was Alistair Campsie on the Cocoa Survey whom I did not meet when I was there but knew from earlier days. I had spoken to his mother before I left. Then there was Jim Aitken working as a surveyor with Rio Tinto Zinc, an appropriate employer for a Lanarkian, the highest point in the Lanark area being Tinto Hill which was visible from my bedroom window when I lived there and from the top of which you could follow the twists of the upper stretches of the River Clyde. I had visited Jim when on tour from Calabar. I was in contact with Dorothy (Aitken) MacIvor who was in Lagos with her husband Charlie. Dorothy was a member of the Lanark Tennis Club in the late 1940s as was Albert Goodere whom my wife and I would meet in Jos and whom we would be delighted to see again in Lagos with his wife Sheila. A cousin, Spud Murphy, who was born in Lanark but whose parents had moved to Stockton, worked with the United Africa Company. He and his wife Sandy spent longer in Nigeria than I did and qualified by the length of their time there to be 'old coasters'.

A hospital bed, particularly as you think you are recovering and have neither company nor books, is a good place to contemplate things until you slip back into feverish confusion. I kept seeing the original advertising verse of Ross the Draper's on the bricked-up first floor window opposite the shop in the Castlegate, not a stone's throw from the plaque commemorating where William Wallace first drew his sword to free his native land.

There are drapers in Lanark named Ross
Whose shop is just south of The Cross
And the number Fifteen, as it always has been
For value supreme, TRY ROSS

In 1940, during the threat of invasion, the name 'Lanark' had been painted out as part of a country-wide effort to deny invading enemy troops knowledge of where they were. I hoped this tiny bit of history would be kept for posterity by the authorities slapping some kind of preservation order on it so that I could show it to my children. As they got older I could give them a lesson in grammar by pointing out the anacoluthon in the rhyme.

I got to thinking that if there were six of us from Lanark in Nigeria (this number does not include Spud Murphy) then if the population of Lanark was 8,000, there would be 0.75 Lanarkians per thousand of its population serving in the colony. If we then related the estimated 5,000 Europeans in Nigeria as a percentage of the British population of 50 million we get something like 0.1 British per thousand living and working in the country. Could it really be that dear little Lanark in relation to the number of people living there had more than seven times the number of its inhabitants serving in Nigeria than had Britain as a whole? Could Lanarkians more than others really do such calculations in their heads as a legacy from the teaching of mental arithmetic as a social skill? Would others be thrown by the catch question slipped in by Miss Cassells in Primary 4 'What's the price of a one and sixpenny hammer?' Was Lanark representative of Scotland or was this high percentage presence some kind of distribution that represented an extremity of statistical probability?

We shall never know the true numbers but without doubt the number of Scots was considerable. There were two Scots Governors-General during my time there. There were many in trade as well as in government service. Andrew Young, the Director of Marketing and Exports when I came out to Nigeria, was a Scot as was John Brown, my boss in Port Harcourt. Historically, Scotland always felt more a part of a Greater Britain, or Britain and its empire, than it did of a United Kingdom and maybe this exodus was a continuation of the movement that took the waves of emigrants to the Low Countries and the Baltic before the post-American Revolution empire. Were there places for which the Scots or English or Welsh showed a preference which did not show up on any distribution graph we tried to draw of the work destinations of the British overseas? Of course there are no figures to confirm or deny this. Was it something in the culture or just an opportunity for ambitious Scots to obtain elbow-room and achieve self-expression or for those who did not share the upbringing of the elite and were marginal at home to test the extent to which the spirit could soar?

Such discussion is not useless as it makes us consider these factors we might not otherwise address. It does not follow that, if we cannot measure something, any consideration without numerical evidence is useless. I always suspect people who like to prove accountability or whatever else they are trying to demonstrate by producing numbers. There are, unfortunately, those among us who measure everything and understand nothing. The qualitative can have its own importance and awareness of it can release us from the tyranny of numbers.

The sun was something else that was always forcing its way into your awareness. It was forever distorting your vision and impinging on your consciousness at a time when you didn't want to see it, making the bush shimmer in its intensity. Sometimes I couldn't see what was out there for the bright, liquid heat. Then it would clear and enable me to contemplate how we all have different reactions to its harmful ultra-violet rays. Some of us who had recently soldiered or sailored in the tropics developed a darkening of the skin's pigment and were able to expose our bodies if we chose to the direct sunshine after careful, prior and gentle exposure. Others without experience of it had to find out for themselves the effect on their skins often to their extreme discomfort. Yet others with a fair skin and those with red hair had to cover themselves for protection. I only exposed my body when swimming in the Ethiope River which was clear and almost fast running or in the evening sunshine on Bar Beach in Lagos. Why couldn't these people who sought a tan ask themselves why Nigerians protected themselves from the sun with umbrellas which served the dual purpose of diverting the rain and providing cover from the sun? If they could be adversely affected by its rays, what hope was there for mere Europeans? Why am I worrying about them when they don't worry about themselves?

Out of another bright-out appeared the face of Jim Walker. He must have been on my mind for I could see him, born and bred a white Jamaican, with his head covered whatever the conditions. He suffered from skin cancer and removed his hat only when he was under a roof. Even those bred to the tropical sun were susceptible to its harmful light. The authorities in London who advised officers going to work in the tropics suggested, nay strongly advised, the acquisition of a sola topee. Shades of British soldiers standing firm at Rorke's Drift in the Boer War and the troops defending the Khyber Pass from marauding Pathans passed in front of me. Then I glimpsed myself bare-headed in Navy uniform in a tropical setting and I knew it was no longer necessary. Why then did I do as strongly advised and buy myself one?' Didn't I have a mind of my own, for Heaven's sake?

Now, the sola topee has a long and magnificent history. I tried mine on only once and vowed I would not wear it again. I did not consider it went with my 'ba' face' as they have it in my part of Scotland, not that I would want people to know that. It didn't go either with with my idea of comfort, light though it might be. My preference was for the bare head except when an extended period in the sun was likely. When I got to Nigeria I was pushed to find many who liked it. Apart from a mere handful of Europeans, the exceptions were Nigerians themselves, many of whom felt it denoted that they had arrived. Chief clerks wore them with dignity and they were to be seen on the heads of people who carried out menial tasks. If I had known that Richard coveted one, I would have passed mine on to him sooner. In the event, after taking possession of it in Ibadan, he wore it with apparent pride and the jauntiness of a man about town on the one occasion I met him wearing it. 'That's my boy, Richard!' I said to myself. I felt proud of him.

A tear of British learning falls upon the fall from grace of the sola topee. Even some of us who had enjoyed the benefits of a classical education and many who had no knowledge of the Latin language, believed that the 'sola' bit was to do with the sun. Some even referred to it as a 'solar' topee, the English pronunciation of the 'r', or the lack of its pronunciation to be more accurate (this is a Scottish interpretation), compounding the misunderstanding. In fact, it has nothing to do with the sun. It comes from the Indian name for spongewood and its pith-like stems, hence the alternative name 'pith helmet'. It is light in weight but overkill in affording protection from the sun, just like the reinforced spine pads on Navy shirts that used to be issued for wear in warmer climes. 'Topee' or 'topi' is Hindi for a hat. The Indian connection runs and runs in the English language. When the British left the sub-continent, they could not leave behind the ways in which it had influenced them.

My protection from the unforgiving sun was a lightweight French-made hat I bought in the Cameroons. It was a size 59, equivalent of a British size 7 and could be folded up and stuffed in a pocket, unlike a sola topee, and it would spring back into its original shape when pulled out. I referred to it as my 'Douala hat'. It was to disappear from my parked car in Lagos just at the time that hats were going out of fashion and the hat-making industry did some joint advertising under the easily remembered slogan of 'If you want to get ahead get a hat'.

CHAPTER 27

Crossing the Rubicon

If expatriates, or indeed anyone else, wanted to get married in Nigeria, it could be done by district officers according to the law. This was interpreted by assistant district officers and senior district officers as coming within their authority with the result that many wedding ceremonies were carried out by them. Unfortunately, it was established as a legal precedent that only those people who had been married by a full district officer, not a senior district officer nor an assistant one, were legally wed. The upshot was the demand by people so affected, it being no fault of theirs, that someone should rectify the matter. Their worry was that they might be disadvantaged at a later date if it was discovered that they had not been officially joined in wedlock, or that their children might receive mental scars if the bastard nature of their birth became known; or even be psychologically damaged themselves in the knowledge they were living 'over the brush'. As a result, it was not unusual to see in the *Nigeria Gazette* a 'Marriage, Removal of Doubts Ordinance' the outcome of which was that many a tortured houseperson found she had been made an honest woman of overnight and many an offspring, albeit by a quirk of the legal system, had any stigma of bastardy removed at a stroke.

Not for us these legal tribulations, for Mary and I were married in St Ann's Church, Ibadan on January 29th 1955. We met a short time before my first interview for a job in Nigeria. We met again on my first leave and became engaged towards the end of it. We visited her parents in County Roscommon and relatives in Galloway. It was during this time she discovered she had rheumatoid arthritis. We decided it would be best if she joined me three months before the end of my tour to see how Nigeria agreed with her condition. That's how we came to be married in Ibadan.

The wedding went off well considering there were no family members present but not without an initial alarm. The ceremony was to be conducted by Alan Galloway who held a post at the University of Ibadan and officiated ecumenically at the university chapel. In the event, the best man elect, Ted Barker, didn't turn up at my house as arranged. I drove to the church and on the way my horn stuck in the blow mode. 'That's all we need' I groaned to myself. Fortunately, I knew where the fuses were and managed to find the one that disconnected the horn by removing each one in turn.

At the church I explained the situation to Alan and we had a short discussion on what Plan B would be. 'Who has the ring?' he enquired. For a moment I was nonplussed. It was as if my memory just refused to work. Then it came to me. I had it in my pocket. I stood alongside Mary and explained the nature of the problem to her. 'Are you sure Ted's reliable?' she whispered, knowing him only from my letters. 'Absolutely,' I said in a hushed tone. I was sure I knew my friend from early Lagos days. Had he changed? 'No' I thought, 'that just isn't possible'. Ted was meticulous to a fault. The awful thought struck me that he might have had an accident on the way or at best had a breakdown. Ted was not a touring officer and was a stranger to bush roads. Was his Triumph Herald in which he cantily tootled around Lagos man enough for the job of withstanding the corrugations in the road? I wanted to give him as much time as possible but time was something we were running out of. We waited.

In the meantime, Phil Knights, on secondment from the Crown Agents, kept on playing the organ as if it was the most natural thing in the world - without repeating the music. And still we waited. I shall forever remember Phil's feat of memory. He eventually gave me a glance and a baleful smile and I knew it was time for the alternative action. The ceremony had been delayed until it could be put off no longer. I asked an old friend from my Warri days and a guest at the wedding, Jim Brown, if he would stand in as best man at this short notice - as if he had any choice given the circumstances. He agreed without hesitation.

Happily, Ted and his wife arrived during the reception none the worse of a hectic journey. We felt for them. Ted, who was a city man - and I use this expression in its very best sense - if ever there was one, accompanied by his wife Vera, had taken the wrong turning on his way from Lagos and arrived in Ijebu Ode instead of Ibadan. He had taken two sides of an equilateral triangle when all he needed was to follow the straight line.

The reception was held in my director's house and the arrangements were organised by his wife Betty Hardwick. It was a joyful occasion. Betty's husband Neville was a gentleman of the old school and one of that special band of agricultural graduates who had provided the core of the produce inspection service in the late 1920s and 1930s through to the present time. His post had been recently redesignated Chief Produce Officer under the Western Nigeria Ministry of Trade and Industry to which the Produce Inspection had been attached at regionalisation. He it was who gave Mary away. Mary chose not to have a bouquet of flowers as they wilted very quickly in the damp heat. Instead, she carried a white Bible to which she attached a small bunch of scented frangipanni flowers she picked fresh just before the car left for the church. These she later pressed and kept in our wedding album.

Mary's arrival more or less coincided with my transfer to Ibadan and the household's transition from a wood-burning Dover Stove to an electric cooker. Her first dinner party was by way of thanks to Neville and Betty Hardwick for their kindness in taking charge of the wedding reception. Richard had not yet mastered the intricacies of the electric cooker. As always, conversion was a painful process. The changeover was traumatic for both Richard and David. When the new electric kettle had been used, it was placed on the cooker without being switched off and eventually burned itself out. Pots boiled dry for the same reason and timings for the cooking process based on years of experience no longer applied. Richard advised dinner would be slightly late. An hour after the appointed time, nothing had appeared. When questioned he could only say 'Give chance'.

I had never seen Richard so close to panic except when we were stuck in the mud in the Cameroons and the grunting of the gorillas in the far distance got to him. "I too feah for dis place" he had said. There are no gorillas in Obinze. Eventually he was told to pass the fish soup the preparation for which Mary had made suggestions. It was very good. After a wait the soup plates were cleared and we waited once more. I could sense Mary's discomfiture. The conversation became somewhat strained but an enforced gaiety had a stress-relieving effect. Then momentary hesitations in the flow of talk would appear again and take on the dimensions of a protracted silence. I was aware at one point of my voice going unnaturally high followed by a laugh that was more like shriek. And I marvelled at how I could somehow stand outside myself and watch myself display a nervousness I didn't normally feel.

Two hours after the expected tabling of the meat, the main course appeared and the rest of the evening, or what was left of it, passed off without further incident to everyone's relief. Mary remembered her mortification and she vowed there and then, she told me later, that she would teach this Richard how to do things properly on the electric stove. Richard was happy to know. Madam managed to establish her authority without interfering in Richard's domain. Prior to her arrival he had not shown any sign of worry about the possibility of a new regime but he must have had some doubts as to what would change. Some wives were celebrated for their fixed ideas as to how the house should be ordered, cleaned and kept secure and no doubt the servants talked about such idiosyncrasies of their employers' spouses. Life must have been desperately insecure and stressful for them as they tried to impose a system they had brought with them. In the event everything on the house front turned out well.

Months later, when we had been invited to the house of the Acting Chief Produce Officer and we had just arrived and taken our drinks in our hands when the lights went out. The Acting Director's servants were old hands, and although the dinner was not ready at the appointed time, they did manage to salvage a meal from the ensuing chaos by ingeniously lighting a fire in the compound and constructing a makeshift stove while our host dug out his paraffin lamps. Dinner was very late. When we related this to Richard, he already knew; such was the efficiency of the bush telegraph. He appeared to take great pleasure from it and said to me feelingly 'Dat nevah go happen for our Dovah stove'. I think he was beginning to miss the excitement of being on the move much of the time.

Part 4

The Social Scene

CHAPTER 28

Quarters

To have reasonable housing was a pre-condition of a satisfied government official. No matter how much you enjoyed being on tour, it was good to come back to a base where there was a social life. The SP17 (Southern Provinces 17) is a type of house that comes to mind. There was a number of standard houses built by the Public Works Department for the use of government servants and the one I am thinking of had an integral garage, an unusual feature for these days and is the only type I can remember. The space could have been more usefully used as an extra room. Not that I lived in an SP17 but it does suggest a multiplicity of types. My first house after rest houses in Ikoyi was a flat in Apapa which looked as if it had been designed by an architect of the City of Birmingham Corporation during the post-war shortages and transferred holus-bolus to Nigeria with the addition of a ceiling fan. Thankfully, it lasted only a few weeks. Things only got better.

I lived in houses built entirely of wood and raised on stilts and in more modern ones of the brick and mortar (or rather concrete block) variety with integral kitchens as distinct from the older ones which had kitchens away from the house. They tended to be smaller than the more traditional houses where you had a feeling of space and freedom. The latter lent themselves to an active social life which was important in smaller stations where people came together in biggish numbers. Most had verandahs where the relative cool of the early morning and early evening could be enjoyed. Another design had a balcony upstairs with a lavatory off. One officer in Akure, who lived in such a house, kept an African Grey parrot on the balcony. It talked only a little but regularly repeated the most familiar sound it knew, that of a flushing cistern.

Furniture was also by kind favour of the Public Works Department. You signed for it when you arrived and had it checked off when you left. There were usually four easy chairs of a standard and basic design which varied with their age. Older ones were made with slats to take cushions on top. They had long wooden arms, long enough indeed to stretch your legs on and wide enough to stand a glass of beer. Later models were more Swedish in design but not so versatile. An occasional table was included in the Marketing Board house I occupied in Apapa and this of an unusually acceptable appearance, incorporating the kidney shape perceived to be the last word in the '50s. Anything outside that, like drinks stools and occasional chairs and table or standard lamps, you as the householder had to provide. A dining table with one carver chair and three ordinary dining chairs and a form of dumb waiter or sideboard completed the official provision. We relieved the bareness of the table by buying locally made dinner mats, woven in Ikot Ekpene under the tutelage of 'Raffia' Smith (to distinguish him from 'Cocoa' Smith and 'Gorilla' Smith). The more creative among us, usually the womenfolk, rang changes with home-made mats using glass or celluloid, an ordnance survey map of the Niger Delta cut into an appropriate size and passe-partout.

Older houses had hardwood or parquet floors. Concrete floors were normal in the more modern houses. To make these easier on the eye and more comfortable to the spirit, it was customary to have them polished with Cardinal polish. This was a brand without challenge in the territory. The servants, usually the 'small boy' applied it liberally on first application and worked it into the concrete. He polished the floor using half a coconut husk which raised a shine and eventually a skin which was much easier to maintain than establish. The colour was usually red but a green variety was introduced during my time there. Some of us aspired to a carpet in the middle to soften the appearance of the room and I eventually achieved this even if I got one cheap because it had a hole in one corner made by rats. I had it patched and the offending corner stayed under a chair.

When we moved from government quarters in Ikoyi to a Marketing Board house in Apapa, there was a decided improvement in quality if not in style. The move coincided with an office move from downtown Lagos to Apapa where a new and more suitable building was made available. At the house long metal windows could be rolled back to give access to the verandah which extended the lounge to accommodate a good number of guests. There were troughs round it to encourage the cultivation of flowers which was a rewarding occupation as seeds germinated in 48 hours. We planted them in half petrol drums cut longitudinally for the purpose and painted on the outside. Minute tree frogs as they were called (but closer to the toad family) balanced on the growing plants and provided a diversion as you sat on the verandah and conversed or communed. There were tiles of a kind of plastic on the floor which had to be kept clean with a proprietary cleaner. The roof covering the house was made of the exciting, new and easily affixed asbestos tiles. It had a self-contained guest wing with separate access which was a boon for departmental colleagues and friends proceeding on or returning from leave through Lagos and a pleasure for us mostly.

To these various quarters would come callers plying their wares and services who would in European circumstances be called upon. Tailors would bring their references which they had cajoled and pleaded for when a good client went on leave 'You go give me good book sah?' They would produce their written reference 'Mr Lawal is the best palindromic tailor in the business' and solicit your patronage. Most references were good ones. One doubtful one I read was 'Joseph Oluwole has worked for me for four years to his entire satisfaction'. A bad one might have read 'He has done me well'.

Barbers would call to give a tropical short-shorn haircut on the verandah. Hausa traders would display their carvings of dramatic heads in king ebony even as your hair was being cut and enjoy the ritual haggling on price, being more likely to reduce the asking price if they had had a bad day at the races. Many of them were excited by, and addicted to, gambling. Others would lay out their delicate thornwood figures or beautifully made crocodile skin bags sewn with a very special leather thonging. On the odd occasion, Indian traders would appear with exotic items for sale like camphorwood tables inlaid with contrasting woods and ivory lamps exquisitely carved from elephant tusks brought in from Asia long before the idea of banning the trade in ivory was even considered - we looked on them as works of art. The creation of each one was obviously a labour of love, such is the intricacy and delicacy of the carving and the story it sought to depict.

Car cleaners would negotiate a regular contract and strip down the car to the barest of paintwork and then put on a polish that lasted for months, coming back to touch it up every Sunday. Others would offer anything from baby crocodiles, whose tails were reputed to be a great delicacy in curry, to salvation from itinerant evangelists. One of the latter typically created theatre by inviting a young assistant to read from the Bible 'Boy, makee read de verse from Revelation twenty two'. And the assistant intoned '...they shall be his people and God shall be with them, and be their God. And He shall wipe away the tears from their eyes'. At this point the evangelist took the index finger of his right hand across his eye and shook it towards the ground going through the motion of casting away copious teardrops. Your quarters were part and parcel of the passing show.

CHAPTER 29

The Steward

The steward was the senior servant of the colonial house and continued to be so in what was in effect the post-colonial era. Richard was no exception. All other servants knew he was the man to be consulted about decisions, who passed on instructions and who generally considered himself responsible for the smooth running of the house. Mary allowed this perception to continue while ensuring that things were ordered in the way she wanted it. Wise women, and men, showed trust toward their servants and never held on to the keys to such places as the drinks cupboard as some unhappy expatriates did. Even the cook in his specialised domain realised that he had to defer to the steward if interests conflicted.

Most managed to find an accommodation of sorts. My first cook, Nathan was passing good but could not work harmoniously with Richard and eventually had to go when the heated arguments disturbed the tranquillity of the evening. My second, an ex-service Cameroonian called Max with an immense sense of humour, received a call to his village where he was to assume a senior role subsequent to the death of his father, and this provided Richard with the opportunity to press for the combined job of cook/steward. During the probationary period which we agreed, Richard produced some very palatable food and it was obvious that all the time he had spent in the kitchen had not been wasted. He called for assistance and that was when I took on David Aggreh as a 'small boy'. David was a willing but slow learner in Richard's view. He couldn't have done so badly for David would stay in my employ until we left Nigeria.

As he instructed David, I seemed to note an extra vigour in the example that Richard showed him. Polishing the floor with the half coconut husk, he demonstrated with unaccustomed vigour how he wanted the job done from that moment on. Sometimes Richard's patience was sorely tried as when David failed to draw the sinews of the turkey as instructed. This was a very simple process. The feet of the bird were jammed in the top of the kitchen door and the sinew-drawer merely had to clasp it with his arms, take his feet off the ground and the sinews came away readily. This creative piece of improvisation was my sole contribution to the efficient running of the kitchen.

Richard complained to me in his exasperation 'Dis damn small boy, he never de heah (understand). Not one time I tell him, not two time, not t'ree time; one, two, t'ree, four time I tell him '.
Then, turning to David he said 'How many time I tell you?'
'Four time sah ' said David.
'Na so ' Richard enjoined, turning back to me, his body language signalling that he awaited my very positive reaction to this affirmation of his complaint.
When David passed jam instead of marmalade at the breakfast table, Richard pointed to the jar it had come from and said 'You never see de lettah?'
'Sorry sah', said David to him, 'I make mistake'.
'Go get am one time' Richard commanded.
David was the one who had been to school and could read. It was he who made the entries in Richard's book in which he recorded how he had spent the week's market money, a custom Mary discontinued. On one occasion I queried an entry in the market book for 'chewing sticks' which many Nigerians cleaned their teeth with. David had mistaken 'stewing steak' for the object he was more familiar with. Richard explained 'I tink massa know I no de savvy book'. I was always careful after that to make sure Richard did not lose face and the pretence was always maintained in the presence of others.

Sometimes early in our relationship it was difficult to understand some of his words. Native speakers of most West African languages find it difficult to put certain consonants together unless preceded by a certain kind of vowel. Milk can be pronounced 'meelk' or 'millik'. Richard always had a problem with the combination of 'r' and 't' and and usually omitted the 'r' altogether. He laboured over the pronunciation of words like 'dirt'. Nzeocha, the departmental driver, often talked about the 'fan bellit'. He must have recognised that this was not the standard English pronunciation as he sometimes referred to it as the 'fan bet', the unfamiliar combination of consonants requiring an adaptation of pronunciation for communication purposes. In similar fashion native English speakers have difficulty with African language pronunciation. The Yoruba town Ibadan, for example, is pronounced in the way the French would speak it with a nasalised ending - something the average English-speaking tongue seems to find difficult.

When Richard was at market one day, Mrs Richard came to me in great distress with a howling Onyerije obviously in pain and shocked.

'What's wrong Mrs Richard?' I asked

'Dis pikin put stick of matches for her ear'. I looked closely at the ear and I could just see the end of a match-stick inside the ear. If we couldn't get it out of her ear, then it could possibly be serious. I piled the two of them into the car and took them to the hospital where a male nurse wanted to extract it himself. I demurred and asked for the doctor to examine the ear. The doctor was not available being at a bush clinic. So we took them to a private African doctor who managed to retrieve the match-stick to everyone's relief. David, who accompanied us in the absence of Richard, was open-eyed at what the doctor did. 'Doh,' he said, uttering the Urhobo exclamation used in all kinds of circumstances from wonderment to condolence depending on the inflection, 'big stick of matches for small child's ear'.

On another occasion, we tried to spare David Richard's displeasure by not telling him of something David had done when he was out. We heard the most awful gurgling noise outside the kitchen door. On investigation it turned out to be David carrying out Richard's instruction to kill a turkey - turkeys always seemed to get David into trouble. He was twisting the turkey's neck until he couldn't get his wrist round any further and had to let go and make a quick grab for the next turn of the screw. The turkey's head would unwind in reverse spiral describing circles in the process, and it laboriously tried to draw breath which was what had caused the noise that attracted our attention. David was about to repeat the action when he was stopped. Mary my wife it was who, being more elegant and practised than myself in such matters, showed him how to do it properly. David marvelled at the effortlessness and simplicity of the despatch of the bird.

Richard's routine varied with the weather. If it was fine he would give priority to airing the pillows and mattresses which would otherwise have smelt of sweat. Clothes in the wardrobe would equally need to be exposed to fresh air as mould was quick to grow. In the rainy season an electric bulb (if indeed there was the electricity to lead into the wardrobe) helped to protect the clothes. Then Richard would get on with the inside work like ironing. He insisted on having No 3 and No 13 flat irons as the minimum consistent with a well turned out employer. To assist this process he would liberally apply starch to shorts and longs. Mine were usually of 'Kano cloth' or Bedford twill made in Nigeria.

The shorts and trousers had buckles and tapes at the sides to fix to the desired tightness and ballops with buttons. To make it easier I had an ironing table made at the workshops of the Hope Waddell Institution in Calabar under the guiding hand of Joe Blair. How many people I wondered had an ironing table made of solid mahogany? Not many if they had to carry them themselves, for it weighed heavy and did not come on tour with us. Richard was meticulous in his attention to my appearance and an outstanding role model for David in his attention to hygiene. He wore out two scrubbing brushes to my certain knowledge. I felt my starched shorts were his pride.

He was just as careful with his own clothes which he ironed tirelessly. He and David wore khaki jacket and shorts through the day. Early on in my employ when we had reached the stage of having conversations in which he volunteered information, Richard asked what the Scots word was for 'knicker' (shorts) and I jokingly said 'wee breeks' and he referred to them as such from time to time. He wore longs in the evening. He had brass buttons on his jacket from choice. But the joy of both was to get into their immaculate whites if visitors were coming and to show their skills serving drinks and at table. A successful party was planned, not only by the host or hostess but by the steward. He it was who arranged additional chairs or crockery (often a guest's) and extra help in the kitchen or at table on a basis of reciprocity. He had social skills too, for the guests usually knew him and he responded to their banter which he enjoyed. You knew the evening had gone well if he said 'It be too fine'.

If Richard had done particularly well I would give him a penny or two. These were the West African ones with a hole in the middle. He kept them on a string and the string got heavier and heavier until he had to have a spending spree. He would probably been relatively wealthy if he had held on to them for many of them had King Edward VIII's head on them, the only coins ever minted which bore the head of an uncrowned British king. Collectors would clamour I'm sure to have such coins. I had one which I would later use to make a plumb line for hanging wallpaper in a fit of DIY enthusiasm but the coin would disappear with my enthusiasm for home decoration.

CHAPTER 30

The Thunderbox

Performing the natural functions under difficult conditions has long been a favourite focus for writers. Not as the main theme of their work but as something insinuated lightly into the fabric of their tales that strikes a chord with readers because it encompasses their experience at some time in one way or another. First World War stories of the trenches were interspersed with unfinished tales of the tree trunk that gave way when a number of men were on it with their trousers down. Or the explosion in the privy in the comedy act when the performer appears from the smoke with his neck through the hole in what had been the seat saying 'I guess it must have been something I ate'. This universal awareness is not unconnected to the lavatorial jokes beloved of youthful enthusiasts of the bodily functions but is mediated by maturity and education.

It can ascend into myth. So it was in colonial settings for a young wife arriving at her husband's station for the first time. The first test of her moral fibre was her reaction to the tales of the thunderbox. The ritual was that some reference would be made obliquely to it and others would enlarge on it implying all kinds of terrors that lurked there coiled or with hairy legs and pincers. They would elaborate on this theme later with such tales as that of the woman who had just completed a function and was about to close the lid when a black face peered up at her and said 'Good morning madam'. There is a saying in impolite circles that a person of undeserving character 'isn't fit to shovel sh•t'. The nightsoil man rises far above any such categorisation. He has to be the soul of discretion as well as the modest provider of a necessary service.

On one occasion I was staying at a rest house in Aba in Eastern Nigeria. Rest houses in these days were the equivalent of hotels. The ones which came nearest to hotel service as the pampered among us new it, were Catering Rest Houses. These only existed in cities and were only seen once in a while by junior officers, usually when they were going on leave or were returning from it. Those of us who used up-country rest houses had to make do with a building with a roof thatched with palm fronds or made of 'pan' (galvanised corrugated iron sheet), a kitchen with wood burning stove if you were lucky but usually with bare mud walls sometimes cement rendered, quarters for servants and a thunderbox. Come to think of it, Aba was an important market town, surprisingly without a Catering Rest House. After my first visit to that place I received a letter from the District Clerk asking if I would use less sand in future as the nightsoil man had found excessive weight on his head and neck when carrying the bucket. My dilemma on my second visit was to mitigate any odour while minimising the labour for the nightsoil man. The problem was heightened by the fact that something in my Sunday dinner the previous day had disagreed with me. Such were the dilemmas with which the touring officer was confronted and to which he had to bring to bear all his ingenuity, experience and education in search of a solution. The more thoughtful 'small house' controllers provided wood shavings which were much lighter but unfortunately not in abundant supply like sand despite the surrounding forest.

At a more public level, provision was made in Calabar for a concrete table to be built out over the creek on columns some 20 feet high with 12 circular holes in the concrete to accommodate a maximum of 12 persons at times of maximum demand - an alfresco communal convenience observable by all and sundry from numerous, if distant, vantage points. Designed and built by the Public Works Department (PWD), it was the epitome of functionality. Presumably the long drop and exposure to the rush of wind it created, helped to accelerate the decomposition of the waste matter in the water.

For people who enjoy a close-knit social structure, it represented, I suppose, an opportunity for a chat on happily met occasions. Not so on a device at the fore-end of ships observed at Sapele (renowned for the mahogany named after it as used in post-war UK railway carriages) from which one of the natural functions had to be performed nearly half astride a precarious and solitary perch not unlike the leadsman's chains ('by the mark twain') on ships of pre-sonar vintage which had to navigate narrow and shallow channels. There was a similar drop from the point of performance to the Jamieson River as from platform to creek at Calabar. Canoe traffic crossing the river was aware of the danger and skirted round the possible arc of flying turds with a dexterity and urgency born of perceived necessity.

When it came to leaving our government quarters, it was necessary to have the inventory checked and a signature that all was in order from the representative of the appropriate department before we could go. Among the items were 'Goree jar and pail' - the heart of the thunderbox. And a reminder that while we might be in West Africa, many of the items of equipment we used were designated by Indian names or so we thought. In fact, while Goree has a suggestively Indian ring to it, it is just as likely that it derived from the 17th century French military and trading post of Gorée, an island just south of Cape Verde, the most westerly point of the African continent. It was the first slave harbour to use a real currency as opposed to cowrie shells or manillas and may well have done a good line in the export of glazed pot jars right down the coast of West Africa.

When Queen Elizabeth II visited Nigeria in 1956 Warri was on her itinerary (did you know by the way that when a Scottish admirer in Edinburgh climbed a lamp post to remove one of the I's to reflect historical accuracy at her coronation - there never had been a Queen Elizabeth I of Scotland previously - he was charged with treason?). Her visit there was preceded by instructions from government officers seconded for the purpose who advised on arrangements that should be made to accommodate the needs of the royal party.

I remembered at the time that I had read somewhere that the only advice that Edward, Prince of Wales and subsequently Duke of Windsor, ever received from his father was to relieve himself at every available opportunity. If this was such a problem then when travel was relatively restricted with the added benefit of en suite facilities on the royal train, how much greater the problem in a country like Nigeria at that time with sometimes long distances by motor car between facilities deemed suitable. Her Majesty and attendant ladies were not clothed to perform the functions in the Nigerian manner and no one would have expected them to do so. It was only right and proper to ensure that any excessive tweaking of aristocratic sphincters was kept to an absolute minimum even in the line of duty.

I did wonder whether the zeal to ensure the comfort of the royal party was triggered by some administrator's knowledge of some such tale of the manner of departing this life as that of an eminent mathematician and astronomer, Tige Brahe, who was too embarrassed to excuse himself from his emperor's festive table and died of a burst bladder. God forbid that the bad dream of one of the Queen's entourage expiring in such a way should come to pass. Someone would have to carry the can. And the ultimate nightmare scenario that such an eventuality should befall our dearly loved young queen would be almost too unbearable even to contemplate. She would be consigned by history to join those scions of the blood royal who had drowned in a butt of malmsey, had died from a surfeit of lampreys or had declined to the point of death believing they were frogs rather than be remembered for presiding decently over the prolonged decline of Britain as an economic and political power while retaining the trappings of greatness. What would happen to any officer found responsible for failing to foresee and plan against such a contingency can only be imagined. The successful completion of the visit was marked, I believe, by the sighs of relief, whether loud or contained within a seemly silence, on the part of those responsible for its passing off without any obvious hitches.

I had an acquaintance, Bob Rapson, who had a certain responsibility for coordinating the visit and he received an MVO for personal services to Her Majesty. When he checked up in whatever book gives the order of precedence in such things he found that his gong, the MVO 5th Class, came between Master in Lunacy and a less familiar decoration. The upshot of his or someone else's intervention was that the Resident Warri's entire annual vote for maintenance of permanent and semi-permanent buildings in the station (never very big in truth) was applied, it is said, to the decoration of his bathroom and lavatory in anticipation of the short visit.

I cannot say that his facilities included a thunderbox ('shunkie' or 'cludgie' are the more onomatopoeic Scots expressions that come to mind, the former being closer to the exact meaning) as I seem to recall that flush lavatories were installed in Warri quarters where the Public Works Department was expert in building concrete septic tanks just a foot or two above the water table. If I had been able to say that we had thunderboxes in Warri, then I could have recounted that Louis X1V, *le roi soleil*, had dignified them in an earlier era by holding court from his *chaise percée*, giving symbolic emphasis to the identification of the state in his person - *'L'Etat c'est moi'*. (Scottish intellectuals please note that 'erse dichter' is not a Gaelic poet but was, in its French translation at this epoch, a royal servant who performed his humble duties under the *ad hoc* throne of his king).

CHAPTER 31

The Dinner Party

During my first week in Nigeria I was invited together with another recent arrival to have drinks with Andrew Young, the Director of the Department of Marketing and Exports, the executive of the Nigeria Marketing Boards. He it was who interviewed me on the 'milk round' when would-be employers came to the universities on an annual visit to look for suitable recruits. He first went to Nigeria in 1927 in the Department of Agriculture and was instrumental in setting up and running the Produce Inspection Service within that department. Now he was Director of Marketing and Exports but retained his interest in the quality aspect of the Board's products in his capacity of Chairman of the Produce Inspection Board. He was also appointed to the post of Chairman of the Cameroons Development Corporation.

He was to have the good fortune to survive a plane crash at Tripoli when a well known Nigerian chief sitting just in front of him, the Orimelusi of Ijebu-Ode, was killed. If he gave us a message it was that what is normal in Nigeria is not quite the same as in Britain. The adjustment would have to be made by us and that quickly. He also warned us against a certain type of European. He would rather sit down to a meal with his African cook, he told us, than some of the Europeans who arrived on the Nigerian scene. We had been recruited, he said, because he felt that we had, among other things, the character and ability to discriminate among people and issues.

Nowhere was this adjustment truer than in the ways in which people socialise and this of course means the ways in which they entertain, eat meals, observe rituals associated with dining and generally enjoy each other's company. Eating is one of the ways by which relationships are established and maintained. And eating in Nigeria was very different from the way it was done in

Auchenshuggle or Brighouse. Nowhere was this more evident than at the dinner party, not to be confused with other evening get-togethers. Certainly not with the extended drinks party where 'finger chop' or 'small chop' was provided for a fairly large gathering and only the older ladies had chairs to sit on. The majority stood and conversed in informally well-dressed groups which would change their composition in the course of the evening as guests circulated assisted often by introductions, where necessary, from their hosts or willing others. The food consisted of goodies like anchovies on toast, devilled eggs and various canapés which were available in sufficient quantity to make dinner later a matter of choice rather than necessity.

Nor was dinner to be confused with knee chop which in terms of intake of calories closely approximated that of the dinner party with cold meats, salads, home made crisps and other relatively substantial fare available at a buffet table. A knee chop gathering was a highly informal affair where guests might be invited to remove their jackets and ties and were seated sometimes in the most unusual ways like sitting on a pouffe made in traditional Oyo leatherwork based on traditional prayer mat designs of the kind on which it was customary for the faithful to kneel upon when bowing in prayer in the direction of Mecca.

The dinner party proper was by far the most formal. Guests were received by the host(s). In the rainy season the man of the house or a servant would carry a golf umbrella to your car and accompany you to the shelter of the house (there were no gutters on the houses, the rain cascading from the roof straight into the storm drains). Only on the most formal of occasions would jackets be kept on, guests being invited to divest themselves of their 'coats' on arrival. Stewards and 'small boys' would be decked out in their best whites and would pass drinks to the seated guests. Drinks would vary from pink gins to gin with orange squash and soda, to whisky and its various additives if preferred. One or two hosts with good sources might proffer gin and French or gin and Italian (vermouth), a drink that would be combined at a later date in a more profitable same bottle, never mind the individual taste - a triumph of marketing over substance.

In the course of conversation it was not unusual to see people remove flies from their drinks and place them in ashtrays and go on to finish them. It was something one got used to in sticky climes where insects were abundant. The operation was performed with an ease and nonchalance, even elegance, born of practice. Flying beetles were another distraction, certainly away from the cities. They needed a distance to gather speed before becoming airborne rather like a plane taking off at La Paz in Bolivia where the elevation is so high that engines lose much of their power at take-off and require an extended runway to enable the requisite amount of 'lift' to be achieved to become airborne. When the flying beetles eventually got off the ground they didn't seem to have the radar apparatus to avoid things like hanging lamps which they would hit with a thud and fall in temporary concussion to the floor leaving the lamps swinging as they came to when they would repeat the process, perhaps hoping to avoid stationary hanging objects on a second essay into the air in a slightly different direction.

During mating times, flying ants would swarm in the evenings and windows had to be kept closed as they made for the light and fluttered against the glass and fell to the ground to couple or do whatever else was their pleasure. Problems arose only when there were no windows and the ants flew in through the jalousies which we had to shut in a hurry. They were prized as delicacies by the servants who scooped them into any convenient container for later frying, in palm oil of course, and consumption. Manna comes in different forms in different countries.

When the steward informed the lady of the house that dinner was served, guests would be called to table and invited to sit down in appropriate places, these being as far away from spouse or partner as possible with every lady a man on either side as far as possible as is right and proper. Knapkins were starched, folded into all kinds of pleasing configurations and ironed to hold the shape. This was the setting in which I felt it would be

196

appropriate to say a Latin grace *Sit nomen Domini benedictum, per Jesum Christum salvatorem nostrum, Amen.* None of it. The atmosphere of what I imagined to be an academic dinner without the gowns was destroyed by the arrival of the soup in bowls with lids to keep it warm and nary the sign of a grace except in the most devout households. Guests were asked if they preferred light or dark (sherry) and glasses were filled according to taste. The fish course, garnished to provide matching and contrasting colours, would arrive perhaps laid out decoratively on anodised trays, an innovation of the early fifties, and guests helped themselves to a portion, the newcomer feeling perhaps that it was equivalent to being a vandal to destroy the symmetry of such a masterpiece.

It would be wrong to say that hostesses vied with each other in novelty of table decoration. Flowers grew luxuriantly in the Nigerian climate and the way in which they were mixed and shaped was a miracle to the male mind. Even bachelors contrived to have choice floral centrepieces. My own *pièce de résistance* was the blushing hibiscus that grew in my compound in Warri. Under normal conditions it opened white in the morning and by the evening had turned red. The manager of G.B. Ollivant, Eric Mintie, an old hand of an old established company on the coast, let me into the secret of adding a subtle interest to the meal by cutting a couple of heads in the morning, putting them in the refrigerator and removing them just before guests were seated, making it the focus of the table. As the meal progressed the flowers changed colour from white to red.

When the servants had taken away the plates of the fish course, the plates for the main course were put in front of the guests from the left hand of course. If the dish was a hot one, everything had to be on the table quickly to prevent anything going cold (a relative condition in these circumstances of high temperature and humidity). While the senior steward went round offering the meat to guests, handles of the serving spoon and fork at the optimum angle for the diners to take hold of them, he would be followed closely perhaps by the steward of a neighbouring officer with vegetables and the small boy, resplendent in his whites like his seniors, with any additional vegetables or sauces. Cooperation among servants was normal and one imagined some kind of meeting among all the servants every morning to find out whose employers were dining where and negotiating the necessary support perhaps even calling in accumulated credits if the occasion was one of real importance. The empty plates would be cleared with a practised alacrity and the sweet would be offered prior to coffee and brandy.

Conversation gathered momentum over the brandy and continued until the hostess invited the ladies to retire to the main bedroom and dressing room. Since rooms were spacious but few, guests often many, the weather usually fine and post-prandial lavatory facilities limited, the men were asked if they would 'like to see Africa'. On this cue the men adjourned to the compound and amidst a collective micturition lit only by shafts of light escaping from the house, had the last word on conversations they had started at the dinner table. In Nigeria, men were by tradition the movers and shakers, a tradition nevertheless under siege from a generation that grew up during hostilities and gave women not only more freedom but a new sense of worth.

Many found the job of housewife irksome, especially when there were servants to do the housewifely things. Intelligent women sought a challenge and custom had decreed otherwise. Career women, who were relatively few, had greater satisfaction from their work. Sometimes wives found an outlet for their talents in the cities where their particular skills were more likely to be needed. It was customary for them to provide support for their husbands in whatever duties they had, not least in entertaining guests and relieving them of the task of overseeing the household whether or not they had other work. Nigerian women, if the market traders were anything to go by, had an established authority in their particular role which many of the European wives must have envied.

CHAPTER 32

Leaves

The social scene, as far as Europeans were concerned, was punctuated by people going on leave and being replaced by new faces. By the end of a tour of duty, expatriates began to feel the need of a holiday and to look forward to visiting their friends and relatives whom they had not seen for 18 months to two years. The arrangements that had to be made for this were quite extensive. You had to prepare handing over notes for your successor, go over them with him and effect introductions to all and sundry if he arrived prior to your departure date. There were the loads to be packed. One of the useful items I had acquired (from the same disaffected Canadian from whom I had bought the canvas camp bath during my first days in Lagos) was a brass-bound Christie trunk which took things like bed-linen and clothing and was completely air-tight. Arrangements had to be made for storage with the Public Works Department.

You had to make similar arrangements for the car unless, as I preferred, I left it for friends to use. I recall that my car which I had left in Calabar with Dan McKeown looked cleaner than I had ever seen it when I got back to collect it. Then there was the house and furniture to be checked off in preparation for the next occupier. After that you had to get to Lagos where the plane or ship left from, and find accommodation until its departure. Unless of course you were in the North and travelling by air in which case you had to get to Kano where there was an international airport. Then you had to pay the servants for the period of your absence and give them a point of contact to find out when you would be back in the country. Even without that their grapevine worked efficiently to advise them the when and where of your return to Nigeria. Their ability to obtain all the information they felt necessary, including details of your next posting even before you were advised, never ceased to amaze me.

If some of us were exhausted after a tour, even as we were enjoying ourselves, it was for a variety of reasons. The reason usually trotted out was the lack of the kind of food to which we were accustomed but this was nonsense as far as most of us were concerned. We exulted in the difference. Sometimes there were people who found the food disagreeable, but they were unlikely to come back after a tour of duty if indeed they lasted that long. Then there was the argument that the discomfort of the constant humid heat and the inability to get a good night's sleep had a cumulative and debilitating effect on the system. If that was the case, why did the change to a temperate climate have an immediate effect? While there were those among us who had periodic bouts of malaria or some other tropical ailment and needed a period of recuperation, I felt that the reason for the exhaustion was mental rather than physical.

Some of us were exposed to a number of irreconcilable pressures which was probably the source of stress even if we did not recognise it as such. There was the constant battle against unprovable corruption which resulted in a kind of cat-and mouse game. Nearly all officers at some time or other found an underlying venality among certain members of staff who expanded the custom of mutuality to include doubtful methods of going about their duties. In produce inspection, certain inspectors tried to defend not meeting the daily target for gradings set to reduce their ability to withhold services or otherwise delay the delivery of the service. Their supervisors and myself sought to counter any move that might delay inspection and be used to extort illicit payments over and above what might be considered a traditional gift for a service rendered or the acknowledged illicit fee that replaced it. It was easy enough to say that if one Nigerian paid another to do something he was paid to do in any case, then it was crass stupidity on the part of the payer. The nagging idea in the background that it was wrong raised the question as to whether you were living out a lie by ignoring it or not spending more time trying to eradicate the practice, if not the underlying reasons for it.

There were other little dilemmas. If you were a government

official, did you put loyalty to your employer before principle or doctrine when the two were in conflict? I became increasingly sceptical of the monopoly of the marketing boards when the world was rapidly returning to a market system, perhaps because I had settled into a routine by this time and was able to give more thought to the works of the economists I had read at university and my professor Alexander Gray or because it was possible to look at things from the outside when on leave. Questions were already being asked about similar monopolies in the United Kingdom with regard to such commodities as milk and coal which had been subject to central control in the war and to the tenets of a centralising and a well-meaning but inflexible Labour government after it.

The system of Boards, I was more and more convinced, was an honest attempt by civil servants not necessarily skilled in political economy, to put right a system which had discriminated against the African merchant aspiring to have a piece of the commercial action and which had been indisputably manipulated by the larger expatriate companies that made up the Association of West African Merchants. A market system would rely on a course of dealing over a period that enabled trust to be built up between the growing band of African merchants and potential overseas buyers. The problem was not with the economics but with the creation of this trust which, on the part of overseas buyers, was related to adherence to the norms of business as they saw it and African merchants who were still prone in some cases to break contracts, as already perceived by the buyers of non-board produce, very often for reasons of under-capitalisation or overtrading.

There were those who claimed that if the boards were not necessary, then neither was the produce inspection service. This I challenged for a number of reasons. Its usefulness was acknowledged by the produce merchants themselves. I particularly valued in this regard the views of significant officers of the companies with a vested interest in the quality of their chocolate and the ethics of its production like the Rowntree-Fry-Cadbury local representatives and their visiting chairmen -

Adrian Cadbury was one who was years later to have a prize-winning article on ethics in business in the Harvard Business Review. These companies had bought their own cocoa before the war and were now mere licensed buying agents of the Cocoa Board and relied on inspection to get the quality of cocoa their organisations needed. A cocoa broker from New York on a visit to Nigeria gave me an external confirmation of the need for continuing inspection. Indeed he suggested I would easily find a job among cocoa brokers in New York and would assist me to obtain a placement if I wished. My own experience in Lagos of adulteration of cocoa and its destruction either by burning or by dumping in the Iddo Pool convinced me that an inspection system was still required. The palm produce buyers were not quite so adamant but also favoured the maintenance of the inspection system.

Whatever the cause of the exhaustion, many officers took proprietary medicines or tonic wines like *Sanatogen* which claimed to feed the nerves, for the last months of a tour of duty. Others preferred to take cigarettes or similar substance to keep them going. There was an insidious tobacco advertisement at this time which urged you to 'let Capstan take the strain'. There was a brand called 'Pirate' that was made in Nigeria and enjoyed extensive sales. Cigarettes were kept in a box and offered round on a regular basis even by non-smoking hosts.

Occasionally, someone returned to Europe feeling better than they did when they arrived. So it was with Mary. By the end of her second tour the rheumatic pains that she had continued to suffer disappeared completely and doctors put it down to the effects of the humid heat. She was later in our second leave to be diagnosed as having a defective mitral valve in the heart. After that leave we would be returning to Nigeria for one last tour, myself by air and Mary later by sea.

CHAPTER 33

The Club

Expatriates are people who have imposed exile upon themselves. Being away from the mother country or the fatherland tends to make their hearts grow fonder and to ascribe to the land of their birth qualities they would never have imagined it possessed had they not left its borders or shores. It is only to be expected that such people will want to associate with others of similar origin to celebrate their shared uniqueness and to obtain mutual support in the face of real or perceived adversity. Hence the significance of the thriving Caledonian Societies, Yorkshire Societies and so on. Whether the toast is 'Caledonia' or 'The Broad Acres' or whatever, people want to celebrate their identity. It gives them a feeling of not being alone. Drinks like Atholl brose and food like roast beef and Yorkshire pudding heighten this feeling, all the more so for its only being available on such occasions.

In Nigeria they came together in the club. My introduction to it was the Ikoyi Club. Ikoyi was the island off the island of Lagos connected to another island, Iddo and all already joined together by bridges, where the desirable low density residences were concentrated. For many, the Club was the focus of their social activities. It was the only place where golf could be played - it had an 18 hole course with sand greens known as 'browns'. It was also a difficult place for Nigerians to become members. It had its black members but they were few in relation to the white faces. In other words it was exclusive, not only of black faces but also of the artisanal white ones. I was taken there as a guest but never had occasion or desire to join even if someone had proposed me. Frustrated Nigerians eventually set up their own club, the Island Club, which became exclusive in its own way but was not knowingly discriminatory.

In Port Harcourt, the club took in most people and had that uncomfortable air from time to time that exists when the English pretend they are all John Thompson's children (anglicisation of *'Jock Tamson's bairns'* meaning a group of people united by a common sentiment). In other words the class system reared its ugly head. The direct language of the construction managers and the more refined language of the colonial servants, and the differing attitudes their words expressed, sometimes led to misperception and acrimony. At the risk of my being accused of stereotyping, there is no one more adept at the art of putting people down than the archetypal English public schoolboy whose command of biting sarcasm is unsurpassed; nor is there anyone more ready to take offence than the self-opinionated man of working class origins inflamed by his culture of booze as an expression of his manhood.

One social explosion came when a Senior District Officer made what was interpreted as a devastating comment to a construction hard man who had an arm round his neck before he could get out of his chair and broke his jaw. Port Harcourt club had the saving grace of a thirteen hole golf course with greens, the only one in Nigeria in these days. It was sown with Bahama grass which grows sideways rather than upwards and can be kept closely cropped. To sow you get handfuls of the stuff and chop it into small pieces, sow it broadcast on the ground and nature does the rest. Except of course that greens need to be tended with care and consummate skill.

We had a mixture of people in the Calabar club, but it was a smaller station with a greater degree of social control. The atmosphere was good and this was reflected in a series of social functions. On club night we dressed up in white mess jacket and black trousers complete with cummerbund. These latter were the standard black or green which was the colour for Nigeria. The club in Warri was similar to the one in Calabar in that the members were a close social unit and cooperated in all manner of activities but was more informal on special nights. The club night in Warri was enhanced by the odd cabaret act put on by volunteers in the station. I remember a pair who called themselves 'The Western Regional Production Board Brothers' doing a skit on the Western Brothers in their distinctive drawl as heard on radio immediately post-war. One of their acts I remember included a song

Then there's D.O. Western Ijaw
He's somewhere up the creeks
We don't know what he's doing
He's been there for weeks and weeks.
All his troubles will be over in nineteen fifty six
Not to Warri, chaps, not to Warri.

The D.O. was Bill Pratt, the District Officer on a tour of the creeks. 1956 was the projected date of independence for Western Nigeria (it was actually 1957) and the last line a play on the Western Brothers' concluding catchphrase 'Not to worry, chaps, not to worry'.

They came to the club night from all the remote stations by road and/or creek. Jackie Cooper, Lt-Cdr Royal Naval Volunteer Reserve (rtd) of the Nigeria Marine based in Forcados (a very remote station by this time in its history) arrived by launch and would warm to the occasion as the evening wore on. He would take on himself the responsibility for lining up the champagne bottles and then give naval fire orders as he popped the corks one after the other calling out 'Always keep one in the air or the bastards'll get you'.

The Warri club overlooked the river where seagoing vessels tied up. At Christmas, Santa Claus in the person of Harry Whitaker of John Holt's Transport, arrived at the Club by canoe for the children on the station, clad in traditional garb. He received a welcoming cheer from children of all ages. Such people as Harry were deserving of public recognition for such activities and the fact many remember him after all these years is testimony to the fact that that recognition was given. To be remembered by people who cared was more valuable than official recognition. Particularly where there were families it was a real morale booster.

The Sapele Club, only forty miles away with a plywood factory and timber industry with its saw doctors and shipping people did not have the same atmosphere. Entertainment tended to be films or otherwise was of the housey-housey kind. Nevertheless the Sapele club kept open house for touring officers as did the small club in Aba. In the latter I met a judge on circuit, Mr Dove Edwin, who originated from Sierra Leone and who enjoyed a game of snooker. When he missed an easy pot he would call out 'There's no justice here'.

If anything killed the clubs it was the improvement in living conditions. With the growing practice of women accompanying their husbands, and latterly joined by their children, on their tours of duty to the coast, couples might go to the club but they had an alternative social milieu in their own homes. Whether this opened up the membership to those excluded is open to doubt. What is incontestable is that the clubs initially played an important role in the social life of a station. Events may have overtaken them but they provided an opportunity to bring people together who would otherwise have felt divorced from their roots.

They also developed an attitude of superiority which was inward looking and ring-fenced. By that very fact the clubs tended to become exclusive, thereby creating and perpetuating a problem until they had outlived their usefulness. Of course there were exceptions, not least among many administrative officers who actively sought to bring in people who had been excluded, but those who had been excluded now had other places they could go where they could develop their own interests and celebrate their own culture. There might now be a need for specialised clubs for particular activities but 'The Club' as a centre where people fell back on the support of people of similar origins was as dead as old Marley himself and became a refuge for those whose prejudices prevented them from indulging in a wider interaction with local people

CHAPTER 34

The Five Events

The club's activities also reflected social attitudes in the United Kingdom. Among the ruling elite of the United Kingdom and its official representatives overseas there had long been a prejudice against trade. All this despite the fact that the economic well-being which supported their activities and life-style came from the very trade they despised. It might well have been an attitude derived in Nigeria from the perceived unsavoury nature of the so-called 'palm oil ruffians' about whom we have already spoken, but the roots of the prejudice go back to the days when 'gentlemen' did not soil their hands with it. The public schools geared to preparing the sons of the aristocracy and the emergent middle classes for careers in the army and in administration of the empire perpetuated the view.

It was made worse by successful businessmen aspiring to become 'gentrified' rather than evolving a mode of living that grew out of their business culture and setting their own style of behaviour with their own values embedded in it. This was silent witness to the deep roots of the class system in Victorian times and the legacy it had left. Although this attitude had been changing, particularly under the influence of recruitment into the service of officers chosen for their personal qualities and education and perhaps brought up in regional counter cultures, and later, of ex-servicemen whose war experiences had created a confidence combined with an education and maturity that gave them a sense of intellectual equality, it persisted to a degree in the minds of a number of people in business and administration and was exemplified in what was known in Calabar as 'The Five Events'.

This was a series of sporting contests the outcomes of which indicated which of the two sides, the government side or the trade side, prevailed. It was administered as part of the activities of the club. A good-going rivalry was guaranteed as the perceived attitude on the government side generated an equal and opposite reaction on the part of those not paid from the public purse. It was originally confined to the expatriate community but was extended to include Nigerian nationals who were becoming a bigger proportion of government employees and indeed of the firms. Nigerians excelled at games like football and tennis but were excluded in games like golf that they had not yet embraced. Lest I give the impression that it was entirely a government versus trade or an 'us and them' situation, members of the two groups interacted in all sorts of ways. The tradition had probably outlived the circumstances it had arisen from. At the highest level, the general managers of the companies found common cause with the Residents in charge of provinces and later, when Nigeria was divided into autonomous regions with a relatively weak centre, with the people in the regional and federal secretariats. In small stations all participated in the social scene.

Choice of the teams would be made by persons chosen in theory by the Resident and the senior General Manager but in practice by reasonably competent individuals nominated by them. My own position was an odd one as I was officially a government officer but concerned with trade.

'I don't know where we should put you McCall; you have a foot in both camps' the Resident, Cuthbert J Mayne, said to me.

'I don't mind which side I am on, sir' I replied, 'it's only a game'.

'Don't you believe it', the Resident declared, 'it's an important tradition'.

In the event I was put in the government team. Preparations went ahead with teams being selected with great forethought. Who should we play against the scratch player and cousin of Jimmy Adams, a well known golfer of his day (and known as the champion runner-up) and partner. Should it be a weaker pair so that there was a better opportunity of winning a later match? Who could best handle James Akinbiyi's top-spin service? Who should open the bowling against Brian Thwaite, who had been a Cambridge University cricket blue, with the best chance of containing him? The Resident insisted on playing in the cricket match. I knew from experience that he was not averse to calling out 'Drop it' to someone in the outfield when he skied a ball. Whether he wanted to enjoy a little longer at the crease or just wanted to test the mettle of the fielder involved I do not know but suspect the latter. I would have been mortified if I had been in the opposing team when the ball came in my direction and I had muffed the catch on hearing the Resident's call to spill it.

There was a feeling like the aftermath of a rugby match against Wales or Ireland at Murrayfield when the results were known. Win or lose, it was an excuse to have a special celebration. If someone had excelled, it had been customary at one time to donate a bar stool to the club, allegedly fashioned to fit the backside of the donor. Whether a cast was taken before it was made was not a question that came to mind at the time and I suppose there is no one to answer it now. The custom was dropped as the bar became crowded with stools and none of my contemporaries were required to leave their mark. So I would never know how the template was made from which the stool seat would be fashioned.

It was interesting to see that as companies prospered the conditions under which their expatriate staff worked got better and better while the government officer's lot remained much as it was. Air conditioning and dehumidifiers came to the company houses to make living a little more comfortable and to facilitate a good night's sleep in the high humidity of the oil palm belt. It also meant that those who lived in them were more likely to catch colds and feel the effects of the heat as a result when they emerged from it. This gave us poor relations in government service a comforting feeling of *Schadenfreude* for those of us who had to spend our nights in less well appointed houses. With the advent of the Shell D'Arcy Exploration Company drilling to establish if there were oil deposits in commercial quantities and finding it by all accounts, it was obvious that 'big bucks' were going to be spent in the region and dramatic changes ensue if it were to be found, not all of them to the advantage of the people of the area who relied on the local eco-system for their livelihood.   It would also swing the balance of advantage in any future events against the government side.

I wondered if there was just a connection between the fact that a Resident's son had joined one of the companies was a sign of the times and also that the son of one of the company managers had become an administrative officer?   Was some kind of role reversal taking place? If so, there was not much of a mileage to be had from it as Nigeria was assuming responsibility for its own affairs and exercised more and more direct or indirect control over who did what. While there would be a need for experienced officers for some years to come, there was not much of a future for a relative newcomer. In the companies, it was even further advanced and bore witness to the fact that commerce was more often than not at the forefront of change as it had been in the days of the change from slavery to a 'legitimate' economy.

CHAPTER 35

Luvvies

A calabash is the dried and hollowed out shell of the bottle pumpkin and other types of gourd trees. They come in different sizes but are still used for particular purposes irrespective of how big or small they are. They are used as containers and as vessels for food and drink. The shape is imitated in the manufacture of clay pots. I have seen big ones balanced on the heads of women carrying water and other loads for long distances, small ones by a potter when water was needed in the process of throwing a pot, in the kitchen for adding water to a culinary creation, in the process of starching and ironing clothes (by taking water from it into the mouth and spitting it out as required on to the garment), and for adding liquid to achieve the right consistency in the making of indigo dyes. On a sadder and exceptional note, calabashes were used to dispose of newly born twins less than a hundred years ago because they were supposed to be the result of malign witchcraft. Again, on a practical note, I have seen a hardened clay pot-bottom turned upright on top of a calabash full of loose earth and the sides of the pot built downwards in coils before being smoothed off following the sides of the calabash and then rimmed.

The prime use of the calabash is a social and celebratory one. It is for holding palm wine which is the liquid that betokens hospitality, lubricates friendships and serves to bond groups on occasions of significance like weddings and funerals. It is the fermented sap of the raffia palm made by tapping the tree at its crown and letting the sap drain slowly into the calabash, or more frequently these days, into glass bottles. In a couple of days it is ready for imbibing, a milky, frothy, strong liquid with a unique, yeasty taste. Unlike whisky, it does not improve with keeping and indeed loses its attractiveness after a few days. The calabash can be decorated with line drawings or paints, or sometimes a combination of both and with carving. The artistic aspect is appreciated as well as the practical, particularly for more important occasions. One of these occasions occurred on a visit to the lower Cross River stations.

Outside of the educated elite, weddings in Nigeria were noticeably different from those in the United Kingdom. Brides like to look their best wherever they are. It goes without saying that different countries will have different ideas about how to dress for the occasion, how to do the hair and what rituals are to be observed. We do not always think of marriages elsewhere as being differentiated by what constitutes the body beautiful. But this concept also varies with where you are. The pencil-slim figures who parade the catwalks of Western Europe would have no appeal in parts of Nigeria. When I was in the eastern part of the country in Ibibio territory, I was invited with another expatriate whose local popularity was the reason for the invitation, to visit a wedding celebration near Okopedi where the bride had just come out of the fattening house in which she had spent some time to enhance her beauty. To me she seemed gross but there was little doubt about the dignity with which she carried herself.

In this peasant society the man who could afford a fat wife was a man of wealth. The longer a girl remained in the fattening house the wealthier her father appeared, the fatter the girl became and the more flattered was the husband-to-be. So the fattening houses of south-east Nigeria were like the expensive finishing schools of Europe - the higher the cost, the greater the father's reflected glory and the more equipped the girl to find a well-heeled husband. As part of the celebrations we took palm wine poured into glasses on this occasion from a large and highly decorated calabash. We drank the wine in honour of the the bride-to-be and felt the warmth of collective joy. The spirit of the water goddess was invoked to look favourably on the life of the young woman. We made our contribution to the assortment of gifts given by well-wishers as a token of our appreciation of the invitation and took our leave at what we felt was an appropriate moment.

Like any other fermented drink, palm wine can be taken to excess. When my assistant director was on a tour of inspection to Warri, he dined with me. His steward, who accompanied him, was given hospitality by Richard. He over-imbibed and was subsequently unable to stand.

'I'm less than pleased, Ian, that your steward plied mine with drink' Jack Fleming complained the following day, 'he was absolutely drunk and incapable of carrying out his duties later.' Jack was a fellow Scot originally from Glasgow. Until then I had assumed that he was able to cope with such a condition even if he disapproved. 'I hope', he went on, 'that you will ensure that it doesn't happen again.'

I was furious. He had sat in my house and drunk my whisky and could have had much more if he had wanted. He had the good sense not to. 'Jack sir,' I said, trying to put some respect into my words, 'you had exactly the same kind of temptation as Justin (I think that was his steward's name) but you knew when to call a halt'

Jack looked at me with his blue eyes that always seemed to go right through you.

'You have a responsibility as an employer to ensure that hospitality isn't overdone by your servants. You know how excessive hospitality can be here. As your senior officer I feel you could have done better'.

When I inquired of Richard how it had happened and recounted the bare bones of my deputy director's complaint, he merely said 'Every peson know how much palm wine he fit take for belly'. For me that said it all.

Amos Tutuola, a Nigerian writer, drew on his Yoruba tradition to write a book called 'The Palm Wine Drinkard (sic)'. It had appeared a year or so before the incident with Jack's steward. It is an unsophisticated fantasy untouched by the creativity-inhibiting process of much higher education. In it, the principal character is searching for his dead palm wine tapster before he gets to heaven (there is an intermediate stage which is of this world). It takes the reader through devilishness and cruelty, macabre humour and imagery, possession by the spirits and jousts with the harbingers of death to provide a picture of the writer's mind and origins in all its grisliness and grotesque inventiveness. And all this is done on the memory of three hundred and seventy kegs of palm wine drunk every day. Such a compelling tale of unbridled imagination is it that the 'willing suspension of disbelief for the moment that constitutes poetic faith' is a state of mind that is easily induced.

The clay pots which are copies of the shape of a calabash are usually made in sizes to which the natural calabash cannot grow. Instead of a calabash the pot makers often use metal formers round which they coil the clay. Some sizes are used for the storage and carriage of various items, but their principal function is for the transport of liquids. No need for the women who carried calabashes on their heads to have exercises in deportment. They would be a fine example to many European women today and to women in some countries to whom dignity and elegance are strangers. Sometimes the laws of gravity seemed to be defied as the women still managed to proceed graciously with a pot tilted to one side while observers like me waited with bated breath for it to fall.

The calabash has given rise to miniaturisation of the species to be grown as a decorative plant with all manner of variants in terms of the shapes of the fruits. Maybe the god responsible for palm wine in all its facets has sent the message that 'everything in moderation' should be the watchword and that the miniaturisation of the calabash is a first symbolic act on his part to encourage all his followers to a more abstemious behaviour. Then the inspiration might be lost that begat the talent of Tutuola.

I still have a painting I bought from the artist himself when he called at my house selling his productions. It is a typical creek scene in the Delta portraying a canoe propelled by a lone paddler in a forest of mangrove rising out of the mud and water. The dug-out canoe and its sole occupant - who is probably a fisherman - are somehow in stark contrast to the apparent stillness of the encompassing water and land because of the sense of movement they together convey. The artist has captured in oils the essence of the creek in all its loneliness; he has imparted

214

the ubiquity of the vegetation once it has been able to sprout leaves from the gnarled and unpromising roots that sustain it. There is just a suggestion of hidden dangers lurking in the brackish waters.

It is high tide evidenced by the apparently endless water out of which the mangrove grows. One expects something resembling a floating log to appear at any moment, in reality a crocodile in its least aggressive mode (as far as humans are concerned) as this is its time for fishing. It highlights the difference from low tide when the water level drops and the mangrove looks for all the world like it is sprouting from stilts. There is a shoreline on which the water oozes rather than laps but it is a shore you don't step on. Any weight sinks in the mud unless it can be spread across an area. The stench is horrendous. This is where the crocodile feels most at home with its tail securely in the mud and may attack anything that comes within its domain provided it is not sleeping as it often is, with its jaws open which should in itself should be a warning to travellers, albeit going about their daily business, to be circumspect in their actions. The so-called 'crocodile tears' which the reptile sheds results from the squeezing of the tear ducts when it opens its mouth.

The artist has drawn on the intimacy of his own upbringing and experience to interpret a scene that might be repeated hundreds of times at that moment throughout these sluggish waterways. He has chosen to paint a familiar subject based on a traditional activity - God knows how this activity will be affected when there are the inevitable oil spills from the growing number of oilfields being identified in the delta. Yet he has used modern materials to produce this very acceptable and evocative painting. Is there, one might ask, an indigenous Nigerian art form that draws on local sources for its production as well as its inspiration?

We have to go back to the discovery of the Ife bronzes in 1911 to give us a clue to significant indigenous productions. The first was unearthed in a sacred grove by a team of German archaeologists and is reputed to be the head of the sea-god

Olokun. In parallel were found a number of terra cotta heads. The find caused great excitement in art circles in Europe because of their classical form which gave rise to widespread speculation on links with the ancient world. Interest was revived in 1938 when more bronze heads were uncovered when foundations were being dug out for a new house near the palace of the Oni of Ife.

More speculation followed. If indeed it was a local flowering of the art of *cire-perdue,* that is, where the cast is made of wax and then melted away just as the metal has hardened, then it was not something that was handed down as a result of generations of its practice and development. While cire-perdue bronze working was known to the people of Ife, the style of the bronze heads was not. In this respect it was high noon without dawn with an equally sudden sunset. There were still badly weathered terra cotta figures to be seen in some of the shrines around Ife in the 1950s, each of them sacred to a demi-god or *orisha.* It was the claimed birthplace of the Yoruba nation; indeed in Yoruba mythology the birthplace of the world too.

There was an oracle known as the Ifa whose priests would divine the oracle's wishes, on behalf of a person seeking its guidance, whether for preferment or revenge, by scattering sixteen palm kernels on a board and reciting a story from the appropriate permutation from the 1,680 possibilities determined by the way the nuts fell on the board. One can only imagine the years of apprenticeship needed for a priest to understand and memorise that number of stories. The carving on the cups used for this and the board itself represented the very best in Yoruba art, but this craft is no longer practised either. Other Ife productions included the making of decorative beads.

Leo Frobenius, who led the 1910-11 German expedition which discovered the first Ife bronze, speculated that the number sixteen had significant implications for the Yoruba as in their mythology, Yemaya, the goddess of moisture, gave birth at the same time to sixteen divinities including Shango, the mighty god of thunder, who was reputed to have ridden across the heavens on the backs of goats and to have shown a preference for the ram as a food.

He saw links with the Mediterranean, presumably through the connection with the Hausa states, with this god and Ammon, the ram-headed god of Egypt; he also connected Ife which was rebuilt in 16 wards in 1882 with the Etruscans who built their temples in sixteen different quarters and divided the horizon into sixteen parts for purposes of divination. While the link may be tenuous, the idea is seductive. The more mundane decorative bead-making was also still being practised in the area when I was there. The aggry bead of hard glass had apparently been made, from an early date, in the territory of the Yoruba.

The *cire perdue* process of casting bronze was also a mark of the brass workers of Benin. It is generally agreed that the Binis learnt this from the Yorubas with their connections through their Northern neighbours the Hausas and the old caravan trade routes with ancient Egypt whose influence is said to have been strong. It was earlier believed that the influence was Portuguese but, while themes were adopted from them, there is a good case made through the ornamentation with snakes, grotesque faces and lizards of an Assyrian or Phoenician connection and, more tenuously, a Graeco-Roman one. There was still a body of skill among the brass and bronze workers of Benin but it was dying out for the reason that Benin work was done for the glorification of the Oba and his barons who have been shorn of much of their power and who apply their wealth to other, more modern, attractions.

Perhaps the applications of more recent skills is the way forward for the new generations and that the artist from whom I bought the painting and his like were in the vanguard of a new tradition. The old tradition had its own style based on roots very different from the European classical concept of proportion and perspective. In almost every imaginable situation - the houses, the towns, the farms, the markets, the sculpture and painting - the straight line is conspicuous by its absence. It is not a Nigerian concern. Proportion gives way to rhythm, Elspeth Huxley suggests to us in *Four Guineas,* and the ideal to the grotesque. The mental picture derives from different ways of thinking, influenced by the perceived world which in turn is influenced by the *orisha* of storm and war. Inevitably, this is reflected in art with its symbols of terror and revenge.

If the traditional arts were decaying, the performing arts seemed to be in good health. Not as a spectacle people paid to watch, but as an integral part of the social life of the people. The Urhobo stilt dancers were traditional and vital in their own communities. Drumming was a way of life in many communities of the south of the country and provided the rhythms and the cadences for the dance which sprang from their everyday activities. Its expression was uninhibited and left little to the imagination, the symbolic and the interpretative being conspicuous by their absence. Miming was in the same tradition; not the formalised mime taken to a fine art by artistes of the French school, but a sense of drama that drew on local people and events. It could have a spontaneity that provided an additional flavour for the audience who in a sense were also participants making responses to the cues as they emerged in a new situation.

As a consequence Nigerians had a highly developed ability to mimic and Europeans could be the butt of their plays. I was on the receiving end of this when I was mimicked by a local wit in a remote village. He had made grass into spectacles and tied plantain leaves round his legs to represent my knee hose and then proceeded to interpret my actions in a way bystanders thought excruciatingly funny. He was obviously castigating the palm kernel traders for the poor quality of what they had brought, the store buyer for not being more careful in what he accepted or in keeping records, the produce inspector for not ensuring the others brought produce of an acceptable quality and, through his playing the part of myself, the produce officer for his inability to control such a band of incompetents.

An accompanying member of staff said he was a half-wit, presumably a polite way of taking any sting out of the performance, but such was the exaggerated emphasis of his portrayal that I was left in no doubt as to who it was meant to be. Those in the immediate vicinity found it good entertainment and tried without success to keep the smiles from their faces. If mimicry and intelligence have any correlation, then he was the brightest half-wit I have come across. I conclude that if the grass roots can produce such characters, then the theatre, if I may use the word in its widest sense, is not lacking in talent to draw upon.

But it is in the written word that Nigerians really distinguished themselves. An older writer like Amos Tutuola, drawing on his own traditions, had a tale to tell which caught the obsession with death and spirits and the macabre humour and grotesque imagery of the African mind. It was, however, younger and more educated writers like Wole Soyinka - much later to become a Nobel laureate, who were already making a name for themselves and developing a genre that would focus on well-crafted stories calling on the Nigerian present. Chinua Achebe and Ken Saro Wiwo would become icons who symbolised the freedom of thought that would be one of the few freedoms to exist in the later Nigeria under military government. Like the other modern arts they reflected the Nigeria of their times in all its vigour and enterprise and were to be a beacon for other aspiring writing talents in the land who would distinguish themselves in the years to come. Names like Ben Enwonwu in sculpture and Rotimi Fani-Kayode in painting would also inspire the next generation.

CHAPTER 36

Sweet Pass Kerosene

If there is anything that makes Nigerians stand out for me it is their use of the spoken language. It may not be the Queen's or King's English, although there are those among them who speak that language better than many of the native English speakers. But the average Nigerian brings to the language a colour and expressiveness that enriches it and at the same time differentiates it. It was striking on first arriving in Lagos how some words and expressions in English seemed to have a certain resonance. Lorries doubling for buses would carry slogans painted on the sides or at the top front of the cab. The hard lot of the male of the species was reflected in the phrase 'Strive on o man pikin' (*pikin* is another of these words that derive from the Portuguese and comes from 'pequeno' meaning little or child) and awareness of the eternal verities in 'Water finds its own level'. The only exception seemed to be the Albion lorries of the Public Works Department, some of them thirty years old - they never seemed to wear out and were the easiest of all vehicles to maintain (and built in Glasgow). The slogans would have brought a welcome brightness to the drab image of the Public Works Department but for regulations that forbade the defacing of government property and these included the painting of such slogans.

When labourers were riddling cocoa on the beaches to eliminate small pieces of trash prior to inspection or at the time of bagging it, they did it with what they called a 'shiftah'. In the process of 'shifting' the workers would riddle the contents to a rhythm they created themselves as they shuffled the cocoa about to remove everything but the beans - *daa-di-di-daa-di-di di-di-daa-di-di-daa di-di* accompanied by their own words which on one occasion, the firm's representative told me, meant 'The produce examiner grades the beans and we do the work, today, tomorrow and next tomorrow'. Now, a phrase in general use like *next tomorrow*, meaning 'the day after tomorrow', somehow conveys a sense of the closeness and importance of that day. Another commonly used phrase, *one time,* meaning 'immediately', has a no option ring to it. The word *dash,* referred to earlier, conjures up a vision of something special soon. When my steward Richard was feeling sorry for himself, he would associate my discomfort with his in a particularly mosquito ridden area by 'We too suffer for dis place'- the breadth of the concept of suffering being expanded to take in feelings of a less painful kind. Or perhaps the truth of the matter was that he did not have a classification for degrees of pain. Reports of civil servants complaining about their 'suffering' when ascending Mount Cameroon on an Outward Bound type training course had to be interpreted in that context.

A report in the local Lagos paper of a cricket match, Elder Dempster v Dyaks, in which I played, recorded that our captain had had to retire due to a 'wrap *(*sic) on the balls' reflecting complete indifference to a separate style for the written word. When an assistant produce officer reported a misdemeanour on the part of one of his staff, he started off his report with 'As I was standing behind the office trying to ease myself....'. David, my small boy, went to a church school where they taught him politeness. He always referred to the room containing the thunderbox as 'the stool room'. Euphemism has no place in spoken or written language and accuracy in spelling is not highly rated. It is what is said that is important and if it is necessary to reduce it to writing, the same words suffice.

One of the nicer things about the Nigerian press was the custom of announcements of local marriages with text written by someone in the bride's family. The page or part of a page usually featuring this was edged by a thin line to indicate it was a paid-for notice and presumably a disclaimer by the paper of responsibility for anything that might appear. Language is tied to the spoken word, warts and all, even if it appears in print. If the spoken word is not always used accurately, that is how it comes across in the written version; it is the overall image it creates that is important. One notice that comes to mind is one with lines round it reporting the marriage of Miss Odusanya to Mr

Arogundade (names made up for I forget what they were) at St Saviour's Church, Lagos where the ceremony 'was conducted by the Reverend G. D. Princewill and consummated on the lawn in the presence of 300 guests'. In the sporting world, boxers were called by names like 'Speedy Twitch', 'Ninety-nine Horse Power' and 'Superhuman Paul'. This lent an exaggerated and picturesque dimension to the images of the personalities concerned and somehow gave an added emphasis from elusiveness and boxing skill to raw power. It would seem that the meanings of words are of much less consequence than their sounds; that their total effect, both physical and mental, is of infinitely greater importance than their purpose as a means of rational communication.

I have a theory that the expressiveness of the language as used more than makes up for an apparent lack of appreciation of metaphor. This lack stems, I believe, from the propensity of ordinary Nigerians to think in concrete terms rather than in conceptual ones. Educated men and women have a greater facility for it. I have a record of E T Mensah, a Ghanaian musician whose band played regularly on the high-life scene in Western Nigeria, giving backing to a song about a parcel found on a bus at Ebute Metta, a mainland suburb of Lagos, which when opened contained a dead child. Rather than convey musically an immediate sense of grievous loss and tragedy, the lyric tells the sad tale as a series of actions.

Nigerians perceive things intuitively and rely on sense data; they are non-logical, emphasising the particular rather than the general. Metaphorical expressions like 'Put a tiger in your tank' (give a boost to your engine) or 'Nail your scrotum to the chair' (don't move from the spot) are likely to be taken literally and be seen as an irrelevance at best and as offensive at worst. If an English word is not immediately known, a kind of metaphor may be used but even that will draw on familiar actions associated with the object; so a balloon became known as a *blò-blò*. It is used as an emergency measure where the name of an object is not known or can't be recalled, to articulate a description for it rather than give colour and emphasis to what is being said and perhaps convey a different and more cogent meaning. *Blò-bl̇o,* because it has this particular resonance about it that is more expressive of the action needed to inflate it than the word 'balloon', became the accepted expression for it. It is this idea of stress on the concrete that makes metaphor, supposedly a universal enricher of communication, a non-event in Nigeria. The buzz generated by the general expressiveness of the people more than makes up for it.

The cause of this emphasis on the concrete appears to lie in the nature of the languages themselves which make it impossible for people to think or speak in abstract terms. It is reinforced by their close relationship with the power of nature, with animals and things. The human psyche is affected by this oneness with nature which is personified in representational forms which do not distinguish between people, animals and things that occur naturally. Because these are essential qualities, models and images, and because their existence is implicit rather than explicit in the material world, they are 'of another world'.

Yet their existence is real. Events, ideas, physical objects and places can be understood in terms of these basic aspects of nature. There is therefore no absolute dividing line between mythology and history. It is not their scholastic background that enables educated Nigerians to embrace concepts and abstractions. It is the English language that frees them to do so, as it does not predispose the choices of interpretation imposed on them by their own tongues. Presumably it is similar in former French territories where the French language elevates the educated from the constraining influence, in European terms, of concrete language usage.

The idea of the comparative is conveyed by the use of a descriptive adjective and the word *pass* what is being compared as in 'palm wine is good pass beer'. There is a story, probably apocryphal, of one man who sampled a particular drink for the first time and enthusiastically declared it 'sweet pass kerosene'. The phrase captures for me the uniqueness and expressiveness of 'English as she is spoke'. The superlative is conveyed by use of a phrase like 'good pass all'. Richard sought to establish my hierarchy of culinary preferences by determining how different meals were good pass others until he knew what I liked better than I knew myself.

The same words are used as for describing the present as are used to describe the past. 'He go dis way, he go dat way, he pass de ball and de centre forward score de goal'. It could be a spectator at a football match describing to a blind companion an incident in a game or it could be the description of a spectator relating what had happened to friends who had not been there. That it happened in the past is indicated by the situation which the speakers share. If it were to be spoken out of context, no one would know if it was the present or the past that was being described. The future is described by prefixing the verb with the word 'go' as in *I go take am* ('I'll take it'). Another example is *I go follow de lorry come* ('I shall come by bus'). In this case the verb 'follow' is used to express movement and is used in conjunction with the word 'come' to indicate direction of travel. The opposite direction would be captured by *I go follow de lorry go*.

Depending on the way in which some words are spoken will depend the meaning intended by the speaker and felt by the hearer. Certain words sharing the same spelling are distinguished by where the emphasis is put on them as in *babá* meaning 'old man' or 'grandfather' and *bába* meaning 'barber'. It is also seen in *fáda* meaning *'father'* and *fadá* meaning a Roman Catholic priest. Pitch also has a part to play in understanding. *He go gó* meaning 'he will go' is distinguished from the question *He go gó?* meaning 'will he go?' by a rising pitch on the latter. Apart from the features of stress or pitch, Nigerian pidgin also has similar characteristics to English in that it varies the use of rhythm and rate of speech to mediate meaning. These elements are used to bring closer together utterance of the spoken word and its felt meaning by the hearer.

This mode of speaking arises from the variety of languages spoken in Nigeria and serves as a kind of go-between language to facilitate communication. Nigerian pidgin is a special form of pidgin English and a legitimate medium for allowing social interaction between people who would otherwise be unable to convey meaning by the spoken word without which non-verbal accompanying behaviour is meaningless unless made by a mime artist - and there are few enough of these. Negro slaves from West Africa in the 15th and 16th centuries were taken to Portugal where they adapted Portuguese to create a pidgin or 'fala dos negros'. Since they came from different tribes and spoke different languages, there was a need for them to communicate with each other and this need was met by the development of pidgin Portuguese.

The English themselves spoke pidgin French in the wake of the Norman Conquest until the overwhelming numbers of the native English speakers eventually swamped the Norman-French language as imported with William the Conqueror. During the Scottish wars of independence, more than two hundred years after the arrival of the Normans in the British isles, Edward the First of England, 'Longshanks' to his Anglo-Saxon followers, the so-called 'Hammer of the Scots', was in fact a ruler who was more at home in Norman French, the language of the ruling nobility in England.

Nigerian pidgin arose in the first instance from the need of British traders and local sellers and buyers to communicate with each other. It is strongest in Calabar, Port Harcourt and Warri (situated on the original 'slave rivers' later to be known as the 'oil rivers'). It was a relatively recent development in metropolitan Lagos where the palm oil trade was never great and was part of a trade developed much earlier in the oil rivers and Calabar. Pidgin has, historically, a close connection with commercial affairs and the name itself is said to be a corruption of the Chinese rendering of the English word 'business'. As the different tribes of the Delta developed their own form of English bringing to it structural aspects of their own languages, it eventually spread to others who did not interact to any extent with Europeans, as a means of imparting meaning across different languages. It is a creative form of communication, not a limited form of English and is as much a product of the economic history of the country as the commercial customs and institutions that have evolved.

Like any living language pidgin is dynamic and subject to change. It can have regional variations. At the same time it has retained basic expressions from the early explorer merchants to the Guinea coast, particularly the Portuguese who were active there in the 16th and 17th centuries and indeed dominated trade in these parts for two hundred years which included trade in slaves.

'Salute your master for me' means 'I send your employer my greetings' and can be traced back to pidgin Portuguese. I have heard Europeans use the word 'salute' to send regards to another European, many years after the meaning originally shared with the Romance languages had fallen out of use, showing how easy it is for even a pidgin to influence a major language and in this case to reintroduce an older meaning. In places like Warri where the majority of the population, the Itsekiri, shared their town with substantial minorities of neighbouring peoples like the Urhobos, the Ijaws, the Okrikas and the ubiquitous Ibos as well as Europeans of different nationalities, pidgin was the language of communication.

Before purists talk about a dominant culture undermining a less dominant one through its language, consider that Mother English for her part has been enriched, extended, and corrupted by the American version. Those people who use American words or pronunciations without being aware of doing so are understandably those without a strong local identity, often the less educated or the more easily influenced or simply people who have sub-consciously absorbed an expression like 'hospitalise' for which there was no equivalent single-word verb in the English spoken in England. But the educated are not exempt from the use of such expressions. If you talk about vacuum tubes (rather than *thermionic valves)*, deck and wild card (rather than *pack* and *joker*), morgue (rather than *mortuary*), specialty (rather than *speciality*), envision (rather than *envisage*), résearch

226

(*reséarch*), temporárily (*témporarily*), kilómetres (*kílometres*), rómance (*románce)* dumb down, spat, feisty, guy (the living male variety), cop, oculist or hooker (not the middle of the front row kind) or the glass of whisky but an honest whore, you are wearing the intellectual equivalent of a baseball cap. If you use a majority of these expressions, and there are all sorts of mitigating circumstances if you do, connected in the main with the global dominance of the US news and entertainment media industries, then you are wearing that cap back to front. If the English have an identity problem, is it to be wondered at? Being a basic lingua franca and culturally neutral, Nigerian pidgin does not have such complexity to contend with.

CHAPTER 37

Missionaries

No one could live and move around in the south of Nigeria in the 1950s without coming in contact with men and women who had consecrated themselves to what they saw as the betterment of their fellow beings whether as bearers of the word of God, teachers of the young or carers for the sick. Nowhere was this more evident than in the Presbyterian Church of Eastern Nigeria leper settlement at Itu in the Calabar province, originally a constituent part of the Church of Scotland overseas missions. It was here that a Dr MacDonald first set up a hospice to care for lepers on an island in the middle of the Cross River. After a number of years an area on shore was acquired and the settlement was relocated there. That was where I visited it. I didn't have the privilege of meeting Dr MacDonald but I did meet his cousin the Rev. Bob MacDonald who assumed responsibility for the running of the settlement after his cousin had given up the reins.

As the doctors there came to diagnose the disease at an earlier stage, so the number of cures effected mounted. Pregnant mothers carrying the disease were cared for and the child looked after until such time as the mother was cured. Leprosy is not hereditary and the child could enjoy a normal life even if the mother was at an advanced stage of the disease. Patients were given work producing palm oil and other crops and were paid from the proceeds. The Palm Products Marketing Board was aware of this practice and encouraged it after taking pathological advice.

The colony had 100,000 palm trees grown from seedlings obtained from the Agricultural Department.and a second-hand mill which was replaced later by a pioneer oil mill. Not for the patients there the indignity of dependence. A stock farm was developed with cows, goats, sheep and pigs; a lumber industry was started. It was the first place in Nigeria to grow rice. The patients had allotments where they grew yams, corn, plantains and other vegetables for their own use, and sold any surplus in the market place. There were four 'towns' with houses in straight streets, one town being for women and another for particularly bad cases of the disease. The whole regime was aimed at countering the psychological effects of being shunned with horror by their own people and the low state of their bodily and spiritual wellbeing.

The development of the aesthetic side of the inmates' personalities was encouraged - one of the lepers had made a statue of Edward VIII, the only one ever erected to him, the uncrowned British king who abdicated his throne before his ritual coronation. They had their own social life. A court was built and presided over by a chief and two sub-chiefs to sort out differences. When members of the colony had the requisite number of clear tests they were declared officially free from the disease. They took hard to leaving the settlement where they were bound together by the bonds induced by their affliction and the close friendships they had formed with others as a result of the mutual support they had provided. I felt that I was only now beginning to realise the purpose that lay behind the retiring collections for the overseas missions at the church of my youth.

In January 1951 a record number of 883 patients were discharged cured, a tribute to the staff involved and the new drug 'Dapsone'. The most moving aspect for me was the church service which was taken in three languages - Efik, English and Ibo. When you have heard the voices of over 1,000 lepers singing 'The Lord is my shepherd' with a conviction that would choke the most hardened observer, as happened to me and my assistant produce officer A U Antia on a visit to Itu, it is not something you forget easily. The singing was accompanied by a band whose instruments had been obtained by the church. One story told me by Bob MacDonald was that his cousin had authorised the bandmaster to choose the music at all church activities. One day when officiating at a funeral Dr Macdonald was taken aback momentarily to hear the band strike up 'Will ye no' come back again?'.

When touring up-country it was not an unusual to pass Methodist schools. It was part of the ethos of the religious denominations to develop education as and when they could. This was probably because the government, certainly during the earlier part of its colonial rule, did little to promote it, almost certainly seeing it as likely to undermine good order as students started to read about political affairs for themselves. The Methodists were part of this tradition of providing education. Their schools were distinguished not so much by any notice board as by the distinctive blue uniforms of the pupils. On public holidays they would come round the houses collecting for a cause and give a song in return. I recall that it was children from a Methodist school who sang a song known and enjoyed all over the south of the country - 'Everybody Loves Saturday Night'. They sang it first in sol-fa and then with the words to an accompaniment played on bones like others in at least one temperate country would play the spoons.

It seemed on my travels that the Methodist Church, more than any other denomination, delegated the work to Nigerian nationals and they gave the impression of being very committed. Certainly, they seemed to provide most of the primary schools in these areas in south-east Nigeria which I travelled in my earlier days there, apart from the Cross River area where the Presbyterians and Roman Catholics predominated.

Although the colonial government was initially a poor provider of educational facilities, latterly it did set up a number of secondary schools and the first university at Ibadan. For many years, the only secondary education available had been at the Hope Waddell Institution in Calabar which produced many of the people who were to become leaders of thought in the emerging new Nigeria. They were also to become the people who would be the founders, perhaps retrievers is a better word, of a cultural nationalism and who became leaders in government and business. It was said that Lord Lugard, when Governor of a united Nigeria, discouraged teaching about the Stuarts as it was likely to encourage contempt for authority but that the principal of the institution at the time disregarded that injunction.

I found Nigerians in general liked to talk, and the quality of conversation was high with subjects being discussed like 'Will Hausa become the *lingua franca* of Nigeria?' I have no doubt that this stemmed from good teaching in institutions such as those provided by the religious orders. In a country of so many different tongues, pidgin is the established means of communication across the language barrier. As for the educated classes, English is the medium by which they interact.

The Roman Catholic Church was also strongly represented in the country. If we as latterday government officials served eighteen months to two years before going on leave, the priests and mothers, as the sisters were called in Nigeria, served five to seven years before seeing home again. It is not surprising that they immersed themselves in their work and their charges. The mothers taught in the convent schools and such was their dedication and reputation that expatriate parents, whether of the Roman Catholic persuasion or not, elected when they could, to have their children educated in them.

It was salutary, I felt at the time, for these children to experience living and working with Nigerian children. Not that all expatriate parents believed that Nigeria was a place to bring up children, for the majority still had theirs at boarding school in the United Kingdom. It was perhaps significant that many of those parents whose own parents had been on overseas postings and who had themselves been at boarding schools in England, were the least likely to repeat the experience with their own offspring. Part of the colonial officer's contract was that his children would receive passages twice a year and the parents looked forward with eager anticipation to the holidays as did the children.

The Church was represented widely in south-east Nigeria and the spartan life of the fathers was legendary. Not that they didn't like the good things. It was common practice for a touring officer to bring with him a bottle of whisky in return for a good meal and better company. Sometimes the older priests got into a routine as a way of coping with the long tours of duty. I remember one of the younger ones laughing about his colleagues in Oron on the right bank of the Cross River where the ferry left for Calabar. He warned that they were so fixed in their routine that they did not like it to be broken. If you intended to visit then you had to let them know well in advance so that the routine could be expanded to accommodate you. 'If you happen on them out of the blue' he said, 'they'll just tell you to feck off'.

Strangely, it was only on a small number of occasions I came in close contact with the Church Missionary Society which represented the Church of England in the land, perhaps because I spent, if we exclude my time in Lagos, a relatively short period in Yorubaland where it had early on established most of its missions. The church had appointed its first Nigerian bishop, Bishop Crowther, as early as the late 19th century, and he was active in the Niger delta. I was married in one of its churches in Ibadan, very kindly made available for the occasion. I did attend a couple of christenings in Lagos but otherwise only observed the activities of the Church through the CMS bookshop which filled a gap in the provision of the other denominations.

It was said on the coast that the CMS had been responsible in the early days of the colonial period for the writing in pidgin English of the Book of Genesis and I have heard a number of versions of it. It was written at a time when it was more important, in the view of the authors, to express the concept of the Christian deity in the simplest and most uncompromising of forms to which the readers or hearers could relate than to provide a sophisticated translation suitable only for an educated audience or readership. The following is a short extract from it:-

For de first time no ting be. Only de Lawd he be.

An de Lawd he done go work for make dis ting dem callum Earth. For six days de Lawd he work an he done make all ting. He go put for Earth plenty plantain, plenty yam, plenty bush meat, plenty cassava, plenty guinea corn, plenty groundnut, plenty everting. An for de water he put plenty fish and for de air he put plenty dinda bird.

After six days de Lawd he tire an he done go for sleep. An when he sleep plenty, palaver start for dis place dem callum Heaven. Dis place Heaven be place where we go when we done die, if we no been so-so bad for dis place Earth. De Angel, dem live for Heaven an play de banjo an get plenty fine chop and plenty palm wine.

De Headman of de Angel dey call Gabriel. When dis palaver start for Heaven dere be plenty humbug by bad Angel dem callum Lucifer. An Gabriel he done catch Lucifer an go beat am. An palaver stop one time. An de Lawd he tell Gabriel he be good man too much an he go dash Gabriel one trumpet. An Gabriel he get licence for play trumpet an his drum for Heaven. An Lucifer, he go for Hellfire where he be headman now.

After de Lawd done lookam dis ting dem callum Earth, he savvy no man be for seat. So de Lawd he take small earth an he breathe, an man he dey. An de Lawd he call dis man Adam. De Lawd he say 'Adam!' an Adam he say 'Yessah!' An de Lawd he say 'Adam, you de see dis garden? Dem call am Paradise. Everting for dis garden be for you, but not de tree Európean call Appel for middle of garden, dat no be for you. You no go chop am, or you get plenty pain for belly - you savvy?' An Adam he say 'Yessah Lawd, I savvy'.

An de Lawd he done go back for Heaven for hear Gabriel play de trumpet, an Adam he waka-waka for garden where everting be fine too much. Byamby, de Lawd he come back for Earth an go look am Adam. An he say 'Adam, everting be fine fine, no palaver, you like am?' An Adam he say 'Yessah Lawd, everting be fine pass most ting'. An de Lawd he say 'Whassa matter, Adam, you get small trouble?' An Adam he say 'No, I no get trouble Lawd sah, but I no get mammy'.

An de Lawd he say 'Ah-ha!' Den de Lawd he make Adam go sleep for one place, an he take small piece from Adam side. He

*go breathe - an mammy she dey - an de Lawd callum his mammy
Evie. De Lawd wake Adam an he say 'Adam, you de see dis
mammy?' An Adam he say "Yessah Lawd, I see am - she be fine
pass stinkfish."*

It was said, and it is not surprising, indeed it is to the credit of
the Church officials if such is the case, that for the last few
decades they had been collecting all extant copies of the
translation to limit the offence it must have caused to the
increasing number of educated Nigerians who came across it. It
was not the fact that it was written in pidgin that upset some. It
was the images it tried to evoke through the analogies it used to
create them. The idea of the Bible story might have been
conveyed to an uneducated generation being swamped by a new
culture through expressions like 'Noah he be headman for Elder
Dempster boat', but events have overtaken this attempt to win
simple minds over to Christianity. There were those who said
that no offence was intended and should not be taken. My view
from the vantage point of nearly 60 years on is that the perception
is the reality for people and humankind should act accordingly if
that perception cannot be changed.

The devotion of the missionaries to their flocks was widely
acknowledged. They would have sat uncomfortably with some
people of the lesser cults which found Nigeria a happy hunting
ground for converts. There was a sect from one of the southern
states of the USA which was extending its activities more widely.
One of their pastors asked me if I knew a healthy place in the
Eket Division where the word of God was required. Another of
his kind, visiting from his homeland, claimed in the name of God
to effect cures of those who were stricken of diseases and
afflictions that medical science could not address. I can
remember in Calabar hearing one from the comfort of my own
verandah, his resounding voice rising to a crescendo, exhorting
some poor unfortunate wretch to walk. I heard nothing of
miracle cures.

Despite all the effort and love for the human race put into their
work, and despite their belief in the high moral purpose and

absolute righteousness of their cause, these different manifestations of Christianity could do little to stem the onward march of Islam despite its having as many divisions as the Christian faith. Islam appealed to the leaders in Nigerian society, with the exception of those in south-east Nigeria and to a degree in Western Nigeria where leadership was not invested in one person, in that it was more in accord with their economic needs and did not forbid the taking of more than one wife who would bear them more children who had also a value in terms of their work and their marriageability. The followers in that situation would take their lead from their chiefs. The Muslim brotherhoods which assisted greatly in this success also appeared to have much in common with people's customary faith based on the their tolerance of regional tradition. For example, they practised fortune-telling and the interpretation of dreams. These facts in no way detract from what these torch-carriers of Christianity did, which was in the best tradition of caring for the physical as well as the spiritual and mental welfare of the people who were the subject of their ministrations.

Missionaries certainly did come in all sorts and sizes. If commitment is the most significant determinant of action, then the missionaries were certainly moved to do things, not only the ministers and priests but the many lay people who supported them in an equally dedicated way. Those to whom they ministered had little difficulty accepting the Christian God as Number One provided their own spirits were not proscribed. Many of these spirits were benign, and wise missionaries emphasised the Christian code without directly rubbishing the traditional gods or taking the joy out of their spirituality which many of the earlier ones had done by their narrow interpretation of Christianity.

A knowledge of the history of their own religion would have shown these earlier bearers of the word of God that the early Christians in their own country modified pagan customs to provide a comfortable bridge from the old to the new as in the choice of one of the days after the winter solstice for the commemoration of Christ's birth, a date unknown to researchers in religious matters. The association of mistletoe with Christmas derives from Celtic rites which centred on their sacred oak tree on which the plant is frequently found and is considered to be the symbol of life.

The related sacrifice of bulls was one of the customs that fell into decay with their embracing of Christianity although there are records of such sacrifice continuing among the ordinary people of north-east Scotland into medieval times. The famous bull - the papal rather than the bovine kind - of Pope Gregory 1, which accepted certain Celtic ritualistic practices, facilitated the acceptance of Christian belief by the Celtic religious leaders, the Druid priests, without altogether destroying their spiritual values.

CHAPTER 38

The French Connection

Dan Hood was an international rugby player in his younger days. He would smile deprecatingly if I introduced him as such and perhaps with good reason. For his one and only international appearance was for Nigeria against Dahomey in Cotonou. Dan recalls there was insufficient accommodation for all the team and supporters and some of them had to be slept in the local income tax offices. These had no lavatories inside the building and an abiding memory of the team was having to pee out of upstairs windows. One or two of the accompanying ladies were reportedly in agony by the morning which tells us that this minority were either lacking in initiative or were weighed down by a modesty that far exceeded awareness of the harmful effects of holding one's water. A more generous interpretation perhaps of their behaviour might have been that they had a fear of heights.

How did this unlikely match come to take place? The reason lies in the fact that in Lagos where Dan worked there was quite a French community. The two countries had common borders, the French territories of Dahomey, Niger, Chad and Cameroun entirely surrounding the country. As the result of an agreement between the two countries some 60 years before, each had the freedom to set up a commercial representation in the other's territories. This was not unusual in West Africa. For example, the firm of John Holt (Liverpool) Ltd, long established as traders on the coast but now operating in specialist areas of business under different names, had trading operations for example in Nkongsamba in what was the French Cameroons and where I once made an unauthorised visit to see a friend. It all stemmed from this earlier agreement between the two countries early in the 20th century that their traders would have equal access to markets in the West African colonies and protectorates.

France and the French people and language have always had an attraction for me. Our family has always been francophile as have the vast majority of Scots. I would be delighted to go to a conference many years later organised by the Franco-Scottish Society and graced by the presence of the French ambassador to the Court of St James, to mark the 7th centenary of the *Auld Alliance* between the two countries. When he addressed the Scots in Edinburgh in 1942 Charles de Gaulle enthused: 'No sooner has a Frenchman set foot in this old and noble country than he detects a multitude of natural affinities between your people and our own and he is aware of the thousands of vivid, precious links in the Franco-Scottish alliance, the oldest in the world...'. During the short reign of François II, husband of Mary Stuart, the two kingdoms were in effect joined when all Scots in France and all Frenchmen in Scotland were granted the same civic rights as the natives.

Two major French trading companies were established in Lagos and they had very similar names. One was the Société Commercial de l'Ouest Africain (SCOA) and the other the Compagnie Française de l'Afrique Occidentale (CFAO). Their expatriate employees were by the nature of their work involved in the social exchanges that took place. The companies were also represented in smaller stations and that was where it was impossible to live a separate existence. Because the French presence was minute in relation to the British presence, it was only to be expected that the French adapted more quickly and readily to the British ways while retaining their own unique culture.

Like their British counterparts, many of the French had experience of other parts of the world. They had been in places like Algeria, Niger, Morocco, Upper Volta (now Burkina Faso) and Chad, and spoke of places like Constantine, Ouagadougou, Tombouctou, Zinder and Fort Lamy. They brought their own backgrounds and lifestyles with them. We could often hear radio broadcasts from French territories on my old thermionic valve Pye radio *'Ici Brazzaville, poste national français en Afrique équatoriale'*. Often they were crowded out on the airwaves by American missionaries from the deep south who believed there was a colossal market for conversions in West Africa and worked at it for all their sincere worth.

There is always a rub-off from friends. We learnt respect for wine from the French in our midst. They received their wine not in 70 centilitre bottles but in demijohns. The French are not given to excesses like the British in the consumption of alcohol but perhaps drink more steadily at a lower level of consumption. My experience was that they allowed for two glasses per person at the dinner table and felt no one needed more with a meal. One or two of the young British newcomers were even known to chill their red wine until the restrained horror on the faces of guests indicated something was amiss or some other Brit with more savvy and taste would tactfully but firmly indicate the error of their ways when they had a moment to themselves.

To dine at a French house was a different experience. To be exposed to a *couscous* cooked to an authentic Algerian-French recipe is to have, certainly for a young man not long out from the United Kingdom, a rewarding experience - a bit like having your first *nasi goreng* in a Dutch household with East Indian connections. I wonder as I write if people from other countries coming to the United Kingdom enthuse over Indian curries as the locals do over the very British invention of *chicken tikka massala*.

Many of the friendships forged have lasted the lifetime of the people concerned. My cousin's widow, Sandy Murphy, herself an old coaster, was recently at the wedding of a grandchild of French friends, the de Horteurs, from their Nigerian days. As I key this in she has arrangements in hand to be with them on the occasion of their golden wedding. The world may have changed, probably for the better. Some things are changeless like friendships forged in what was sometimes seen as a crucible of adversity.

Apart from their mighty influence on the English language, the French have long made a contribution to the Scots tongue. The Scottish word Hogmanay denoting the feast of the New Year and now used to describe the activities associated with 'seeing it in', comes from the Old French *aguillanneuf* commonly used likewise to describe either the New Year or a New Year's gift. My paternal grandmother cut her meat with a *gullie* possibly derived from 'guillotine' via the Scottish mercenaries who plied what was then an honourable trade on the continent (French kings were protected by their *garde écossaise* for 133 years in recognition of the Scots' help in assisting in the expulsion of the English from France). That meat could have been a *gigot* straight from the French for a leg of mutton - and still to be seen with that spelling on butchers' boards from Melrose to Mintlaw. It was normally carved on an 'ashet' (*assiette*) which was a plate big enough to contain the leg of lamb. My great-grandfather played the best in the land on his dambrod (draughtboard), from the French word for draughts, and my grandmother would 'pree' something at table (a word derived from Old French) if she wanted to try a small piece.

At school we would be encouraged to do something 'at the toot' meaning 'quickly' from the French *tout de suite*; Scots soldiers who fought in France in the First World War returned with the expression 'tout de suite and the tooter the sweeter'. A narrow alley between houses in my home town is called a vennel in a couple of cases and derives directly from the Old French *venelle*. In my childhood in Lanark anyone who wasted time doing absolutely nothing constructive we called a fouter (pronounced footer), a word that comes from the French *foutre* meaning literally to fornicate but used in Scots as in French in the sense of fiddling about. There are enough examples of the effect of French on Scots, as distinct from formal English, to justify learned research if this has not yet been done.

The French influence persisted in Nigeria in the custom of signing the Governor's book contained in a gatehouse at the entrance to Government House in Lagos. It was signed when you arrived from leave or transfer into the territory and again when you went on leave. It was expected that all government officials would sign the book and those in other occupations had the unwritten option to do so. As it did not appear to serve any particular purpose, I surmise that it was a symbolic gesture of obeisance to the Queen through the person of her senior representative in Nigeria. Those departing on leave would enter their names and what they did where, concluding with the letters 'PPC' meaning of course *pour prendre congé* - to go on leave, literally to take a holiday. Foresters, agriculturists and engineers did not usually possess the refinement of the French language beyond school level - that was the province of those who had studied the 'soft' subjects - but they recognised the letters. They dubbed it 'the PPC book' forgetting that these initials were for departure only.

CHAPTER 39

The Champagne Breakfast

I may have been a willing participant in the fag-end of empire but I cannot let the opportunity pass of acknowledging the style with which the charade of power instituted by the early representatives of imperial authority was perpetuated even as its rule was being wrested from it. I say 'wrested' advisedly as the British government's time-scale for the granting of independence seemed progressively to contract as a result of response to the identification of unrelenting forces calling for change. Nowhere was this charade reflected better than in the custom of the champagne breakfast. Perhaps this seeming oxymoron was in fact a commonplace among the landed classes or the turn-of-the-century equivalent of today's chattering classes.

It certainly was not something practised by the people living in the houses of the wynds and vennels of my home town, nor in the substantial dwelling houses of its somewhat more affluent citizens. There is an expression known to me - 'the wedding breakfast'- which could conceivably be associated with champagne, but that always seemed a nonsense as no one in their right mind would get married or drink champers so early in the day. Champagne lunch perhaps. Maybe it is a custom that scions of the aristocracy who took the 'Grand Tour' of Europe in the second half of the 19th century, brought back from their travels in Germany where the *Sektfrühstück* was a ritual to mark an important event like a fiftieth anniversary or the annual meeting of German wholesalers as they thrashed out the basis of civilised competition for the ensuing year.

The champagne breakfast was given in celebration of an important event and that was associated in the few instances in my experience with the award of a decoration in the Queen's Birthday or the New Year Honours List. It was inevitable that someone you knew or knew of would be honoured in one way or another. The secret was well guarded and invitations would be made by a close friend or colleague of the impending recipient on the morning of the publication of the list, thereby perpetuating the myth of the spontaneity of the event. This information is largely from hearsay as I was present on only one such occasion. So I infer the general from the very particular but also from the accounts of others. The 'breakfast' was just before the normal lunchtime and consisted indeed of champagne, accompanied by tasty bits. Speeches were part of the proceedings, one (at least) of congratulation and another acknowledging the support of colleagues and thanking them for their part in the award which was also in recognition of their contributions.

I am sure that recognition was deserved, the only pity being that there were many more deserving cases who could have been included if only the list were flexible and nominations not confined to senior government officials. A case in point was Harry Whittaker who arrived at the Warri club from the creek on Christmas Day dressed as Santa Claus and bearing presents in his canoe for the children on the station. I have mentioned Jim Brown's work also in the Warri area where he quietly, in addition to his other duties, went about doing simple but effective infrastructural works in the bush. No doubt, if more people had been recognised as deserving, the awards might not have been valued to the same degree. Maybe the greatest of rewards lay in the knowledge of having done the job to the best of one's ability, and that often meant beyond the call of duty.

The titles of these decorations were redolent of empire and the prerogative of the Sovereign graciously to bestow them a gesture within His/Her gift in grateful acknowledgement of the bestowee's contribution to the furtherment of the *Pax Britannica*. If you thought about it, you came up with questions about the honours system itself and what it was it underpinned. That Harry Johnson should have been knighted, the man who had so dishonourably tricked King Jaja into captivity, an action deplored by the prime minister of the day and one that had long-lasting repercussions on the trust that could be put on an official's word in the region, suggests that it is at worst a mockery. Was it a vehicle for giving psychological rewards to those employed by government or to politicians for doing adequately what they were paid to do or perhaps to reinforce the hierarchies the British elite found so dear? Or recompense for serving dutifully in some distant and none too salubrious place? In any case it was based on an outmoded concept as the following examples will illustrate. It has taken journalists over forty years to discover only one or two of the names given to some of these decorations by clever and irreverent officials, which those of us who lived it accepted as part of the linguistic baggage we took along with us:

Member of the Most Excellent Order of the British Empire (MBE) *My Bloody Efforts* {Motto of the Order *For God and for Empire*}

Officer of the Most Excellent Order of the British Empire (OBE) *Other Buggers' Efforts*

Member of the Royal Victorian Order (MVO) *Ma'am's Very Own* (This is a decoration awarded for personal services to the monarch)

Commander of the Most Excellent Order of the British Empire (CBE) *Can't Be Ennobled* (Got as far as he/she can get but did well what he/she had to do)

Companion of the Most Distinguished Order of St Michael and St George (CMG) *Call Me God* (Usually denotes the recipient served with some distinction)

Knight of the Most Distinguished Order of St Michael and St George (KCMG) *The King Calls Me God* (probably served with even greater distinction or did whatever he did for longer or in a more exalted position)

Knight Grand Cross of the Most Distinguished Order of St Michael and St George (GCMG) *God Calls Me God* (A paragon of all the virtues; usually reserved for those in the highest echelons of the service but awarded very sparingly).

The apparent pomposity of the names of the orders is mitigated by the irreverence of the articulators of the alternative titles. At least two of the people I first heard quote some of these have later had a decoration bestowed on them. Will they feel any different now? Will the concept of Britishness be an anachronism in an age when the nation state is fragmenting all over the world and reverting to a pattern which indicates that the last two hundred and fifty years of its assumed permanence have been an extended blip in the continuity of small autonomous societies? Perhaps it is a case of 'back to the future' and the death-knell of the all-powerful state that forces its will on large and reluctant minorities even where the representatives of the people have been 'democratically' elected.

Part 5

More About Work

CHAPTER 40

The Vote

Each government officer with responsibility for a geographic area controlled his own expenditure. Each year he was allocated a 'vote' which was a given amount of money to cover the costs of running the area. The biggest item on the vote was that for transport and travelling. In preparation for the following year every officer with responsibility for expenditure had to make an estimate of financial requirements covering all aspects of his work from the erection and maintenance of permanent and semi-permanent buildings e.g., accommodation for members of staff in remote outstations where appropriate housing was not available, to calculating the annual salary bill, reckoning the mileage covered by officers with cars to determine the cost of running them and estimating the cost of sending staff on leave and transfer.

Staff salaries were easy. Every grade had a scale on which a staff member's salary could be identified. The greatest trouble was in getting the transport and travelling right. First the leave entitlement had to be established, then who was to cover for the staff member on leave or who was to be transferred in his place, then the estimates made on the basis of the transport costs - a long and tedious process for which the officer in charge was responsible even if he had not personally made the estimates. Each head of expenditure had to be correct, for the principle of virement was not applied, that is, there was no transfer of money between heads. Any officer exceeding his vote was liable to be required to make good the amount overspent, even if it meant a monthly deduction from his salary over a number of years. Knowledge of that concentrated the mind wonderfully.

My first estimates in Warri coincided with the regionalisation of Nigeria into three regions with their own Secretariats in 1955 just prior to my transfer to Ibadan. These were sent off on the basis of actual requirement and in my covering letter I had noted that this was the absolute minimum consistent with the maintenance of a satisfactory oversight of the area. These were sent to the new Ministry and were returned approved subject to an arbitrary reduction of 15% which I was quickly able to translate into what I might have to pay back. Representations to my director were followed by a visit to him. He was convinced by my need for further funds based on the integrity of my original estimates and the economies in transport and travelling I had earlier introduced.

Together we went to the Secretariat where officials in the Ministry were already getting delusions of power and refused to countenance any increase. My director then went over their heads to the Permanent Secretary whom he persuaded to overrule a particular official under the Old Pals Act. In government service, I came to realise, minimum funds needed were the subject of negotiation and anyone who included his actual financial needs was naïf in the extreme, the more so if they had been based on earlier economies. A contingency had to be added to take account of the negotiation that would likely take place.

As the year goes by, this year's vote becomes the basis for any negotiation that takes place on next year's when the staff situation is likely to be different as local economies change and area officers muster their statistics and calculations to reflect it. All is well if they can live with the fact that rationality does not apply. It may be rationalised because we like to dress up any subjective decision in rational argument. It is difficult to complain about something if it is shown that it is going against 'rationality', even if that rationality has been firmly based on gut feeling.

Other office work included the production of reports of tours of inspection where problems had to be highlighted and the action taken indicated and whether actions taken on previous visits were producing the desired results. Benin was always a difficult station particularly during the period of high rubber prices in the mid 1950s. Problems ranged from attempts to pass off inferior rubber as of higher quality to claims by buyers that inspection staff were deliberately holding up the inspection of rubber. The

248

upshot of such problems was the production of working instructions that provided little room for interpretation and a visit of the Minister of Trade and Industry, R A Njoku, to Benin to reinforce the message of the importance of quality. A photograph of myself taken with him in Benin appeared on the front page of the *Daily Times*. It was a pointer to the increasing influence of ministers in affairs that until then had been the prerogative of officials and the hidden message of the photograph was presumably that ministers were now controlling the shots.

Once a year an annual report had to be produced which was incorporated in a report for the whole region at headquarters. It included all kinds of statistics on such details as produce graded, the quality, marketing problems, amount of produce graded per member of staff and prosecutions taken and won. I remember thinking I was doing quite well in my first report when I stated in the body of the document that the 26 appendices 'were not inappropriately lettered A to Z'. This arrogance prompted a reply drawing my attention to certain lacunae in the report, this being a device it took time and labour to respond to and ensured that as objective a report as possible was sent in future unencumbered by personal views and clever comments.

What did not appear in the annual reports were these little incidents that constituted learning like when I went out one night when adulterated cocoa was being burned in Calabar. It had been slowly burning for a few days within sight of the office and I decided to cast a nocturnal eye on it. In the process I thought I would see how watchful the nightwatchman was. I found him asleep and called out roughly 'Watchnight!' Immediately he leapt to his feet, machete over his shoulder ready for the blow when he recognised me. I was taken aback but noted that he was alert. I recalled the recent story of the five watchmen employed by the United Africa Company who were found guilty of murdering two men and eating their fingers to acquire more strength. I would be more circumspect in future.

It was pretty obvious to me then that judging performance on the basis of the number of prosecutions taken and won was a pretty poor method of evaluating the implementation of the law. It encouraged the pursuit of the petty criminal rather than the people who were egging them on. In Olympic diving, points are awarded on the difficulty of the dive as well as its execution. In a similar way, prosecution could be considered on the basis of a 'heinosity index' which would bring about a focus on the more serious contraventions of the law if the more serious crimes prosecuted successfully had, say, ten times the weighting of a petty offence.

Before departing on leave and probably transfer, the ground had to be prepared for your successor, who would not necessarily arrive to provide an overlap, to introduce him into the ways of the area. It was therefore necessary and mandatory to make out comprehensive handing-over notes. These were to provide the incoming officer with the 'feel' of the area together with some useful detail on Licensed Buying Agents of the Board, on issues specific to the area, on staff and on inspection and touring problems. For the new incumbent good handing over notes could be invaluable as they accelerated the learning process about the area. It could add to physical as well as mental comfort. One set of notes gave me all I needed to know and more (all forty pages, presumably my 'newness' implied I had to be given every assistance) by advising how to keep mosquitoes at bay with instructions on when to use DIMP and where to smoke like a chimney. Like everyone else I formulated my own rules based on experience. If there was an overlap in handing over, the notes were enriched by insights given as a result of talking into the night over a dram.

CHAPTER 41

The Produce Inspector

He was a man of authority in the community. The local cocoa farmers, and particularly the intermediaries who brought in most of the cocoa for inspection, held him in awe because he could hold up the approval of the quality of the cocoa they had brought to the buying station and therefore the release of the payment for their produce by the company acting as buying agent for the Marketing Board. In effect, this reduced their ability to finance further purchases. The Board was determined to maintain the quality of cocoa from Nigeria and the Cameroons (or that part of them administered under the Nigerian Government) and the produce inspector was the local enforcer, sometimes with an exceptionally heavy hand, of that determination.

Chocolate was originally discovered by Spanish *conquistadores* at the court of Montezuma in what is now Mexico. The cocoa or cacao tree *Theobroma cacao* (Cacao, Food of the Gods) was brought in the first instance by the Portuguese from South America to São Tome, a fertile island just touching the equator off the coast of Gabon, and its cultivation spread from there to other parts of West Africa where it was taken up mainly by Christian farmers, in Nigeria by the Yoruba whose efforts stimulated the economy to the benefit of many at a time when the market for palm oil was weak and prices poor. The earliest attempt to grow cocoa in what was to become Nigeria was made by a Chief Iboningi who established a plantation in Bonny in 1847 with little success as the land of the delta was not suited to the growing of cocoa.

The ancient Aztec and Maya civilisations drank *Xocolatl* (literally 'bitter water') ritually, believing it to have restorative, aphrodisiac and even magical qualities. They often took it with hot peppers as a stew. Later when it was combined with sugar as that commodity became progressively cheaper with the increasing, slave-driven production in the West Indies and in

South America, it assumed a popularity that it has maintained ever since.

Nigerian cocoa had a reputation for constant quality but less flavour than South American cocoa. Its advantage was that it was mild and could blend well with any flavouring a manufacturer cared to use. It was the produce inspector who was the local enforcer of the Board's determination to show that the quality of the cocoa transplanted into Africa, and into Nigeria in particular, was as good commercially as, if not better than, that which grew in its original habitat.

It was the inspector's job to ensure that cocoa was of the right grade, that is, did not contain an undue proportion of under-fermented and defective beans for the grade as defined in the regulations made under the Produce Inspection Ordinance (these give an undesirable taste to the cocoa), or any trash or animal ordure, that every bag weighed the required 142½ pounds without the weight of the bag and bore the allocated identification markings of the Licensed Buying Agent and the identification of the store where it had been graded. The Board Executive had had enough complaints in the past. One of its officers liked to tell the (apocryphal and linguistically inexact) story of the German buyer who was disappointed that the last shipment was 'with goatschitt gemixt; please ensure cocoa and goatschitt are sent separately in future consignments so that we can blend to our own formula'. The Produce Inspector had to be vigilant. It was his steel seal press number that was impressed on the seals which secured the bags as a guarantee of quality and which could be traced back to him. There was also a dropmark on the bags which could connect any consignment to its place of origin. Woe betide him if a supervising officer found he had been negligent. And there was the additional checktest done at the port of shipment which could undo him if it was found not to conform to the grade indicated.

The produce inspector's powers, although not as extensive as those of supervisory and senior staff, put him in a position of influence in relation to smaller local traders and employees of politically less powerful licensed buying agents. This was especially so in one-man stations. There were many stories, unsubstantiated but convincing, of petty tyranny and corruption on the part of some inspectors. There was in some places a recognised scale of (illicit) fees payable to produce inspectors to have the produce inspected and passed. Any traders who refused to pay were allegedly made to wait for such long periods that their cocoa fell below standard. Occasionally a licensed buying agent or his senior employee would complain that these payments were above what was recognised as the norm but would not be prepared to confirm this in court. This was a kind of situation that I was continually faced with. I just could not obtain proof.

The frustration was such that a focus on corruption could become obsessive. I eventually decided that if I could not beat the rotten system, then perhaps if I could go about it in a more subtle way that allowed the straight inspection staff to get on without being cajoled or bullied into slowing down their rate of work. The instance of rubber illustrates the point. I received so many complaints in Benin that inspectors were slowing down the period it took to attend for inspection and the rate of inspection itself - again without a willingness to be a witness - that with the very considerable help of my assistant produce officer I conceived a strategy.

After satisfying ourselves of the amount of rubber a reasonably diligent inspector could grade in a day, allowing for rejections, I issued a standing instruction to the effect that if anyone could not meet this norm they should draw it to the attention of his assistant produce officer. It also implied that such was the importance of the instruction that failure to implement it was *prima facie* an admission of incompetence. This was reinforced by supervisory staff rewarding desired behaviour and penalising that which was not. There was a constant game on the part of some bolder inspectors of trying to get round the instruction and of supervisors aiming to frustrate their wiles. It was as well that there were many produce inspectors who played within the rules, whether written or unwritten. Some were indeed exemplary.

The relative wealth of the produce inspector extended the power he exercised to the social sphere, particularly in remoter stations. Earlier in his career Ade Olusanya (real name best forgotten) realised the power he could exercise in the creek village of Frukama. The girls adored his life style and he had made a number of conquests to the consternation of the elders and the young men of the village. I received a letter presumably written at the behest of the elders of the village or of someone with an axe to grind. It is reproduced below.

The produce officer
Warri

Frukama Town
9/2/54

Sir,

We have the honour most respectfully to forward this my application to you that the produce Examiner at Frukama always fornicated the women in Frukama and for this reason he has no time to go work. Now in this case, he will give the other to the head labourer as to pass the kernels. The action of this produce examiner that is living at Frukama is quite defficient from the other one which you are transfering here. So if you think this matter of his fornication to be a lie, He has paid £8 for the damage. We have the honour to be Sir

your Obedient Servant

Frukama

N.B.
The name of the woman which he has fornicated is called
Olome.

As usual there was no name to connect the authors to the allegation lest they be discriminated against when their produce was being inspected. The inspector was transferred when his time for leave came, as he would have been in any case, to a bigger station where he was supervised and did not exercise the same power. But the long time organising his own time had led him into slipshod ways and his representations were eventually called for when he was found in contravention of the regulations, as to why disciplinary action should not be taken against him. He had to submit these representations in triplicate within 24 hours of its receipt and had sat up all night making his defence. He had told his Area Officer that he was sure he, the Area Officer, 'would not want to see his interest in his work sacrificed on the altar of prejudice'. Such use of metaphor was exceptional and almost certainly lifted from a text he had read as I came upon the identical phrase on at least one other occasion.

Despite an appeal to the Director, he was given a Letter of Warning which meant that if he slipped from grace once more he would receive a Letter of Warning and Severe Censure which would put him at risk of dismissal if he should offend yet again. There were considerable advantages in being a P.I. and later developments showed he did not want to ruin his chances of a rewarding career. There is little doubt that Produce Inspector Grade 11 Olusanya pulled up his socks. His appearance improved. He bought a new helmet of the sola topee variety with fresh-looking red puggaree round it which marked him out as a produce inspector, started to press his trousers and generally comported himself in a way that would commend him to anyone. He seemed to feel the part as well as to look it.

Transfer to a station far from home was sometimes preferred by an inspector. If, as a result of a father's early death, an uncle steps in to assist and educate the family, he is considered a generous and decent person. If an Ibo did not do so, he would be roundly denounced. A clerk or a teacher or a produce inspector or anyone in a relatively profitable or exalted position, and having a good income in the eyes of his fellows, was well and truly fleeced by his impecunious relations. He might well have

255

been helped by them to obtain an education by which he reached his position, and they regarded it as a good investment for the future. They expected him also to use his influence to get good jobs for their children. It was not surprising that some of those from whom the dividends were expected sometimes requested to be transferred as far away as possible from their relatives. This was not that they could avoid their obligations but that they wished to limit the number to whom they made periodic payments. The general view among officials was that excessive hospitality and indiscriminate maintenance of relatives were likely to diminish as the economy grew and commercial and social life increasingly shed the habits of a subsistence economy. It was perhaps no coincidence that a number of inspectors should choose to supplement their earnings with unacceptable demands on those whom they were paid to serve.

CHAPTER 42

Time No Dey

The trouble with colonial administrations is that they think their way is the only one. Imperialism drew for its strength on the arrogance, confidence and self-reliance with which most of its builders and enforcers were well endowed. That they also had a civilising role in their perception provided moral support for their attitudes. That these traits should be reinforced by a belief in the inherent goodness of their motives, and legitimated by the Christian religion which put them on the side of the angels, gave them no reason to question their actions. Muscular Christianity was the accepted model. That view of the way things are constituted clashes with local customs and practices and the hidden assumptions people make. Not that colonialists are the only people who do this; they are just the prime example of not seeing there are other ways of doing and thinking. Plenty of others see the world through the lens of their own culture. We are all prone to it. We only rarely see ourselves as others see us; there is the corollary too that we rarely see others as they see themselves.

This homily is exemplified by an experience I had on the road from Akure to Okitipupa. I was driving along and saw approaching an open-sided, passenger - carrying bus, sometimes called a 'mammy wagon', when from behind the lorry and going across the road in front of me rode a man on a bicycle with a young boy on a carrier over the back wheel. The man was looking behind him with the back of his head facing the oncoming traffic. Instinctively I braked hard and pulled to a stop inches from the bicycle, my heart pounding fit to burst. My initial reaction was to ask him what the hell he was doing.

'Why you done do dis stupid ting?' I cried, 'You never see what come from Akure?'

'Why you holler?' he said, 'I was speaking to my friend'.

His values were different from mine and he was ready to defend them. Relationships are important in Nigeria as in the rest of

West Africa and awareness of them is in some circumstances more acute than that of imminent immolation.

Nowhere do these differences create more problems between people of different national backgrounds than in their relationship to time. In Nigeria, the sun, the moon and the stars marked the meaningful divisions of life for the majority of people. It created a circularity which was predictable and repeatable. It meant that such importations as submitting returns in time and turning up for meetings at a given hour or making payment by a given date were carried out with a considerable exercise of will and against a counterflow born of custom. Nevertheless such unaccustomed practice was perceived to be the way forward for many indigenous power holders whether in business or in the public service.

When a cross-departmental team showed the producers of palm oil in Ughelli how to make the highest quality edible oil in a dugout canoe as their protection against the future removal of lower grades due to the arrival of substitutes for technical palm oil of a lower grade, the people to whom the team were giving their demonstration expressed their thanks with natural Urhobo politeness. On the team's return to Ughelli some months later, the producers were seen to have reverted to the old ways. When asked to explain they simply said 'Na so we used to do am' (That is our custom). They would then receive a lecture to the effect that the old idea of 'time no dey' (time is not important) no longer had a place in Nigerian life. New ideas had to be adapted to within a time scale laid down by the authorities or the traditional social life they and their forefathers had enjoyed would break down.

Similar exhortations were made among cocoa growers - *Tètè ja kórikóri tàbi àdùm* (Yoruba for 'cut out black pod early') was an injunction frequently given, the implication being it was a function not always carried out at the optimum time but when the farmers had time to spare from other duties. They were reluctant too to bury the pods that had contained the cocoa beans after harvesting. This was a necessary precaution as these could

258

harbour disease not yet evident and so adversely affect future crops. Black pod was particularly prone to manifest itself in this way. Some had heard that there was a possible market for processed pods in the making of respirators for military and civil purposes and didn't want to lose out on any opportunity that arose by holding on to their old pods.

Rubber producers were urged to coagulate the latex tapped from the trees with the stipulated coagulant, dilute formic acid, rather than by the natural way (meaning not to be coagulated with human urine, this being a practice carried out to save time and money and observed, or rather, smelt, during the period of pressure of demand and high rubber prices on the world markets at the time of the Korean war). In this connection it was remarkable how many rubber buyers became avid readers of the airmail edition of *The Times* because it gave the latest commodity prices. The fear was that an export duty promised when the price of rubber reached a certain threshold at one time believed impossible, would automatically be imposed.

One of my most difficult prosecutions involved the employees of a prominent politician, Chief F S Ekotie-Eboh, only a few months previously guest at the coronation of Queen Elizabeth 11 and conspicuous on that occasion by his colourful dress which included a straw hat, a long train and a boa. Just when the threshold attracting an export tax appeared imminent, his company shipped a large consignment of rubber, presumably in order to beat the possible incidence of the tax, without its being passed by the government inspectors. Part of the consignment bore false seals purporting to show that it had received official inspection. It involved having 100 tons of rubber removed in an all-night operation in Sapele from a ship called the *Hendon Hall*, which had been about to sail, and examining every single bale to sort out the bales concerned and detain them as exhibits. As with Chief Nana Olomu, contemporary of King Jaja, whose place Nana's Town was just down the Benin River from Sapele where his premises were, Ekotie-Eboh was at one with those economists who wanted the market to rule, as it had in Nigeria in the memory of the elders, unfettered by restrictions except those established by the natural authority. There was a time and place for everything, he believed, and this was not the time and Nigeria not the place. He had further political ambitions, it was said.

Chief Ekotie-Eboh's actions reflected the structure of society. He would control everything from his own office-cum-court. If you had an appointment with him he would receive you at the appointed hour, or would create time to see you if you called without an appointment, but discussions would be interrupted frequently by the arrival of extended family or employees, who would hold his attention until a particular item of business was concluded when discussions would resume. He carried on multiple conversations at the same time, switching from a mode of thinking with friends and relatives which took no account of time to one with me or other Europeans which accommodated the need to achieve certain actions within a given time scale.

CHAPTER 43

The Board of Survey

Officials going out to Nigeria for the first time were appointed either by the Secretary of State for Overseas Territories and Administrations, as the post-war euphemism went, or The Crown Agents. The latter made appointments for those concerned with trade and industry or the technical government appointments. Those appointed by whichever office were given a kitting-out allowance and usually obtained gear from the estimable firm of tropical outfitters Messrs Griffiths MacAllister of London who provided such necessary recommended equipment as curry combs, sola topees and zinc hip baths, wicker-covered, not to mention indispensable items like camp beds complete with fittings to hold mosquito nets and folding camp chairs. The last mentioned were supplied with leather seats to prevent the discomfort of jiggers boring through some lesser material and into the fleshy part of the buttocks. The discomfort was nothing to the pain of the cure if the feared contingency did arise. This was the application of the lighted end of a cigarette by a servant to the point of entry, which made the offending insect withdraw from its preferred location when it could be seized and disposed of, preferably by incineration from the same cigarette end and/or by the 'mak siccar' treatment of squashing it beyond all recognition. This process was claimed to be the only effective treatment.

Those dispensing this wisdom comprised a discrete group who were termed 'old coasters', otherwise people deemed by recent arrivals to be worth listening to because of the time they had spent on the coast of the Gulf of Guinea and by dint of having survived there for so long in what had been called long since the White Man's Grave. Others who did not qualify for the designation but had nevertheless served some time in the area saw them, perhaps to their own disadvantage, as know-alls or old farts. The old coasters perceived themselves as seasoned and reliable individuals and considered the term an honourable one which by and large it was.

Another item the tyro official received was a copy of an official publication *Hints on the Preservation of Health in Tropical Africa*. Its covers were impregnated with DDT so that the volume would not be devoured by insects; it did not carry a warning that it could do untold long term damage to the person if handled frequently. It contained useful information on what to do if bitten by a snake. If such a contingency should arise, then your first action was to obtain the body of the snake that had bitten you so that the it could be identified and the appropriate anti-venin administered. Accompanying the 'Hints' was a copy of *Colonial Regulations*. You did not read these with as much relative avidity as the 'Hints'. In fact you didn't usually read them with any seriousness at all until you got into trouble or ran out of reading material. It included a section on the requirement of an officer to perform such tasks as might be required by the Chief Secretary (the Governor's first lieutenant) which in effect meant some minion in the administrative function to whom the task had been delegated. These tasks turned out to include such duties as electoral officer and president of a board of survey. The regulations covering these aspects had been skipped as unimportant when first looked at.

The Board of Survey is part of a system to ensure accountability as established by one's peers. My first board was on the stores of the provincial Public Works Department (PWD) in Warri. A certain percentage of the items had to be checked. Accompanied by two junior staff I set about the job. We chose to check that the coffins in the store tallied with the number in the records. Barrels of high melting point tar were checked and the petrol tanks were dipped. The proprietorial Inspector of Works expressed his disappointment that we had to close down his yard as per instructions from the convening officer while we did so ('You'll not close my yard you f...ing b......s'). Those who read the reports of the boards must have been amazed at the statistical quirk that left unchecked the thousands of pieces of sawn timber stacked in the yard usually because it would have taken an unconscionable time to do so.

Several years later when the brake master cylinder rubber of my car had perished and I had driven many miles with only the handbrake for comfort, I pulled into the PWD yard in Enugu, the capital of the then Eastern Region of Nigeria, for a possible replacement. Unfortunately, in my anxiety to have the repair effected, I drove into the yard through the entrance marked 'Exit' and was met by the same PWD Inspector of Works, who advised me to *'clear out of my f...ing yard'*. I angrily and foolishly drove out after a sharp exchange in which I told him his fortune, and made my way along the many more miles to Onitsha, meeting hazards natural and unnatural on the way.

The timber wagons became a source of anxiety, for the drivers drove like devoted henchmen of the Earl of the Black Waistcoat himself. They were reluctant to use their brakes which were air operated and slowed the huge vehicles with such effectiveness that the logs tended to move forwards against the cab. These logs were so big they must have been hundreds of years old. It was, sadly, the beginning of the wasting of Nigeria's forest assets driven by the increasing American commercial influence in the timber trade and the advent of the chainsaw. Self preservation decreed that the driver touch the brakes as little as possible to avoid being crushed and that oncoming drivers must 'go for bush' to ensure their long life on the land the Lord God had promised them.

That I am here to tell the tale confirms I made it. Onitsha, in the person of Able Baker, a former neighbour in Calabar and now provincial engineer in Onitsha, came up with the goods and I was able to carry on driving in safety. Onitsha had then the biggest market in Nigeria and almost certainly in Africa, where the latest cloth designs, gudgeon pins, household gear and gadgets from the four corners of the earth and of course brake master cylinder rubbers for a Standard Vanguard could be obtained. It was said that anything in the world could eventually be had in Onitsha market.

I could have sworn I saw the look of recognition in that PWD man's eyes in Enugu.

CHAPTER 44

Warm Beer at Five

Nigerians on the whole are a hospitable and chatty people, certainly in the south of the country. This is seen not only in the family and social life in general but is carried over into the world of work. This world is punctuated by events which have an associated ritual like celebrating the wife of a colleague having 'put a child to bed' (having completed the process of parturition) or recording appreciation of a colleague on his departure to another station or job or perhaps overseas to further his education. This was extended to Europeans and took the form of an invitation to join the staff in an occasion to mark a significant event like completion of a tour of duty or transfer elsewhere. If the officer's wife was on station with him, she too was invited together with a number of his known friends.

Such events would take place at about five o'clock. It could be held in a local hostelry or in the office. It was characterised in my case, outside the special circumstances of being stationed in a city like Lagos, by the arrival of staff from outstations which of itself was flattering as many had to travel long distances by various means of transport to attend. The fact that they might have something better to do in the evening was not something to cross the mind at the time. It was also an occasion on which everyone got dressed up whether in traditional dress or modern. To turn up in shorts and an open necked shirt was not on. A necessary respect had to be shown for the formality of the occasion and for the people who organised and supported it.

If held in the office, the place was not recognisable. A transformation had taken place. Colourful cloth appeared from somewhere to decorate the walls, and trestles were set up and the tops hidden by an appropriate cover. On top, someone had stood bottles of beer at close intervals and a bottle of whisky was put beside the guest of honour. Nuts and other accompaniments to such an occasion were placed within reach of everybody and the scene was set.

A master of ceremonies had been appointed by prior arrangement and it was he who called the participants to order and set events in motion. The MC was likely to be someone from the immediate office who had worked closely with the honoured guest and who was of standing in the community. He would launch proceedings with the usual reminder why we were all there and invite everyone outside while the daylight was good enough for a group photograph to be taken with the guest of honour in the middle of the front row. This would later be given to him with the names of all the staff added which I thought was a nice touch.

Return to the tables was the signal for the speeches to begin. The MC would resume by enjoining everyone to start and everyone helped himself to beer and passed the nuts round. He would then launch into an encomium on the officer who was leaving - so flattering that if it didn't make you glow, it made you blush if you were the officer concerned. If you were cynical you might ask yourself if he was going to ask for a reference before you left. He would end with a toast to the guest's health. The officer would respond by trying to make suitable references to the various people who had come, some at great inconvenience to themselves, to grace the occasion and sit down to a round of clapping. He could be excused at this stage for feeling a glow of satisfaction in what appeared to be a job well done.

The glasses would be recharged as the beer got warmer. The guest would then take the lid off the bottle of whisky and shake a tiny drop on the floor to symbolise the casting out of the devil - a harmless custom I am tempted to practise whenever a bottle of whisky is opened - and invite the others to have some. Then the speeches would begin again. If they were organised then you could fool me, such was the spontaneity of the speakers. I have always felt that a European in a corresponding job wouldn't have as good a command of spoken English. And the speeches are eulogies, so much so that the glow of satisfaction can burst into a fire of self-importance.

But there is a balance. If you are made to feel good in the first instance, then when a speaker gets up and proceeds to address your perceived faults in a friendly way, the starkness of the contrast somehow underlines the message. It was always a source of amazement to me how many of my staff took a magazine called something like 'Practical Psychology'. In my case my faults included 'being accustomed to command but not to consult'. I wonder if my belief in the consultation process stems from my time in Nigeria. That was not so. My father's example was always one which sought consensus even if he did not always achieve it, so I must have learnt bad habits elsewhere. Concrete examples would be given - how I rushed into a prosecution when one of my junior staff had, unasked, advised caution 'and he lost the case'. The twilight occasion would end with a presentation. I was given two books on one occasion - one by Maria Corelli, a highly regarded author in Nigeria and a book on the life of Mahatma Ghandi which somehow symbolised the aspirations of Nigerians everywhere. In Lagos, on the very last of these occasions, my wife and I received, as a parting gift, traditional Yoruba robes and headgear. The Alapa of Apapa had arrived!

It was all very well for Burns to have said 'O wad some powre the giftie gi'e us, to see oorsel's as ithers see us'. It took a Nigerian, or a number of them, to remind me that my Scottish brethern would have ensured that I didn't get above myself. If one's gas gets too high it has to be put on a peep (i.e. reduced to a minimum flame). The classic Scottish put-down is 'I kent his faither'.

CHAPTER 45

Hazard

Danger can be put into a number of categories. I prefer to talk about (a) real dangers, (b) dangers which are relative to knowledge, skill and experience and (c) those which may be neither of these but may be perceived as such.

Neil Waldman, a colleague of mine in Warri, was originally a Development Officer who, in the course of his duties, had had to wade waist deep in waters that left him with bilharzia which is a disease from which there was only a fifty-fifty chance of survival. And that was with a knowledge of how it is acquired. It is caused by parasitic worms entering the body through the anus and spreading into the bloodstream. Three times Neil's coffin was made ready for him and three times it was not needed. That is real danger as is contracting malaria despite taking the necessary prophylactic medicine and the other precautions.

Another danger also caused by a parasite in the blood is trypanosomiasis or sleeping sickness - an affliction contracted by rank bad luck, but thankfully not prevalent among Europeans although it was widespread in the Southern Cameroons. If blackwater fever or some other affliction is contracted as a result of neglect of the basic precautions or failing to take and send off a blood sample for test on the slides provided to all officers, then the danger could probably have been avoided and comes into the second category of relativity to knowledge and experience which an individual can apply or ignore.

Yet another health hazard was filaria, an uncomfortable condition reputedly caused by the filaria fly depositing an egg under the skin and hatching into the guineaworm which proceeded to parts of the body other insects cannot reach. The treatment for it was with a drug called bannicide and that was a depressant. My senior in Port Harcourt, Frank, would occasionally appear in the mornings wearing dark glasses and say, hand over brow, 'My filaria is bad today'. Filaria blocks the lymphatic vessels and can be excruciatingly painful. In the worst cases elephantiasis can develop. These bouts of Frank's filaria coincided with his having imbibed a half bottle of gin the previous evening. Another colleague at regional headquarters, being unaware of the sociological truth that if you don't take a person at her/his own valuation you kill the relationship, said on one occasion 'Come off it, Frank. You were pissed as a newt last night' and Frank, who was lovable and Welsh, burst into tears. I later heard that he had died of cirrhosis of the liver.

Richard arrived at the breakfast table one morning with half a snake dangling over the end of his machete which he proceeded to put in front of my nose and inform me he had killed it in the kitchen. Kitchens were usually apart from the house, certainly in outstations, and connected to it often by a covered way. He was suffering again and was in no way comforted when I consulted a chart showing that the snake was a calabaria and quite harmless. He treated them all as poisonous and his demeanour was a signal to me that he felt I should do the same and cut them in half if I got the chance.

'You nevah remember how de snake done blind de Forest Officer dog for his compound?' he asked. This was quite true. Alan Roxburgh's dog had been bitten by a spitting cobra but it had not been nearly as bad as Richard was making out.

'The dog didn't die, Richard. He see again after some days.'

What Alan had done was to give the dog an eyewash with water. If water wasn't to hand in such circumstances, beer, human urine or any other harmless liquid was the antidote.

Richard went on 'A man done die for Obinze when snake done bite him. I done see him die. I beg massa, makee kill all snake. I too fear am'.

On another tour of duty, he would remind me that I had the skin of a python shot in my compound in Warri. I had it cured as a memento of the time and always thought it would make a striking pair of ladies' shoes. On yet another occasion he told me off, not for the first time, for having a safari camp-bed of the type that just cleared the ground - much beloved of matloes on aircraft carriers in the Pacific - this after I had wakened up in the rest house in Nwaniba with something rubbing along my back through the canvas and had instinctively pulled my legs up to find instant sweat pouring down them. The higher (and heavier) camp beds with wooden frames, of the kind I had been advised to take to West Africa, would have avoided this incident but would not have removed the snake from the rest house. The urge to travel light with a familiar bed was a strong temptation. I knew I didn't have to take up my own bed and walk but old habits die hard particularly when they are associated with a pleasurable activity.

The same Richard, whose athleticism could be called in question, was on one occasion transferring from a launch to a canoe at Itu and instead of stepping lightly in, he put one foot squarely on the gunwale of the launch and the other firmly on the thwart of the canoe which began to distance itself from the launch under pressure of the current, and his legs went wider and wider apart until he fell into the water. I called out to him in as loud a voice as I could muster 'Can you swim?'

'I de try-o' (I can't swim but I am giving it a go) he gasped, even as he thrashed his arms to keep afloat. His upbringing in the Owerri province, far from clear water of any depth where he could have learned to swim, had not prepared him for this. Perhaps it was better to be hauled out of the Cross River than run the risk of getting bilharzia.

Natural hazards are one thing and their most harmful effects can be minimised. One can avoid going into the river where the hippopotamus is. We were staying one night at a rest house near Mamfe in the Cameroons. It looked on to the Upper Cross River and in the night we could hear the rumbling snorts as they cavorted just under the water. The whole building seemed to shake. This allied to local tales of how people had had their canoes upturned by them was an encouragement to be cautious rather than bold. The fact is that it is not the families of hippotamus that are dangerous according to the Mamfe cognoscenti. It is the lone hippo - a theory I disproved to my entire dissatisfaction when the canoe carrying my assistant and myself had to be paddled for dear life to the safety of the shore. The pullers, who were local, were not singing from the same hymn-sheet as my informant.

The presence of crocodiles had the same effect. A friend in Akure, Garson Miller, who was walking a trace for a new road, witnessed some locals with a captured crocodile. He told how one of his staff had poked a crocodile with a stick when its feet were tied together over its back. It brought its tail round with such force that it would have broken the man's legs if he had not moved just out of reach. Experienced people know what to do, from negotiating crocodile infested waters to coping with sandfly bites that have gone septic. For them the situation is not only predictable but manageable. It is no different in that respect from other occupational hazards. Anyone can have the bad luck to succumb to disease or have his number come up when negotiating the natural perils. To that extent I am a fatalist.

Not so predictable were the man-made hazards. There was the ever present menace on the roads of 'mammy wagons' and lorries carrying all sorts of loads. Many drivers were accustomed to drive with the right foot on the running board and the left foot on the accelerator, robes billowing from the cab in the slipstream created by the speed of the vehicle. This kept him cool in the hottest of days and also facilitated leaping out if danger materialised. Many of these lorries carried produce as well as passengers. Passengers were classified and positioned in the lorry according how much they paid. Number one position, or first class one might say, was beside the driver; very few could afford that luxury. Then in front of the bags of produce was seated accommodation for ten or so passengers, a kind of business class. If the loads moved forward because of having to brake suddenly, these passengers were at risk. The equivalent of economy class was at the back of the vehicle where the passengers had to stand. Such was the abandon with which these lorries were sometimes driven that any attempt to anticipate their movements was destined to fail in favour of pulling off the road to let them whip past.

A favourite slogan painted on the cabs of the lorries was 'Trust in God'. Never was such an invocation more appropriate. The propensity of Nigerians to kill each other on the roads might well have added another dimension to the Malthusian view of population curbed by wars, pestilence and moral restraint to hold down the gap in the situation where it grows at a greater rate than the resources needed to sustain it. Not for this large minority of indisciplined drivers the prohibition of the empty petrol drums which were supposed to deter them from taking their vehicles on to the road being tarred for the first time. That the surface was not yet firm meant little to them. The tarred surface would save the wear and tear on the lorries and facilitate their passage. They would plough through the drums to reach the smooth surface leaving tyre marks on the freshly scraped and tarred strip of road until an Inspector of Works hit upon the idea of filling the odd drum with concrete to ensure compliance.

A year or so before my arrival in Calabar, a young assistant manager with G.B.Ollivant, a husband and father, blew himself up as well as killing a valued customer. He had had a complaint that his gunpowder was damp and he took a handful 50 feet away from the magazine and put a match to it to demonstrate to his complaining customer it was indeed dry. Gunpowder grains are so fine that they leave an inperceptible trail via the fingers which cannot contain them completely. In this sad instance they ignited a fine line right to the magazine.

Accidents involving gunpowder on the west coast of Africa have been frequently reported right back to 1652 when a Mr. Bowles of the Guinea Company was blown apart in an explosion of a powder chest on which he was sitting smoking a pipe of tobacco in the mistaken belief he was sitting on a chest containing gold. Nigerians wanted gunpowder down the years not only for hunting for the pot or for money it could bring in, but also to celebrate any happy event, to ward off any evil spirits which they believed pervaded their life space or to win the favour of the gods for the deceased on the occasion of a funeral. It was a flexible product with a number of applications to suit the particular needs of the user.

Danger can also lurk at home. A departmental colleague, George Pole, had, a year and a half before my arrival in Calabar, the disconcerting experience of having a servant go berserk and kill his (the servant's) mother-in-law with a machete. When George went to the aid of the wife and others who were also being attacked, the madman hit out at him with his machete and severed his thumb. It was only the intervention of a neighbour with a rifle who shot the man before he could kill anyone else that saved him and the man's wife and children from almost certain death.

It has taken me a long time to realise that a person's perception is the reality for that person. Perhaps I should have been more tolerant of some people's irrational fears like that of juju; even more so the fear of harmless creatures like the praying mantis with its forelegs seemingly clasped against the wall in supplication and geckoes and lizards that clung to the walls and ceilings and only infrequently lost grip and fell with a wet smack to the floor or occasionally on the person. I had a spring on my bedroom door in Warri and the closing door one bedtime must have cut a lizard nearly in half. In the morning it already stank. Some hazards work both ways. It's easy to say nearly sixty years on how one's attitude to others' foibles should have been.

Stories circulated widely in the United Kingdom at the turn of the century of people's health being ruined even if they survived their time in the delta. An old lady, remembering a gentleman who had resided some years in Fernando Po (once a British possession) recalled how he had 'returned a wreck at forty and shook so violently with ague as to dislodge a chandelier, thereby destroying a valuable tea service and flattening the silver teapot in its midst'. Perhaps, if he had taken the normal precautions, as informed and responsible people do, he could have given the lie to the old saying

Beware and take care of the Bight of Benin
Although few may come out there are many go in.

It was the discovery of a native American remedy for malaria, quinine, transplanted to India in the 19th century and grown in plantations there for industrial processing, that equipped the white man to master the principal disease of the tropics and prepared the way for the later explorers, military adventurers and colonists to establish themselves there. But it was the commercial enterprisers who were the driving force that brought these others in their train. They all had a vested interest in the treatment of malaria and the use of prophylactic medicines. Later developments in public health and hygiene further helped Europeans in their efforts to limit the risks of an extended stay in the delta swamps and surrounding regions.

CHAPTER 46

The Administrative Hierarchy

My first meeting with an administrative officer was a few days after my arrival in the Catering Rest House in Lagos. How normal and post-war he seemed to be after the tales I had read about life in India and other places born of stories like *The Consul at Sunset* by H E Bates. He was the most junior of all the administrative personnel, a recently appointed officer who had not yet been on an outstation and might never be as more and more administrators were moved into Secretariats and the duties of District Officer were progressively seen as a local matter to be performed by local appointments. He represented a generation that had experienced such a change in outlook from those who had not left Nigeria during hostilities that they made life slightly uncomfortable for them by saying 'why' not 'yes' if he received an instruction he did not understand or thought foolish. That is not to say he did not have much to learn from those who had spent their working lives in the country or indeed that he did not want to show them respect.

What he had was a healthy curiosity bred of an attitude induced by the war or by a regional culture with different values or by intellectual conviction. This particular representative of the administration had a grammar school education and a good degree from Oxford. He was a product of the wider trawl in recruitment for administrative officers than had been the case pre-war. One or two of the administrative officers exhibited an apparent superiority complex and thought roughnecks in commerce a lesser breed, but the vast majority were gentlemanly and dedicated officers. A colleague whose uncle had been a Governor-General of the Sudan and who had had a brother or cousin in the Indian Civil Service, on being subjected to a superior harangue from one of the former, responded unkindly and perhaps inaccurately, by stating that the said brother or cousin had had power of life or death and had not the kind of responsibility of some minor Nigerian administrators who booked people into rest houses already full.

Gradually my contacts with administrative officers extended, particularly in the early days when I toured my area extensively, at the level of District Officer (DO) and ADO or Assistant District Officer. They were the point of contact when I was on tour. As a Produce Officer in the Department of Marketing and Exports, my area spanned a number of administrative areas. When I was moved to another area, my contacts with administrative officers expanded. Some ADO's had a boyish, public school tradition which included the singing of rugby songs that contrasted starkly with the sharp minds some of them exhibited. Others showed a versatility which could have taken them on the boards with ditties such as

> *My ambition was always to go on the stage*
> *And now my ambition I've got am*
> *They say that in pantomime I'm all the rage*
> *I'm the hole in the elephant's bottom*

In larger townships there would be a District Officer (DO). Sometimes they were called 'The Local Authority'. Like ADO's they had a responsibility as magistrates for minor offences, more serious offences being subject to the jurisdiction of Magistrates' Courts with a Supreme Court as higher court for the worst offences and as a court of appeal. Their first responsibility was as an administrator. A Senior District Officer was yet further up the hierarchy and was responsible for a 'division' of which there would be two or three in a province. The DOs and ADOs reported to him. This simple classification was obscured by the appointment of many of these officials to ministries when strong regions were established with a relatively weak centre in 1955 and the more senior officers became Permanent Secretaries and the like in the various Secretariats, responsible to ministers.

Perhaps the most important official that non-administrative functionaries came in touch with was the Resident. He it was who had responsibility for a whole province which could be the

276

size of, or bigger than, one of the smaller European countries. He would make a point of getting to know all the officers on his station and indeed throughout his jurisdiction. He would set standards of behaviour without seeming to. He was said to have a substantial entertainment allowance - I'm sure I knew the figure once upon a time and it didn't seem all that much - and he certainly did have frequent drinks parties, even the odd dinner party. Some complained that he saved on his entertainment allowance by plying guests with Empire sherry which one would have thought was something to be promoted in the circumstances.

The resident's wife would support him in what he did. One Resident's lady, Mrs Diana Curwen, hoped that the younger officers would invite her and her husband to dinner which was one way of getting them to do things properly, i.e. following the ritual proprieties ('Butter with supper, yes: with dinner never'). They responded by giving them experiences they would remember like an excruciatingly hot curry preceded by strong pink gins and dinner parties where different courses were served in different houses to allow the cooks concerned to concentrate on one course only and demonstrate their art.

When I was taken into hospital in Ibadan with malaria, over three hundred miles away from my station, she demonstrated her concern clearly. The fever caused a haemorrhage of the anterior chamber of the right eye, leaving me with eyes that didn't match until 20 years later when the offending one would be removed to ensure the other did not become infected, and a beautiful, plastic one fitted. I don't know why I was surprised that she should write a charming letter to me wishing me a speedy recovery. When I returned to the station she took a continuing interest in my getting back to normal.

Graciousness is a quality I have come to admire and I hope I have acquired a modicum of it. Her presence permeated the Residency. We learnt that no one left until the senior lady present made her excuses, a custom extended to all official, semi-official and even departmental occasions which some of the more recently appointed officers and wives did not bother to heed, observing their own latter-day decencies in excusing themselves. I could not get over the fact that the Resident as representative of the monarch on the station was served first at table. The newly created regional administrations had Lieutenant Governors in charge and embryonic regional parliamentary institutions.

The Chief Secretary and His Excellency the Governor ('H.E.') completed the administrative hierarchy. They operated at the highest level. In naval parlance the Chief Secretary acted as 'Jimmy the One' or first lieutenant being accountable for the running of the Civil Service and perhaps standing in for the Governor if he was indisposed. He would receive important visitors and lunch them or dine them or whatever depending on the circumstances. It was said that when Stanley Matthews brought an English football team to play against Nigerian teams, he was invited to have lunch with the Chief Secretary acting for the Governor. 'Tell me Matthews,' he is reputed to have said, 'what do you athletes eat to keep yourselves fit?'.

'Nothing like this, sir' Matthews is said to have replied nodding in the direction of the poor looking meat swimming in fatty gravy.

Once in a long while the Governor would visit the provinces and everybody would be on their best behaviour. Schools and organisations would be mustered for the occasion. My superior's wife paraded her Girl Guides on one occasion when it rained in tropical fashion as it is inclined to do. The ceremonies were rather protracted and she complained to His Excellency that her guides were getting soaked and inferred he should be getting on with it. 'I too Madam am under orders' he said.

But the hierarchy I have described above was becoming less and less relevant. With the establishment of self-government in Western Nigeria, the post of district officer at all levels of seniority were abolished and decision-making at official level concentrated on the secretariat in Ibadan with local politicians taking greater responsibility for local affairs advised by these officials who were aware of the process of government. This concentration in a secretariat often provided officers with an overall viewpoint that highlighted the much narrower view previously held by identifying with a particular area. Indeed, officers in the bush very often were fully committed to the district they administered and grew strong links with the local people. Local needs had often been at odds with the broader policy issues determined or executed in a central secretariat.

Concentration into ministries gave a focus and direction to their activities which they previously had not had. The need to be seen as acting within the same policy framework put an emphasis on cooperation with others rather than operating on their own in a much smaller pool. The biggest and most significant change was the greater authority of ministers who increasingly determined policy which administrative officers had to facilitate. These administrative officers, and their counterparts in other government departments, had over the years developed a greater humility than their predecessors, embraced a more modern concept of service and exercised a greater duty of care for those less powerful and privileged than themselves.

Today's values are vastly different from those of earlier times. I do not see why anyone should today have to apologise for the colonial period any more than the President of the USA should apologise for slavery or the London government for its neglect of those affected by the Irish potato famine (which was repeated in the Highlands of Scotland, a fact not always acknowledged) or the British royal family for the atrocities perpetrated on the Gaelic-speaking peoples on the order of their Saxe-Coburg-Gotha ancestor, William ('Butcher') Duke of Cumberland, after the Jacobite uprising; or, for that matter, the leaders in the Westminster parliament today for the Highland clearances, a 19th century example of ethnic cleansing which left a legacy of land-holding iniquities in which fewer people own more land than in any Latin American countries and hold it in a feudal manner imposed after the collapse of the clan system.

It was the outcome of a number of factors facilitated by the development of new navigational techniques spearheaded by the Venetians and the evolution of ships that could sail quickly and safely against the wind. The wider spirit of inquiry that sparked off the great exploration of the seas was followed by the arrival of a capitalist economy and later of a mid-Victorian economic confidence and overweening moral certainty which drove the makers of empire until a gentler and more questioning generation arrived to undermine that certainty.

The American investment bank partner is the late 20th century equivalent of the colonial administrator; he is the man who moves into weaker countries and tells them how to behave. Let us hope it provides people of the calibre of those administrators who stayed on to assist in the transition to self-government in Nigeria. Then, perhaps, some good may come of it. But that implies a primary commitment to principle rather than to shareholder value.

CHAPTER 47

Thinking Man's Dilemma

Gift-giving is a means of symbolising relationships the world over. In traditional societies it can take a number of forms. In its simplest form in Nigeria it is a handout usually solicited by someone young who accosts you and invites you to 'dash' him. At the next level up it is an invitation to give something for which something is given in return. This is the traditional level in which there is a two-way obligation which some expatriates did not have the sensibility to recognise and insisted on conducting themselves as if they were at home. *Dash* is not all that different from words in other languages like *baksheesh* (Egyptian), *mordida* (Mexican Spanish meaning 'the bite'), *tangenti* (Italian) sometimes referred to in its intention-to-influence form as *bustarella* or little envelope and *slush* (American English). There is an expression which sounds more innocuous and apparently less demanding that comes from the Cameroons where they called it *smol wata* (pidgin for small water). There is usually a reciprocity involved that makes the word 'bribe' often inappropriate as a translation.

Those who take an inflexible, moral position irrespective of the situation are either blind to the local culture or are trapped in a way of thinking from which they cannot escape, making value judgments on another culture in terms of their own. Certainly there is an ethical dimension but it rests on an understanding of the motivations of the giver. There is sometimes a problem distinguishing when there is merely a mutual consideration and when there is intention to influence.

Gift giving in general in Nigeria was determined by relationships. These have a primacy and compulsion in West Africa and certainly in the south of Nigeria where most of my work took place. You can be doing your job to the best of your ability and lo and behold a gift arrives from someone who thanks you for your help and courtesy. Good manners dictate that this is acknowledged and perhaps reciprocated at a later date. For the colonial servant it was the subject of a dilemma. For did it not state somewhere in Colonial Regulations that any gifts given in the course of the performance of an officer's duties should be handed over to the Chief Secretary to the Government?

Such rules were no doubt made with the intention of preventing officers from being suborned with gifts of some value by someone who wished a particular outcome on a given issue. It had the effect of relieving some officers of the responsibility of thinking issues through even where the present was of minimal value. It was black or white. A gift was a bribe. You accepted one or you didn't accept one. For them there was no bending to local values - automatic, mindless decision making was officially sanctioned in the absence of a definition of what constituted a gift. The reluctance or inability of some to accept the ambivalent nature of the process of gift-giving in the Nigerian context compounded the problem. There are people who need specific rather than general guidelines. Some just cannot cope with situations of perceived uncertainty and that poses problems for them when exposed to a culture very different from their own.

The problem was that the relationships necessary for sensible functioning could not exist under such circumstances. A provincial engineer who had great difficulty in working with contractors when he applied the easy solution of refusing or sending back gifts, told me he found these problems disappeared when he started to accept them without its affecting in any way the decisions he made. A senior colleague, the same one indeed who invited two of us to coffee and a drink after dinner shortly after our arrival in Lagos, and ushered us out almost as soon as we got in, told me that a certain Lebanese businessman buying cocoa on behalf of the Marketing Board asked him to release for shipment, and therefore payment, a consignment of cocoa suspected of having been adulterated. When he returned to his car there was £200 in notes on the seat. He immediately returned to the businessman, threw the money on his desk and informed him that every man had his price and his was £30,000 paid into a bank in Cuba (intended as irony). Apparently the reply he received was that the sum was too high. The point of recalling this uninspiring exchange is to demonstrate that all gifts were put in the same category as this one in terms of intention and effect by those who automatically rejected a gift.

When I was Senior Produce Officer of an area which included Lagos/Apapa and the main cocoa-producing belt centred on Abeokuta, I refused a number gifts, graciously I hope, which arrived well before Christmas time. On one occasion on which a gift had recently arrived, Richard my steward was in obstructive mode.

'What's this?' I asked

'A turkey, sah.'

'Where did it come from?'

'A man come in motocar and bring am'.

'Send it back' I instructed, 'you know what I say about these things'.

'I never know where I send am'

'Who go bring am?' I demanded, warming to the occasion and reinforcing a seriousness by saying it in pidgin.

'He never leave his card' Richard averred by way of explanation.

It was his way of telling me I was being a bit boorish in my behaviour. So I continued to feed turkeys for weeks with my own guinea corn until nearer the holiday when I in turn would give them away.

To the African business mind the line of demarcation between legitimate gift giving and bribery is a clear one. If one offers a gift to a government officer to influence him, that is corruption. But if someone receives afterwards a gift for services rendered, that is a commission or tangible acknowledgement. If one-sided or greatly unequal in value, or given with the purpose of inducing favourable treatment, then such gifts become bribery and should be handed back or handed in. The Anglo-Saxon mind also distrusts the Nigerian use of personal ties and connections because their reciprocal nature means using up old 'credits' or accumulating new 'liabilities' depending on one's 'balance sheet' of reciprocal transactions. The value attached to the use of personal connections is not always an economic one.

When a friend or relative intervenes on behalf of a particular individual, he will have several costs, one of which might be the cost of capital; there was too his personal 'ties/connections' capital. For these services he expects a form of payment now or in the future. Such is the way people look after each other in a collective society. Thus, while there is one line drawn between payment and bribery for a European doing his work in a Nigerian context, the dividing line may be drawn differently for the Nigerian businessman. Morality is not absolute. It is not always easy to determine the best course of action. Ethical decisions are not always clear-cut. That may be why people who dislike uncertainty like rules to work by.

Instead of issuing instructions on handing over gifts received by government officers in carrying out their duties, it would have been smarter for the old Colonial Office to have given those being offered appointments in Nigeria a testing interview to establish whether they were able to adjust to a different culture and possessed the character to address these dilemmas, perhaps supported by training and education in the ethics of decision making in a cross-cultural setting. Or is that bringing turn of the millennium solutions to 1950s problems?

CHAPTER 48

Justice Embedded

In these days when we see and hear talk of televising the dispensation of justice, it begs the question why this should be so. Presumably it is because the due process of law should be seen to be carried out in the interests of people in general so that they can have confidence in it. Our systems in Europe, and in those countries whose legal systems are derived from Europe, the law has become so specialised and remote from everyday life that it is good that attempts should be made to demonstrate that it is an integral part of the social system.

Magistrates' courts in Nigeria were embedded in the community. They were built at places convenient to the bulk of the population and were usually of single storey construction with overhanging corrugated iron roof to afford protection from the sun and open sides, a three foot wall going round three sides of the building. When cases were in progress, the public could go inside for the full hearing or, as the vast majority of interested spectators did, spend some time leaning on the wall outside and listen to the proceedings before passing on to other activities. Justice was being seen to be done in the formal court just as it had been seen to be done even in recent times, when a district officer carried out his lesser magisterial duties on tour at a table out of doors.

One of my responsibilities was for the prosecution of contraventions of the Produce Inspection Ordinance and the regulations made under it. I had assistants who prosecuted the less serious cases like failing to keep required records, failure to protect produce in transit from the elements and minor attempts to adulterate graded produce. A crisis occurred in 1951 when substantial quantities of cocoa were found not to correspond to description when it arrived at the purchasers' premises and were deemed to be 'not of merchantable quality' when examined by an expert arbiter. Adverse outturn reports were treated with the utmost seriousness.

I was expected to take cases involving any significant loss to the Boards and this included major attempts to adulterate. I was amazed how some miscreants had developed a dexterity in cutting open the selvedges of bags sewn with unbroken twine and sealed, removing part of the contents for resale, making up the weight with cocoa trash and sewing a knot inside the bag to make external identification difficult; it also reflected a very considerable manual dexterity. It was usually possible to detect some of these on the checktest at port but such was the process of sampling the bag with a sampler designed for the purpose that it depended where the sample was drawn from. Any consignments on the borderline of the marked grade would have a bag or two examined for tampering, usually by finding the internal knot on what was supposed to be continuous twine sealed at the end with an inspector's own steel seal press and number. If a consignment was suspect, all the bags in that particular consignment would be turned out and tested and half the cost debited to the Licensed Buying Agent by law as 'moieties' to encourage their commitment to the purchase of good quality cocoa.

I preferred to pursue these cases of 'ghost' shipments where lorry loads were tallied in to the Boards stores, recorded as having been accepted and credited to the account of the Licensed Buying Agent concerned (who would normally be completely innocent of involvement) but never reflected in the physical stock. The shipments so tallied in would in fact be resold, inspected again and sold to the Board eventually finding its way on to the terminal markets. It was an intellectual form of theft and the most reprehensible. As the Board Stores, certainly at Apapa, were the biggest single span buildings in the country each containing up to 10,000 tons of produce awaiting shipment by sea, the problems in obtaining corroborative evidence could be difficult and expensive.

As a gazetted produce expert I could also be called upon to give evidence in civil cases. We had wide ranging powers including those of entry and seizure 'at any times which were reasonable'. A colleague who entered premises by force and seized cocoa one night, for it was during the hours of darkness that such actions were mostly perpetrated, found himself charged with breaking and entering and convicted. On appeal he was cleared, but only after asking for a lawyer other than Crown Counsel which agency of defence was widely considered the kiss of death.

Another colleague found that the defence in a case was being conducted by H O Davies who defended Jomo Kenyatta in the Mau Mau trials and liked to recount that the eminent counsel referred to him as 'my learned friend'. I was impressed by the way the magistrates quickly got the bones of the case and gave judgement accordingly, very often in the presence at the wall outside the court of interested parties like representatives of different Buying Agents or a Buying Agent himself whom I might recognise and whose presence I would acknowledge with a nod and who would reciprocate with their eyes.

For all this court work we received not an iota of training and my two years of Mercantile Law were of little help. There wasn't even the practice of 'sitting with Nellie' - watching others do it and discussing with them points arising from their actions. In court I made mistakes in procedure and had to be called to order by the magistrate. If you made mistakes you were expected not to repeat them and become a model of competence just like many a district officer had had to do in the early days in the discharge of his duties as a magistrate. That was why you had been recruited. As a result I felt I had to mug up on things like the law of evidence and I remember buying a copy of Kenny's *Outlines of Criminal Law* and dipping into it from time to time to give me the kind of background that might be needed at some time.

There was one Crown officer who appeared regularly in cases in Lagos and must have been one of the few Europeans at that time to appear on a regular basis in the Magistrate's Court. He always deferred appropriately to the bench and encouraged his witnesses to do likewise. 'Bow to His Worship, bow to His Worship' he would urge many an anxious witness *sotto voce*. He himself would crave the magistrate's indulgence to enquire whether he objected to snuff. On receiving the Court's permission he would shake some snuff on the back of his hand and sniff it into each nostril. Having received his 'fix' he would proceed to do his utmost for the Crown. If the ruling of the court was to the liking of the bystanders, they would demonstrate their approval until required by the court to be silent.

CHAPTER 49

Tobacco Beetle

In West Africa it is not only people who are assailed by bugs. One of the things that concerned the Marketing Boards, and the Produce Inspection Service in particular, was the problem of maintaining the quality of stored produce in adverse weather conditions, difficulties of evacuation and the peculiar infestations that could appear when storage was necessary for longer periods than were desirable. Even perceived infestation, where no harm was actually done, could affect the price paid if arbitration was called for by the buyer. So it was with palm kernels which could be suddenly infested by the *necrobia rufipes* known more familiarly as the red-legged ham beetle. It gave colour to the dullness of the kernels and added a bright movement as it legged it round a bag in quick darts that defied any attempt to remove it or do it in. It did not harm the kernels but buyers did not like them.

Groundnuts could similarly be invaded, in this case by *trogoderma* infestation, which left the nuts in a weevily condition and if left too long before fumigation or evacuation, could be of unmerchantable quality when they arrived at their destination. Just as great a problem with them in value terms was seepage of the valuable oil content of the nuts caused by the weight of the upper bags in a stack exerting pressure on the lower layers, or drying out by harmattan winds, and here the solution was to get them moved as quickly as possibly to their final destination. But the biggest headache of all was with cocoa. Given the care taken in planting the young cocoa trees, looking after them assiduously in their early years until they bore their fruit, cutlassing the grass around them, cutting out black pod and swollen shoot, harvesting the pods at the most favourable time, and preparing the cocoa beans for the market merited meticulous attention to the process. This last activity of preparing the beans for market included removing the beans from the pods, burying the pods to prevent decay and possible creation of harmful bacteria, and fermenting the beans in banana or plantain leaves, turning them regularly to ensure all the beans were properly fermented over a controlled period, drying, and picking to remove trash and animal ordure (dry pellets from goats), spreading ready for inspection and grading by the Produce Inspection Service, bagging in suitably marked bags, weighing and sewing ready for sealing and storage locally until evacuated to port by lorry or sometimes barge. It was only right that every care should be taken that it arrive at the buyer's premises overseas in the very best of condition. That was the objective achieved after years of experience and experimentation and remained the basis of the Nigerian crop's reputation and why it became the custom in the terminal markets to quote prices for best fermented Lagos/Accra cocoa rather than benchmark quality against other countries of origin.

Inspection was carried out by taking a sample of beans from a parcel of cocoa thoroughly mixed with shovels. A produce inspector would draw a sample from the whole parcel from which he would then select randomly 300 beans which he would proceed to inspect one by one by cutting the bean in half longitudinally and classify them to establish the grade of the cocoa by calculating the percentage of underfermented, mouldy, weevily and germinated beans before they were sewn with continuous twine and sealed as the guarantee of quality. In store, before transport to the port of shipment, they were required to be protected from infestation by the *lasioderma serricorne*, the tobacco beetle. This was done by the placing of sticks coated with a combination of heated and slightly diluted funtumia rubber which gave a tackiness to the sticks which were then called *até strands*. If the tobacco beetle was around, it tended to stick to the strands and gave an indication of the degree of infestation should it take place. The rubber used was a local wild variety, not to be confused with the *Hevea Brasiliensis* or para rubber which is the cultivated species of rubber grown for industrial applications.

The problem was greater in the vast warehouses at the ports, but principally at Apapa, the port of Lagos, from which the majority of the cocoa crop was shipped. By the time they arrived at the port the bags could have been in storage for a number of weeks.

In addition to the provision of até strands, the stacks were 'sealed' with a spray at port warehouse that, in its pattern of dispersal of insecticide, left in theory no spot unprotected. The insecticide was a mixture of risella oil and pyrethrin, the latter imported from Kenya. Unfortunately the insecticide only prevented further infestation and had no effect on beans already infested. If the build-up of infestation was unacceptably high, the cocoa concerned had then to be removed to a fumigation chamber specially constructed for the purpose where the tobacco beetle was killed off by an appropriate fumigant.

But there was still a problem. Once fumigated, not only were the tobacco beetles killed off but so were the predators that kept them in check. If cross-infestation from new arrivals in the warehouse took place after fumigation, the rate of infestation took off at an even faster rate. For that reason, priority shipment had to be given to fumigated stocks. The irony is that the tobacco beetle cannot survive temperate climates. Regular shipment would eradicate the infestation but shipping companies like, indeed need if profits are to be made, to fill their ships. To do this means that waiting for a full shipload cannot be avoided.

'Didn't know they grew tobacco in Nigeria' you might say. And a good statement of a question it would be. For tobacco is grown far from where the cocoa trees grow. Tobacco is grown in the centre and north of the country. Apparently, so the entomologists of the West African Stored Products Research Unit informed us, the tobacco beetle attaches itself to cowpeas which are grown in the north and mostly sold in the south of Nigeria and no one has yet found a way to stop the cowpeas acting as a carrier on their way to or through the cocoa growing country.

Perhaps in a quiet moment when you are having a cup of hot chocolate and smoking a cigarette, more likely admittedly if you are French, you will remember having read this and marvel at the connection between the two.

CHAPTER 50

Harmattan

It has to be experienced to be appreciated, this desiccating Harmattan wind. Yet another wind to join the Mistral, the Sirocco and the Golf as creators of temporary changes in climate. Before we know it there will be a Volkswagen car named after it.

This Harmattan most resembles the Sirocco but makes its effect felt from a north-easterly direction rather than the south or south-easterly direction of that wind. In the latter part of the year, clouds of dust from the Sahara are blown into the sky and can blot out the sun. While it can be devastating to people, produce and goods in Northern Nigeria where it is like a thick, cold mist, reminiscent of an east coast haar in Scotland or seafret in eastern parts of England. The cold dryness is so different from the normal weather in the south of the country even in the more innocuous form that it takes there, that it can create all sorts of havoc. A report in the Nigerian press noted on a date in December 1956 that the temperature at Cape Wrath in north west Scotland (latitude 59°N) was higher than that in Lagos (latitude 5°N).

The physical effects of the harmattan could be seen, heard and felt. The unaccustomed dryness in a region where a humidity in the 90's and a temperature of similar proportions (35° Celsius) was normal, did a number of things. It made life pleasant for those of us without air-conditioning. It also occasioned unfamiliar sounds. Joints on wooden furniture, even when seasoned before manufacture, would crack and split and ghostly sounds would emanate from the oddest places in the night. So long as the air is drier than the wood, the latter will give up moisture to it. As soon as the amount of moisture in the wood is the same as that in the air, the wood cannot get any drier in that condition of atmosphere, no matter how long it is left. If, however, for some reason the air becomes drier, as is the case when the harmattan arrives, then further loss of moisture from the wood, together with further shrinkage, must take place. Drawers that could once be pulled out easily were now difficult to open. Stored produce could have its oil content lowered and hence its value reduced necessitating some kind of remedial action. Groundnuts bought during the dry harmattan season gained about ¼-½% in weight between purchase in Kano and delivery in north-west Europe. Wise buyers put their maximum effort into buying the nuts during that season as it could mean they increased in weight when stored in the high humidity of Lagos or Port Harcourt. It affected people too. Their skin would go dry and lips would get chapped. A bonus was the blooming of the harmattan lilies which lined many a drive in residential compounds (an English word derived from the Malayan *kampong)*. They brightened up an often dismal scene.

The harmattan time was the gardening season. These harmattan lilies together with cannas and portulacas and perhaps zinnias were the basics of flower gardening in Nigeria. Charlie McIvor, a friend who worked with the John Holt Company, always referred to the basic red portulacas as 'government flowers' because of the number of government offices which had masses of them planted outside presumably to keep the weeds down. Gardening in Nigeria should always be done with gloves despite the discomfort in the heat. Working with the soil anywhere can seriously damage your health. My own was affected only mildly. I began to get an irritating itch on one finger which could not be identified by the local medical officer. It began to spread and leave long weals on the fingers. When I returned on leave to Scotland, I was sent to the Eastern General Hospital in Leith where there was a tropical diseases unit. The doctors there immediately diagnosed canine hookworm. The treatment was to freeze it with ethyl chloride which did the worm no good. It put up a fight in its host against the cold which meant an uncomfortable day or two only and then all was well. To let drop the fact that I had had canine hookworm was a good conversation stopper.

Mary's love of gardening and its facilitation by the relatively cool conditions of the harmattan had one unfortunate outcome.

While tussling with some plant or other she damaged her back. It turned out to be a slipped disc. The upshot was that she had to undergo lumbar traction at Agodi hospital in Lagos. She had to wear a plaster of Paris corset from top to bottom of her spine. The restriction this put on her breathing became alarming and she had to be cut out of it in the middle of the night while staying at the house of friends. To have to wear a plaster cast in the damp heat of the tropics is a tribulation I would wish on no one.

The psychological effects of the harmattan were positive. People laughed at the various things it did. Schoolchildren, for whom this was a joyful time, would touch each other lightly on their lips dried out by the lack of accustomed moisture and blood would begin to flow but was easily stemmed. Any aberrant behaviour was blamed on it. When the first traffic lights in Lagos were installed, taxi drivers who disobeyed the signals and were charged, pleaded in mitigation that the Harmattan made them do things they didn't want to do.

Decisions made during the harmattan were better reviewed when normal weather resumed. By and large it was a happy time rather like when the first rains came after a particularly trying dry season when people would exult in the wetness and hold their heads up to the downpour in a welcome to the stimulating freshness of the air, laughing and joking as they did so. Only, in these conditions it stimulated physical activity like playing tennis more vigorously or encouraged the indulgence of pulling up a blanket at night.

If the cocoa main crop is light, the tick bird has deserted the backs of the goats, the music of the licensed drummers has changed rhythm from all previous nights, the iroko tree has shed a limb, the cockerel in Igwe Kalu's compound has failed to crow, the newly coiffed hair sticks up on end and the ladies in white have not turned up for their trysts, it is no one's fault. It must have been the harmattan.

CHAPTER 51

The Black and White Keys

The perceived wrongs that have been perpetrated in the cause of justice, the unintended offence that may have been given in interactions between people of different cultures, the doubtful causes that have been embraced for the noblest of reasons and the mutual misunderstandings induced by ignorance that may have occurred, were all probably the kinds of sources of inter-racial conflict that MacAulay felt could be avoided when he talked of the best tunes being played on the black and white keys. The Gold Coast visionary, that is, not the MacAulay who wrote 'How Horatio Held the Bridge'. Such a consummation presupposes a sympathetic understanding of each other's culture and a suspension of judgment allowing a mutual respect to develop.

In Nigeria, some tried, some did not bother and some just did not know. Prejudice operates both ways but the onus is on those who are educated or have by dint of other qualities reached a state of grace, to show others by example. That education is presumed to include insights into one's own culture as well as that of the other party. There were individuals, both black and white, who exemplified all that was best in human nature in the way they behaved to others and as a result promoted harmony between the races. It is not to be wondered at that the ideal was not always achieved for not everyone is disposed by upbringing to have the attitudes and values that lead them to that comfortable state, nor did the history and politics of Britain's colony and protectorate of Nigeria lend itself to good race relations. There were still a few who had to learn that a black man may be a gentleman and a white man otherwise. There are many for whom the world past the end of their nose is foreign parts

At the official level, there was no longer supposed to be discrimination in terms of race but history has undermined this. Segregation of Europeans and Africans was necessary from a health point of view, so the old argument went. But it has older historical roots. Under the regime of indirect rule given effect by Governor Lugard, local chiefs in the North were to be left to administer their fiefs under the guiding hand of a District Officer, which presumed no Europeans would upset the traditional relationship between ruler and ruled. As a consequence, Europeans would live in quarters away from a chief and his people. Rulers like King Jaja of Opobo in the south of the country required European traders to live apart from his people so as not to influence them in undesirable ways. Separate residential areas were laid out and that for Europeans termed the 'European Reservation' changed in my time to the 'Government Reservation' to take account of the policy of Africanisation. This inevitably led to many educated Africans, who were neither European nor government employees, seeing it as a slur on themselves that accommodation of a kind they had become used to and which reflected their current status, was denied them. Having had to listen to late night drumming, apparently without cease, from my quarters in Calabar, I shudder to think what it would have been like had I been closer to the source of the music - unless of course I had become 'hooked' on it.

While integration was beginning to take place and in some ways was quite advanced, it was possible from time to time to see black colleagues being treated differently from their European counterparts. I recall a senior colleague in Ibadan going round the Europeans in an invited gathering asking *sotto voce* if they would like a café cognac and having their coffee liberally dosed in the kitchen while the African guests (with one exception) did not get the opportunity. It always seemed to be the same Europeans who declined the offer. When I think of it I am often minded to discriminate among guests at home by offering those who want to add water or other adulterant to their drink, a grain whisky, reserving the single malt for those with more cultivated taste buds. But my early upbringing taught me not to discriminate among guests and that everyone under my roof should have the best the house had to offer. Discrimination was also practised by some Africans, doubtless the expression of a frame of mind that had developed during the colonial period and

296

felt in some way to be an appropriate way to declare their opposition to it.

During the visit of Her Majesty Queen Elizabeth II to Warri during her tour of Nigeria in 1956, the Royal Rolls Royce, an acquaintance informed me, broke down en route although driven by the government mechanical engineer in situ who was required to drive HM in place of His Excellency the Governor's (HE's) regular driver as a precaution against such a contingency - no doubt the decision to dispense temporarily with the services of the regular driver was a spin-off from the very British belief that an engineer was someone with a facility for mending broken mechanical items with his hands and also a symbolic act to demonstrate the reliability of the white races, and in this case, the Anglo-Saxon race. Indeed, Her Majesty, from the knowledge she obtained from her training as a mechanic in the Auxiliary Territorial Service (the name for women's branch of the army during the war), would probably have had at least as much idea of on-the-spot repairs as the man who had been allocated the task of driving her.

That old attitudes take a time to change was reflected in all manner of things. The wife of a senior colleague referred to the Anglo-Indian wife of another colleague as a *chichi* which had a strange, old-fashioned, prejudiced, out-of-touch ring about it. It was well known in the department that there was a shop in Oron displaying the same unusual but striking name as one of our assistant directors and I myself had seen it. People drew their own conclusions. In the days when wives only came out for the school holidays, it was not unusual for some Europeans to take local mistresses. In a sense there had always been a kind of integration in the liaisons that were formed between men and women of a different colour. Some formalised the relationship in marriage but that was the exception. Those senior African staff who had studied in the United Kingdom, usually in London, sometimes returned with English wives. There was a residual resentment against mixed marriages on both sides and only the children can suffer from such prejudice. It seemed that, as far as the European community was concerned, the further down the social scale you went the more did that lingering prejudice persist. Indeed, some officers in government who ascribed such prejudice to people were asserting an ancient superiority. Snobbery was a stronger social force than racism among some of the old guard, racism being an indicator of class, albeit modified considerably by the inclusion of specially selected personnel over the last quarter century. It was with the latter in mind that the American philosopher George Santayana said 'Never since the heroic days of Greece has the world had such a sweet, boyish master'.

On the positive side, interactions multiplied across the communities and more and more friendships were formed at the personal level, often as a result of people who could be considered as role models having given a lead in the preceding years. People mixed easily on the field of sport. Another colleague who had played rugby for East Midlands enlivened the Akure scene by turning out to play soccer with a local team in Akure at the age of 43. His grey hair won him the nickname of *'Babá'* (Grandad). At the institutional level the Island Club in Lagos, set up by Nigerians who found it impossible to penetrate the Ikoyi Club dominated by Europeans, maintained specifically it was not discriminatory. It was frequented mainly by Africans whose interests were either politics or business which excluded a number of others whose concerns lay elsewhere. It was at least as enjoyable as the Ikoyi Club which had a vast majority of European members.

One institution that set out with the specific objective of bringing the races together was the Lagos Dining Club where a mixed membership met regularly in a spirit of goodwill to enjoy each other's company. I attended on one occasion as guest of Adeola Odunsi, one of the African Licensed Buying Agents of the Western Nigeria Cocoa Marketing Board. Each member brought a guest to the meetings of the club and so extended its influence to those of like mind. A moving spark in its formation was Sir Kofo Obayomi, a man of honour and wisdom as well as of multifarious interests. Initiatives of this kind require to be responded to.

The certainty that characterised the British in the colonies had been slowly eroded since Lowes Dickinson said just before the First World War that the virtue of the Englishman was that he never had doubts - about his superiority to the black man, about the moral imperative that he had a God-given right to be in his country and that he had a duty to do his best in that situation for the people for whom he was responsible. Questions were being asked, I discovered in many discussions, even before the Second World War, that challenged this blind attitude. Even those who spoke with the accent of the superior ones were more sympathetic as far as the African was concerned and more humble than their predecessors.

Early administrators had had an army background and unquestioning minds, perhaps easily conditioned by Cecil Rhodes's injunction to his countrymen never to forget that they had won first prize in the lottery of life by being born English. With the development of a tradition whereby the best people for the job were appointed as the authorities saw it, so did a greater understanding of, and sympathy for, African views and aspirations grow. The aggressiveness that was a necessary accompaniment to the spirit of empire was gone. Such doubts as our superiors in their own wide experience had, were increased by a post-war intake many of whose values were not those of the old establishment but who brought new values to service in the colonies or chose to think for themselves and drew conclusions from their experience in other colonial settings during the war.

Thoughts of this kind were reinforced by the forces driving decolonisation, for example by the experience of Nigerian troops both in the Western Desert and in India and Burma where they saw local people with more decision-making authority than themselves; by the withdrawal of the British from India and the need no longer to protect the bases which protected the sea routes to the sub-continent; by the ejection of the French from Indo-China after the defeat of Dien Bien Phu, the British withdrawal from Palestine, the humiliation of Suez and the quicker march to self-government in the nearby Gold Coast soon to be designated

Ghana. Each constitutional change - and there were four constitutions between 1948 and 1960 - gave a further impetus to the Nigerian surge to independence and caused the British government to reassess a number of times, i.e., to shorten, the period within which self-goverment would be granted. It was accelerated by the belief on the part of a significant number of Nigerians that the benefits of British rule were now outweighed by the promise of greater ones that would result from their ceasing to be a subject people.

Some, like the officer who was designated the Local Authority in Sapele, still maintained that the key factor would be the Colonial Secretary's decision as to when it would happen. The truth of the matter was that the British minister's hand was continually being forced from within Nigeria and his choice of date was restricted to that period within which failure to withdraw posed a greater threat to life in terms of law and order than the enforced continuation of colonial status. The ministers of the Crown preferred to call this movement 'nationalism' and hinted at agitators. They spoke of it in such a way that it had a faintly disreputable ring to it, especially if the fact that the leaders had usually been in jail for their activities was mentioned in the same context, a fact which made them martyrs for the cause of independence and gained further support for it.

There was also an external influence on the speed with which independence was granted in the end. That was the so-called Cold War and the US fear of colonies falling to Communism if independence were not granted at an early date to a government well disposed to the West, with the associated fear of loss of the huge petroleum potential of Nigeria. The ghost of Senator McCarthy, the scourge of all liberal thinkers on East/West relations and witch hunter supreme of those he perceived to be engaged in un-American activities as he saw them, still haunted the minds of American administrators. A programme intended broadly to facilitate the training of Nigerians for autonomy, envisaged when many thought there was time to do it at leisure, was not so much thrown into disarray as overtaken by the speed with which the transformation of expectations of Nigerians took place and the pace of the events that unfolded as a result. Nigerians did not care if efficiency was surrendered in the process. Their ability to celebrate the diversity of their own culture, to create and to write their own history and learn from their own mistakes were more important in their eyes. If political stability was threatened by such developments, it was a price that had to be paid.

Of one thing I am sure. I am glad that I did not have that absolute certainty of my country right or wrong, of the unquestioning moral certainties that were part of the cultural baggage of the earlier men who made the empire and had been handed on to a few contemporaries, even if such suborning attitudes on the part of myself and others of like mind weakened the fibre of empire and hastened its demise. By this time, I had no doubts about what the British government should be doing. When a group of Greek Cypriot merchants hissed and remained seated when 'God Save the Queen' was being played after a cinema performance in Ibadan, I was resentful that my angry reaction was at odds with my intellectual convictions just as I felt when the same national anthem was played and derided by many at Murrayfield on the occasion of a rugby international between England and Scotland. I had a friend in that Greek Cypriot community and knew what his feelings were about colonialism in his own backyard where there was also a backlash against the colonial regime and was the root cause of the booing. Friendship and cultural identity were in separate compartments and I found I could live with the dilemma they induced.

While the best tunes may be played on the black and white keys, you have to know the chords to play to harness the harmonies. There was little point of anyone whose ideas did not go along with the desirability and inevitability of self-government to attempt to change the views of the vast majority of Nigerians, if we exclude the Northerners who feared a coalition of the south would be to their disadvantage when the majority of oil was thought (wrongly it turned out) to be in Ibo country and trade was dominated by the Yoruba people. True friendship between black and white survived such political upheavals. When the politics had run its course, there would be a knock-on effect on the economic and commercial situation. It was to have a profound effect on what the Marketing Boards had been trying to do since their inception and the Produce Inspection Service had been trying to do over a period of thirty years.

I decided to leave my work as a government official in Nigeria when I was asked if I would like to consider leaving the service. I was thirty four years of age and had been aware for some time that something like this was bound to happen. Rather than be one of many with my kind of experience, I hoped that I would find work that I enjoyed by being among the first from the colony to leave. The alternative would have been to have stayed on with the possibility of getting preference in some kind of official function in the United Kingdom. When I discussed this with Mary in the light of our decision on our previous leave to make one more tour, we concluded that it would be better to attempt to carve out a new career sooner rather than later. It only dawned on us slowly, having done the analytical bit, that we would be leaving behind much that we cherished.

EPILOGUE

Epilogue

Our last tour in Nigeria finished in February 1959 when we set sail from Apapa on the M.V. Accra. Our friends were at the dockside to see us off and it was a very moving moment. There is something final about a departure of a ship and the slowly increasing gap between those on board and those on the wharf when it sets sail, something that wrings the withers and renders you unable to speak or control the trembling of the lower lip.

The journey home was in a sense a journey into the unknown. It was a beginning as well as an end. We would miss what we had been doing. Mary would not forget her charges and friends at the Corona School in Apapa which she started as a class for a few in a friend's verandah. What school would have a parrot in class which would periodically say 'Lift me wing and tickle me ribs'? It moved to bigger and more appropriate premises as the numbers swelled and took on an international flavour with English, Nigerian, Japanese, French and Dutch children. Chinua Achebe, in his classic satirical novel *A Man of the People*, makes reference to one of his countrymen speaking with a Corona School accent. So Mary and her colleagues in the Corona Schools – setup under a trust established in 1955 – must have made a lasting impact. Nor would she forget her original pupils and staff at St Saviour's School in Ikoyi. I would miss colleagues involved in the creation, collection, inspection and distribution for export of the country's produce as well as a group of good friends outside that particular circle. We would both miss Richard and David and would worry for them and other friends during the civil war when all communications would cease.

On looking back on what I had achieved, I knew that I was a very small part of an organisation that had seen a progressive increase in the amount and value of produce grown, inspected and sold for export through the 1950s. Groundnuts peaked with the huge efforts to evacuate accumulated stocks from their Northern pyramids. The tonnages of special grade palm oil for edible purposes had increased many times over the same period and more than compensated for the loss of markets, through

304

competition from other lubricants, of lower grades of technical palm oil which had been progressively eliminated. Nigeria was first in the world among producers of oil palm products and had managed to compete with plantation production from other West African countries and from the Far East by the introduction of 125 oil mills and about 5,000 hand presses despite the difficulty of breaking down customary processes and local opposition to mechanical devices. It produced 50% of all palm kernel exports. Cocoa had experienced a similar take-off both in quantity and in quality. Good fermented Lagos/Accra was now the standard against which all other cocoa was judged in the terminal markets. Nigeria was the number one producer of cocoa in Africa and accounted for about 14% of world production. Today Nigerian cocoa sells at a discount to Ghanaian because the market was deregulated and entrepreneurs, unfamiliar with cocoa trade, let quality slip. The country was second just behind Senegal among producers of groundnuts and this represented about 30% of world groundnut exports, only a small amount being processed locally in Kano. This improvement would have to continue as there were other vegetable oils from other parts of the world which provided considerable competition. Its production of cotton made it an important textile producer, certainly for West African markets. Additionally, it was the world's largest producer of columbite.

In terms of gross domestic product per capita, which is the usual measure of success in an economy, Nigeria was at this time on a par with countries like South Korea, Thailand and Indonesia. In addition to the success of cash crops in export markets, Nigeria had the potential to become a big producer of hydro-carbon fuels and it looked as if the earlier optimism of the *Nigerian Eastern Guardian* would be well and truly justified. It had to progress economically to maintain the living standards which had been achieved. The country's population was increasing at more than a million and a quarter annually. That meant it had to do even better just to stand still. Politically, the country had been left with a federal constitution and a parliamentary system constructed as far as possible to avoid the conflicts of differing dominant groups in the North, West and East. What it could not do was to remove the differences in culture, social organisation and language that existed among them and the inherent potential for conflict. There was, however, a rich pidgin English based on the structures of the languages of the Delta that was increasingly being used outside these areas and could one day become a *lingua franca* that would overcome the differences of language among ordinary people who could belong to one of nearly two hundred and fifty ethnic groups. It was to become a legitimate subject of academic research in Nigeria and in some states soap operas were later to be played out entirely in pidgin. The elites had English as a second language.

The potential of Nigeria was such that it could become the leading country in West and Central Africa with the largest population and a wealth of untapped resources, not least those of its energetic and aspiring people. Just as the time of our departure from Nigeria marked an end and a beginning for us, so would it be in a year's time an end and a new beginning for the new country. It would bring to an end the era of colonialism that had succeeded imperialism and would herald a new chapter in British-Nigerian relations. Hopefully, there would be progress. There was a strong agricultural base and a network of trading partnerships which, with proper management, could develop further and outlive the discovery of oil which has a limited life.

There would not be the problem of settlers that has blighted relations in East and Central Africa since the holding of land by foreigners had long been forbidden by law. There was no history of entire peoples having been eliminated as in North and South America or in the Pacific. While there had been centuries of trade in local products with Europeans, the country had not been taken over in the early 20th century as a business to be milked dry as was the Belgian Congo for example. There was an educated elite capable of taking the reins of government if it had the will to do so. Mistakes were undoubtedly made but we could leave with our heads held high.

Imperialism comes in many guises. Even as this is being keyed, the US President is in Japan trying to get the Japanese to spend more and open up their markets to the beneficial effects of free trade, code for the extension of the reach of Wall Street investment banks and the Fortune 500 industrial companies. Simultaneous reports reveal that the US government is bullying foreign governments to protect the global interests of American bio-chemical industry in general, a recent instance being an unexpected rethink of impending New Zealand laws for the labelling and testing of genetically modified products, as a result of US threats to pull out of a free trade agreement. By and large, the latterday individual administrator in the old colonial system tried to interpret an arrogant system with a moral code, fairness and integrity, characteristics which were reflected in the work of officers in other government departments.

Some colonial servants used to say, more out of bravado than anything else I suspect, that it would be a happy day when they shook the dust of Nigeria off their feet. But the dust of Africa was ingrained. I would look back on these eight years and make judgments based on lessons I had learnt there. In Europe and the developed countries in general, people are rushing, mostly through no fault of their own, to meet commitments determined by the date and the clock - a most un-Nigerian activity. They fall easily into habits that are hard to break. A phone call when the recipient is having soup and a roll at lunchtime can be responded to in different ways. Either the soup cannot be allowed to get cold and the call has to be short, or the conversation can be extended as circumstances decree and the soup reheated. What are microwave ovens for if not to assist the second of the alternatives? And this would be a Nigerian response in a latterday context.

When I meet someone I know on the street, I am not the one to break off the conversation. It is too precious to cast off just like that. I wait for others to give the cue that it is time to discontinue the talk. It is their ulcer and perhaps their blight. Interaction is what keeps relationships in good repair as most Nigerians could tell you if they thought about it. It is implicit in their lives. Those of us who live in Western Europe tend to see ourselves as being in communities rather than of them. As a result we are often sufficient unto ourselves with hardly a thought for the people next door which is not a problem in Nigeria. We see self-sufficiency as a positive quality rather than one that is the enemy of community. It is likely there is a strong correlation between the breakdown in community and the growing incidence of love lavished on pets and mental illness in Western countries.

I am privileged to have spent these years in West Africa. They reinforced many of the values of my parents and remind me that, in a material world, there has to be time for interacting with others. How could that interaction be maintained in the UK where television was becoming watched to the exclusion of conversation? The old art was being relegated to times between programmes. When I see the obsession with 4 x 4s in tarred, temperate Britain, I could see no justification for them unless used for real off-road work. Otherwise they seemed to me to stroke the self-image rather than perform a useful task. They are making a social statement and represent a memorial to the victory of advertising over self-respect. Self-image in an over-communicated world is the enemy of interaction. As for bull-bars.....!!

Supermarkets promised to bring lower prices to consumers through competition and economies of scale to include everyone in an ever-improving economic and social polity. As the years wore on they would merge and become bigger and bigger until today there is a strong suspicion that they are in an oligopolistic position and are no longer the consumer's friend because the temptation under these circumstances is for the oligopolists to collude to get a quick return on investment by fixing prices. Could it be that virtual monopoly of this kind is the inevitable outcome of unbridled capitalism? The mantra that 'the consumer is king' has been discredited. 'Guaranteed price protection' means the price had recently been increased by a margin that will not need to be considered for some time. If it says 'If you can buy anything marked with our guaranteed prices more cheaply elsewhere we will refund the difference', that means it is a loss leader to bring people into the store and make their profit on other items with a much higher margin; other stores will not compete on these products as it would mean losses for everyone - so they choose a range of their own for this purpose. Only the consumers will lose; such is their belief in the value of the offers made that they do not realise the strategy being effected through them acts to their disadvantage in the long run.

The system of supermarket groups - and those are becoming more and more concentrated as a natural development of competition - is a long way from the perfect open markets of Nigeria in both the physical and metaphorical senses, where the lowest price was for negotiation although some of these big retailers would maintain with unsurpassed sophistry that negotiation is inherent in the system of branding. Worse still, in these huge retail food chains, and that includes the fast food outlets, real human interaction is replaced by employees who have been asked to memorise a series of scripts and sub-scripts and mindlessly recite them at appropriate points in their interactions with us. We respond by developing a set of mindless recipes of our own that we ourselves trot out in such situations. Where is that enchantment in exchange which includes feelings and emotions, and needs to be continuous and reciprocal? No more dash, no more unwritten contracts, no mutuality. How would these people respond who now shower us with gifts and free offers if we were to give them gifts instead? I suggest life would be intolerable for them for they would have no pat answers to resolve their interaction problems. Their problem is ours.

A new religiosity seems to have arisen in the west to parallel the move away from the church and the more formal religions. This is the comfort some, particularly women, find in countering the stress of modern-day living by spending until they drop in supermarkets and other retail outlets. It isn't a problem with the very poor but appears to lighten the days of those who own credit cards. It is tempting to compare this with the teaching of the old religions and the ethic that they embodied and which helped people to handle the problems of life. It invites a comparison with some of the denominations mentioned earlier and indeed with the code of the animists whose culture met their particular needs. The reader will no doubt draw his or her own conclusions and decide which of the approaches is the nobler.

If society is about living in decent community and companionability with our fellow creatures, then that would appear to be threatened by the world of systems where efficiency is paramount or by the virtual world in which we communicate electronically in a situation where the message is divorced from interpersonal feelings. The satisfactions of touch, eye contact and spatial comfort in social interactions are increasingly denied us and people look in vain for reliable hooks to hang on to and instead create a social reality in which form takes the place of substance, image triumphs over reality and marketing over the ability to think freely.

The disjunctive nature of modern life diminishes the interconnectedness of events, activities and beliefs and increasingly flakes away the bonds of association necessary for our social wellbeing. It may even be that The Elocuted One was being prophetic when she said 'There is no such thing as society'. We are in the process of doing things in the name of economic progress which may well produce a society that is not worth defending. The reverence we offer to the market system has sparked a philosophy that puts a premium on individualism and an unwillingness to postpone the immediate gratification of the labour of humankind at the expense of the values of family and of the group.

Unlike the Ibo or Ibibio village, where everyone helped to look after everyone else and acted on behalf of the community and everyone had jobs they performed, organisations are believed to be able to succeed with permanent insecurity and a continuous turnover of employees. The loyalty of workers or management is considered to be of no influence whatsoever. Yet the great success stories of the later half of the 20th century has not been those of the European Union or the United States and the 'new economy'. Rather it has been the success stories of the industrialisation of Japan, Korea and China where the group is more important than the individual. The abolition of the bonds between company and workers is still not universal. Yet Western management continues to chop problems into neat elements and to measure them. That there might be a link between collective organisation and creativity in a world where innovation is a nation's lifeblood, where the world of art and of the spirit are intertwined with the world of work and where what is essential, in the words of Saint-Exupéry, is not visible to the human eye, does not seem to have dawned on it. Given this emerging scenario, the values of a developing country like Nigeria may have much to offer developed ones in the art of living. Can we absorb the lessons before it is too late?

Our return to the United Kingdom in some ways exposed us to culture shock in reverse. How would it be for the immigrants now pouring in from the West Indies and elsewhere? Would they be received like the slave Jaja in Bonny and be given the rights of the country and advancement on the basis of merit in return for their allegiance, so assisting their integration into the community? And the seekers of asylum and economic betterment who were not so-called British protected persons - would they be accepted to allow them to make the very positive kind of contribution that would help renew the spirit of enterprise and industry in the country impaired by the efforts of mobilising the entire nation in two world wars?

Events subsequent to those described earlier have cast a cloud over good memories. Chief Festus Ekotie-Eboh, the likeable rogue whose rubber I had seized, whose employees I had prosecuted and whose management style I admired on account of the easy way he shifted between cultural modes, became Minister of Finance in the federal government only to die from an assassin's bullet in the mid-1960s in the final year of the so-called First Republic. Ryszard Kapuscinski, the eminent Polish journalist and foreign correspondent in his book *The Shadow of the Sun* declared him to have been a thoroughly nasty piece of work. He was the victim of a military coup originally organised to abolish corruption which was said to have tainted Ekotie-Eboh as well as many other ministers and politicians during his years of office. Sadly, the military regimes that succeeded this turbulent period of civilian rule after self-government established a pattern of corruption of their own, that was to become hideous even by Africa's lamentable standards. Nowhere was the truth more evident of Lord Acton's saying that all power corrupts but absolute power corrupts absolutely. Nigeria is paying the price. A new federal capital was built at Abuja where only a small proportion of the billions it cost were spent efficiently, much going into the hands of contractors in league with politicians; a two tier foreign exchange provided dollars at a discount for the military rulers and their cronies; money from the successful oil industry was used to prop up the naira, the local currency, the strength of which was treated as a sign of national virility. The foreign-exchange earning agricultural sector, once the pillar of the economy, was nearly destroyed as palm oil and groundnut and cocoa exporters were unable to compete internationally with such an overvalued currency.

Today, cocoa is the only agricultural crop that contributes to Nigeria's export earnings and that at a level less than half of that it exported in 1951 which was in excess of 400,000 tons. That production made Nigeria one of the premier cocoa producers in the world. Now Nigeria lags far behind the Ivory Coast, Ghana and is even challenged by the Republic of Cameroun as a cocoa producer. In the event, during the period 1960-66, the government appropriated the surpluses accumulated by the marketing boards from the so-called cash crops, which it used to finance the rapid expansion of the public sector and the development of local capitalism, although a significant proportion of the money disappeared into private pockets.

The marketing boards became a vehicle for development during the ascendancy of the military rulers who took over from the civilian government. Millions of peasant farmers were impoverished. In the mad scramble for a slice of the oil wealth, many middle class Nigerians have abandoned nearly all other economic activity and made the country dependant on oil and vulnerable to a shock in oil price and the run-down of reserves. Meanwhile, the peoples of the Niger Delta have watched billions of dollars in oil money flow out from under their soil as they have grown poorer and have been denied participation in the benefits, harvesting only what remains unpolluted in their eco-system. The corner may just have been turned with return to civilian government in the last year of the millennium.

Sam Bleasby, who had in the opinion of some 'gone native' and who, someone suggested jokingly, might have had a *mami wata* he visited at weekends and who never concealed by his actions and choice of life style where his political sympathies lay, lost forever any sense he might have had of being unalone without company. Sam was to die in the Nigerian Civil War, reportedly shot by accident by federal troops who thought he was a mercenary. If he seemed old to me 15 years previously, there is no way he could have looked like a soldier at the time of his death.

Many Ibo civilians perished at this time as they fled from the predominantly Hausa and Yoruba troops who harassed them continuously according to eye witnesses. The federal authorities eventually adopted a policy of starving the Ibos into submission; famine was used as a strategic weapon. Many were reported to have died of starvation, forced as they were to return in their hundreds and thousands from other areas of Nigeria where their education in the mission schools, encouraged by their relatives, had prepared them for clerical and administrative tasks at which they excelled. The massacre of defenceless Ibos in the North at a number of centres may have been one of the more immediate causes of the civil war. The number of deaths in the war has been estimated at between 1 and 3 million, the vast majority of those being Ibos and most of them civilians, many of them children.

Genocide is the term used by some informed commentators. The actions of the warped minds of trigger-happy bullies are often excused by platitudes that people occasionally get caught up in the cross-fire, but this can conceal a much more sinister intent. There are people alive today who witnessed cold-blooded murder. Ibo friends and non-Ibos from the former Eastern Region in which the Ibo people were dominant, have disappeared into limbo. In all this, the British government sided with the

Nigerian federal authorities in a cynical gesture of support for decisions taken earlier in its name, despite the honourable actions of Tam Dalzell MP to bring these atrocities to the attention of the Government and the British people.

The end of the civil war was characterised by a compassionate peace without any display of triumphalism thanks in some measure to the adjustment of the Ibo to the situation in which they are no longer a powerful political force. They were always able to adapt to any situation and could easily assume where necessary a low profile and apparent humility. Their ability to achieve the political power they had exercised earlier was weakened by the creation of new states in which the Ibo people were deliberately marginalised as large minorities.

The problem now facing the country is to heal the long-lasting wounds of peace as well as of war to do positive things for the economy apart from the bonus of petroleum. Off-shore production will shortly account for the bulk of Nigeria's two million barrels a day. If agreement can be achieved on the distribution of the revenues from off-shore oil which until now has gone to the federal government, then the disputes that have raged between the central government, the state governments, the oil-producing states and the people whose land and waters have been exploited by the federal government and polluted by the oil companies, the conditions will exist for the first time for the establishment of peace and prosperity.

Sadly, the Supreme Court has recently ruled that the revenues will accrue to the centre, thereby perpetuating the problem. Only when there has been a major rethink of this judgment will the country, in my view, be in a position to achieve its potential. There is still time to trigger changes every bit as far-reaching as those that took place on the oil rivers just over a hundred years ago. The external influences are already there. It will need the talent of everyone who has it irrespective of their ethnic origins and the language they speak to make the most of it and provide the leadership the country so desperately needs and deserves.

Lightning Source UK Ltd.
Milton Keynes UK
UKOW04f2048090715

254895UK00001B/103/P

9 781447 631071